GACE

Educational Leadership
Secrets Study Guide

DEAR FUTURE EXAM SUCCESS STORY

First of all, **THANK YOU** for purchasing Mometrix study materials!

Second, congratulations! You are one of the few determined test-takers who are committed to doing whatever it takes to excel on your exam. **You have come to the right place.** We developed these study materials with one goal in mind: to deliver you the information you need in a format that's concise and easy to use.

In addition to optimizing your guide for the content of the test, we've outlined our recommended steps for breaking down the preparation process into small, attainable goals so you can make sure you stay on track.

We've also analyzed the entire test-taking process, identifying the most common pitfalls and showing how you can overcome them and be ready for any curveball the test throws you.

Standardized testing is one of the biggest obstacles on your road to success, which only increases the importance of doing well in the high-pressure, high-stakes environment of test day. Your results on this test could have a significant impact on your future, and this guide provides the information and practical advice to help you achieve your full potential on test day.

Your success is our success

We would love to hear from you! If you would like to share the story of your exam success or if you have any questions or comments in regard to our products, please contact us at **800-673-8175** or **support@mometrix.com**.

Thanks again for your business and we wish you continued success!

Sincerely,
The Mometrix Test Preparation Team

Need more help? Check out our flashcards at:
http://MometrixFlashcards.com/GACE

TABLE OF CONTENTS

Introduction

Thank you for purchasing this resource! You have made the choice to prepare yourself for a test that could have a huge impact on your future, and this guide is designed to help you be fully ready for test day. Obviously, it's important to have a solid understanding of the test material, but you also need to be prepared for the unique environment and stressors of the test, so that you can perform to the best of your abilities.

For this purpose, the first section that appears in this guide is the **Secret Keys**. We've devoted countless hours to meticulously researching what works and what doesn't, and we've boiled down our findings to the five most impactful steps you can take to improve your performance on the test. We start at the beginning with study planning and move through the preparation process, all the way to the testing strategies that will help you get the most out of what you know when you're finally sitting in front of the test.

We recommend that you start preparing for your test as far in advance as possible. However, if you've bought this guide as a last-minute study resource and only have a few days before your test, we recommend that you skip over the first two Secret Keys since they address a long-term study plan.

If you struggle with **test anxiety**, we strongly encourage you to check out our recommendations for how you can overcome it. Test anxiety is a formidable foe, but it can be beaten, and we want to make sure you have the tools you need to defeat it.

Secret Key #1 – Plan Big, Study Small

There's a lot riding on your performance. If you want to ace this test, you're going to need to keep your skills sharp and the material fresh in your mind. You need a plan that lets you review everything you need to know while still fitting in your schedule. We'll break this strategy down into three categories.

Information Organization

Start with the information you already have: the official test outline. From this, you can make a complete list of all the concepts you need to cover before the test. Organize these concepts into groups that can be studied together, and create a list of any related vocabulary you need to learn so you can brush up on any difficult terms. You'll want to keep this vocabulary list handy once you actually start studying since you may need to add to it along the way.

Time Management

Once you have your set of study concepts, decide how to spread them out over the time you have left before the test. Break your study plan into small, clear goals so you have a manageable task for each day and know exactly what you're doing. Then just focus on one small step at a time. When you manage your time this way, you don't need to spend hours at a time studying. Studying a small block of content for a short period each day helps you retain information better and avoid stressing over how much you have left to do. You can relax knowing that you have a plan to cover everything in time. In order for this strategy to be effective though, you have to start studying early and stick to your schedule. Avoid the exhaustion and futility that comes from last-minute cramming!

Study Environment

The environment you study in has a big impact on your learning. Studying in a coffee shop, while probably more enjoyable, is not likely to be as fruitful as studying in a quiet room. It's important to keep distractions to a minimum. You're only planning to study for a short block of time, so make the most of it. Don't pause to check your phone or get up to find a snack. It's also important to **avoid multitasking**. Research has consistently shown that multitasking will make your studying dramatically less effective. Your study area should also be comfortable and well-lit so you don't have the distraction of straining your eyes or sitting on an uncomfortable chair.

 The time of day you study is also important. You want to be rested and alert. Don't wait until just before bedtime. Study when you'll be most likely to comprehend and remember. Even better, if you know what time of day your test will be, set that time aside for study. That way your brain will be used to working on that subject at that specific time and you'll have a better chance of recalling information.

Finally, it can be helpful to team up with others who are studying for the same test. Your actual studying should be done in as isolated an environment as possible, but the work of organizing the information and setting up the study plan can be divided up. In between study sessions, you can discuss with your teammates the concepts that you're all studying and quiz each other on the details. Just be sure that your teammates are as serious about the test as you are. If you find that your study time is being replaced with social time, you might need to find a new team.

Secret Key #2 – Make Your Studying Count

You're devoting a lot of time and effort to preparing for this test, so you want to be absolutely certain it will pay off. This means doing more than just reading the content and hoping you can remember it on test day. It's important to make every minute of study count. There are two main areas you can focus on to make your studying count.

Retention

It doesn't matter how much time you study if you can't remember the material. You need to make sure you are retaining the concepts. To check your retention of the information you're learning, try recalling it at later times with minimal prompting. Try carrying around flashcards and glance at one or two from time to time or ask a friend who's also studying for the test to quiz you.

To enhance your retention, look for ways to put the information into practice so that you can apply it rather than simply recalling it. If you're using the information in practical ways, it will be much easier to remember. Similarly, it helps to solidify a concept in your mind if you're not only reading it to yourself but also explaining it to someone else. Ask a friend to let you teach them about a concept you're a little shaky on (or speak aloud to an imaginary audience if necessary). As you try to summarize, define, give examples, and answer your friend's questions, you'll understand the concepts better and they will stay with you longer. Finally, step back for a big picture view and ask yourself how each piece of information fits with the whole subject. When you link the different concepts together and see them working together as a whole, it's easier to remember the individual components.

Finally, practice showing your work on any multi-step problems, even if you're just studying. Writing out each step you take to solve a problem will help solidify the process in your mind, and you'll be more likely to remember it during the test.

Modality

Modality simply refers to the means or method by which you study. Choosing a study modality that fits your own individual learning style is crucial. No two people learn best in exactly the same way, so it's important to know your strengths and use them to your advantage.

For example, if you learn best by visualization, focus on visualizing a concept in your mind and draw an image or a diagram. Try color-coding your notes, illustrating them, or creating symbols that will trigger your mind to recall a learned concept. If you learn best by hearing or discussing information, find a study partner who learns the same way or read aloud to yourself. Think about how to put the information in your own words. Imagine that you are giving a lecture on the topic and record yourself so you can listen to it later.

For any learning style, flashcards can be helpful. Organize the information so you can take advantage of spare moments to review. Underline key words or phrases. Use different colors for different categories. Mnemonic devices (such as creating a short list in which every item starts with the same letter) can also help with retention. Find what works best for you and use it to store the information in your mind most effectively and easily.

3

Secret Key #3 – Practice the Right Way

Your success on test day depends not only on how many hours you put into preparing, but also on whether you prepared the right way. It's good to check along the way to see if your studying is paying off. One of the most effective ways to do this is by taking practice tests to evaluate your progress. Practice tests are useful because they show exactly where you need to improve. Every time you take a practice test, pay special attention to these three groups of questions:

- The questions you got wrong
- The questions you had to guess on, even if you guessed right
- The questions you found difficult or slow to work through

This will show you exactly what your weak areas are, and where you need to devote more study time. Ask yourself why each of these questions gave you trouble. Was it because you didn't understand the material? Was it because you didn't remember the vocabulary? Do you need more repetitions on this type of question to build speed and confidence? Dig into those questions and figure out how you can strengthen your weak areas as you go back to review the material.

 Additionally, many practice tests have a section explaining the answer choices. It can be tempting to read the explanation and think that you now have a good understanding of the concept. However, an explanation likely only covers part of the question's broader context. Even if the explanation makes perfect sense, **go back and investigate** every concept related to the question until you're positive you have a thorough understanding.

As you go along, keep in mind that the practice test is just that: practice. Memorizing these questions and answers will not be very helpful on the actual test because it is unlikely to have any of the same exact questions. If you only know the right answers to the sample questions, you won't be prepared for the real thing. **Study the concepts** until you understand them fully, and then you'll be able to answer any question that shows up on the test.

It's important to wait on the practice tests until you're ready. If you take a test on your first day of study, you may be overwhelmed by the amount of material covered and how much you need to learn. Work up to it gradually.

On test day, you'll need to be prepared for answering questions, managing your time, and using the test-taking strategies you've learned. It's a lot to balance, like a mental marathon that will have a big impact on your future. Like training for a marathon, you'll need to start slowly and work your way up. When test day arrives, you'll be ready.

Start with the strategies you've read in the first two Secret Keys—plan your course and study in the way that works best for you. If you have time, consider using multiple study resources to get different approaches to the same concepts. It can be helpful to see difficult concepts from more than one angle. Then find a good source for practice tests. Many times, the test website will suggest potential study resources or provide sample tests.

4

Practice Test Strategy

If you're able to find at least three practice tests, we recommend this strategy:

UNTIMED AND OPEN-BOOK PRACTICE

Take the first test with no time constraints and with your notes and study guide handy. Take your time and focus on applying the strategies you've learned.

TIMED AND OPEN-BOOK PRACTICE

Take the second practice test open-book as well, but set a timer and practice pacing yourself to finish in time.

TIMED AND CLOSED-BOOK PRACTICE

Take any other practice tests as if it were test day. Set a timer and put away your study materials. Sit at a table or desk in a quiet room, imagine yourself at the testing center, and answer questions as quickly and accurately as possible.

Keep repeating timed and closed-book tests on a regular basis until you run out of practice tests or it's time for the actual test. Your mind will be ready for the schedule and stress of test day, and you'll be able to focus on recalling the material you've learned.

Secret Key #4 – Pace Yourself

Once you're fully prepared for the material on the test, your biggest challenge on test day will be managing your time. Just knowing that the clock is ticking can make you panic even if you have plenty of time left. Work on pacing yourself so you can build confidence against the time constraints of the exam. Pacing is a difficult skill to master, especially in a high-pressure environment, so **practice is vital**.

Set time expectations for your pace based on how much time is available. For example, if a section has 60 questions and the time limit is 30 minutes, you know you have to average 30 seconds or less per question in order to answer them all. Although 30 seconds is the hard limit, set 25 seconds per question as your goal, so you reserve extra time to spend on harder questions. When you budget extra time for the harder questions, you no longer have any reason to stress when those questions take longer to answer.

Don't let this time expectation distract you from working through the test at a calm, steady pace, but keep it in mind so you don't spend too much time on any one question. Recognize that taking extra time on one question you don't understand may keep you from answering two that you do understand later in the test. If your time limit for a question is up and you're still not sure of the answer, mark it and move on, and come back to it later if the time and the test format allow. If the testing format doesn't allow you to return to earlier questions, just make an educated guess; then put it out of your mind and move on.

On the easier questions, be careful not to rush. It may seem wise to hurry through them so you have more time for the challenging ones, but it's not worth missing one if you know the concept and just didn't take the time to read the question fully. Work efficiently but make sure you understand the question and have looked at all of the answer choices, since more than one may seem right at first.

Even if you're paying attention to the time, you may find yourself a little behind at some point. You should speed up to get back on track, but do so wisely. Don't panic; just take a few seconds less on each question until you're caught up. Don't guess without thinking, but do look through the answer choices and eliminate any you know are wrong. If you can get down to two choices, it is often worthwhile to guess from those. Once you've chosen an answer, move on and don't dwell on any that you skipped or had to hurry through. If a question was taking too long, chances are it was one of the harder ones, so you weren't as likely to get it right anyway.

On the other hand, if you find yourself getting ahead of schedule, it may be beneficial to slow down a little. The more quickly you work, the more likely you are to make a careless mistake that will affect your score. You've budgeted time for each question, so don't be afraid to spend that time. Practice an efficient but careful pace to get the most out of the time you have.

Secret Key #5 – Have a Plan for Guessing

When you're taking the test, you may find yourself stuck on a question. Some of the answer choices seem better than others, but you don't see the one answer choice that is obviously correct. What do you do?

The scenario described above is very common, yet most test takers have not effectively prepared for it. Developing and practicing a plan for guessing may be one of the single most effective uses of your time as you get ready for the exam.

In developing your plan for guessing, there are three questions to address:

- When should you start the guessing process?
- How should you narrow down the choices?
- Which answer should you choose?

When to Start the Guessing Process

Unless your plan for guessing is to select C every time (which, despite its merits, is not what we recommend), you need to leave yourself enough time to apply your answer elimination strategies. Since you have a limited amount of time for each question, that means that if you're going to give yourself the best shot at guessing correctly, you have to decide quickly whether or not you will guess.

Of course, the best-case scenario is that you don't have to guess at all, so first, see if you can answer the question based on your knowledge of the subject and basic reasoning skills. Focus on the key words in the question and try to jog your memory of related topics. Give yourself a chance to bring the knowledge to mind, but once you realize that you don't have (or you can't access) the knowledge you need to answer the question, it's time to start the guessing process.

It's almost always better to start the guessing process too early than too late. It only takes a few seconds to remember something and answer the question from knowledge. Carefully eliminating wrong answer choices takes longer. Plus, going through the process of eliminating answer choices can actually help jog your memory.

Summary: Start the guessing process as soon as you decide that you can't answer the question based on your knowledge.

7

How to Narrow Down the Choices

The next chapter in this book (**Test-Taking Strategies**) includes a wide range of strategies for how to approach questions and how to look for answer choices to eliminate. You will definitely want to read those carefully, practice them, and figure out which ones work best for you. Here though, we're going to address a mindset rather than a particular strategy.

Your odds of guessing an answer correctly depend on how many options you are choosing from.

Number of options left	5	4	3	2	1
Odds of guessing correctly	20%	25%	33%	50%	100%

You can see from this chart just how valuable it is to be able to eliminate incorrect answers and make an educated guess, but there are two things that many test takers do that cause them to miss out on the benefits of guessing:

- Accidentally eliminating the correct answer
- Selecting an answer based on an impression

We'll look at the first one here, and the second one in the next section.

To avoid accidentally eliminating the correct answer, we recommend a thought exercise called **the $5 challenge**. In this challenge, you only eliminate an answer choice from contention if you are willing to bet $5 on it being wrong. Why $5? Five dollars is a small but not insignificant amount of money. It's an amount you could afford to lose but wouldn't want to throw away. And while losing

$5 once might not hurt too much, doing it twenty times will set you back $100. In the same way, each small decision you make—eliminating a choice here, guessing on a question there—won't by itself impact your score very much, but when you put them all together, they can make a big difference. By holding each answer choice elimination decision to a higher standard, you can reduce the risk of accidentally eliminating the correct answer.

The $5 challenge can also be applied in a positive sense: If you are willing to bet $5 that an answer choice *is* correct, go ahead and mark it as correct.

Summary: Only eliminate an answer choice if you are willing to bet $5 that it is wrong.

8

Which Answer to Choose

You're taking the test. You've run into a hard question and decided you'll have to guess. You've eliminated all the answer choices you're willing to bet $5 on. Now you have to pick an answer. Why do we even need to talk about this? Why can't you just pick whichever one you feel like when the time comes?

The answer to these questions is that if you don't come into the test with a plan, you'll rely on your impression to select an answer choice, and if you do that, you risk falling into a trap. The test writers know that everyone who takes their test will be guessing on some of the questions, so they intentionally write wrong answer choices to seem plausible. You still have to pick an answer though, and if the wrong answer choices are designed to look right, how can you ever be sure that you're not falling for their trap? The best solution we've found to this dilemma is to take the decision out of your hands entirely. Here is the process we recommend:

Once you've eliminated any choices that you are confident (willing to bet $5) are wrong, select the first remaining choice as your answer.

Whether you choose to select the first remaining choice, the second, or the last, the important thing is that you use some preselected standard. Using this approach guarantees that you will not be enticed into selecting an answer choice that looks right, because you are not basing your decision on how the answer choices look.

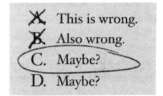

This is not meant to make you question your knowledge. Instead, it is to help you recognize the difference between your knowledge and your impressions. There's a huge difference between thinking an answer is right because of what you know, and thinking an answer is right because it looks or sounds like it should be right.

Summary: To ensure that your selection is appropriately random, make a predetermined selection from among all answer choices you have not eliminated.

Test-Taking Strategies

This section contains a list of test-taking strategies that you may find helpful as you work through the test. By taking what you know and applying logical thought, you can maximize your chances of answering any question correctly!

It is very important to realize that every question is different and every person is different: no single strategy will work on every question, and no single strategy will work for every person. That's why we've included all of them here, so you can try them out and determine which ones work best for different types of questions and which ones work best for you.

Question Strategies

⊘ READ CAREFULLY

Read the question and the answer choices carefully. Don't miss the question because you misread the terms. You have plenty of time to read each question thoroughly and make sure you understand what is being asked. Yet a happy medium must be attained, so don't waste too much time. You must read carefully and efficiently.

⊘ CONTEXTUAL CLUES

Look for contextual clues. If the question includes a word you are not familiar with, look at the immediate context for some indication of what the word might mean. Contextual clues can often give you all the information you need to decipher the meaning of an unfamiliar word. Even if you can't determine the meaning, you may be able to narrow down the possibilities enough to make a solid guess at the answer to the question.

⊘ PREFIXES

If you're having trouble with a word in the question or answer choices, try dissecting it. Take advantage of every clue that the word might include. Prefixes and suffixes can be a huge help. Usually, they allow you to determine a basic meaning. *Pre-* means before, *post-* means after, *pro-* is positive, *de-* is negative. From prefixes and suffixes, you can get an idea of the general meaning of the word and try to put it into context.

⊘ HEDGE WORDS

Watch out for critical hedge words, such as *likely, may, can, sometimes, often, almost, mostly, usually, generally, rarely,* and *sometimes.* Question writers insert these hedge phrases to cover every possibility. Often an answer choice will be wrong simply because it leaves no room for exception. Be on guard for answer choices that have definitive words such as *exactly* and *always.*

⊘ SWITCHBACK WORDS

Stay alert for *switchbacks.* These are the words and phrases frequently used to alert you to shifts in thought. The most common switchback words are *but, although,* and *however.* Others include *nevertheless, on the other hand, even though, while, in spite of, despite,* and *regardless of.* Switchback words are important to catch because they can change the direction of the question or an answer choice.

10

⊘ FACE VALUE

When in doubt, use common sense. Accept the situation in the problem at face value. Don't read too much into it. These problems will not require you to make wild assumptions. If you have to go beyond creativity and warp time or space in order to have an answer choice fit the question, then you should move on and consider the other answer choices. These are normal problems rooted in reality. The applicable relationship or explanation may not be readily apparent, but it is there for you to figure out. Use your common sense to interpret anything that isn't clear.

Answer Choice Strategies

⊘ ANSWER SELECTION

The most thorough way to pick an answer choice is to identify and eliminate wrong answers until only one is left, then confirm it is the correct answer. Sometimes an answer choice may immediately seem right, but be careful. The test writers will usually put more than one reasonable answer choice on each question, so take a second to read all of them and make sure that the other choices are not equally obvious. As long as you have time left, it is better to read every answer choice than to pick the first one that looks right without checking the others.

⊘ ANSWER CHOICE FAMILIES

An answer choice family consists of two (in rare cases, three) answer choices that are very similar in construction and cannot all be true at the same time. If you see two answer choices that are direct opposites or parallels, one of them is usually the correct answer. For instance, if one answer choice says that quantity x increases and another either says that quantity x decreases (opposite) or says that quantity y increases (parallel), then those answer choices would fall into the same family. An answer choice that doesn't match the construction of the answer choice family is more likely to be incorrect. Most questions will not have answer choice families, but when they do appear, you should be prepared to recognize them.

⊘ ELIMINATE ANSWERS

Eliminate answer choices as soon as you realize they are wrong, but make sure you consider all possibilities. If you are eliminating answer choices and realize that the last one you are left with is also wrong, don't panic. Start over and consider each choice again. There may be something you missed the first time that you will realize on the second pass.

⊘ AVOID FACT TRAPS

Don't be distracted by an answer choice that is factually true but doesn't answer the question. You are looking for the choice that answers the question. Stay focused on what the question is asking for so you don't accidentally pick an answer that is true but incorrect. Always go back to the question and make sure the answer choice you've selected actually answers the question and is not merely a true statement.

⊘ EXTREME STATEMENTS

In general, you should avoid answers that put forth extreme actions as standard practice or proclaim controversial ideas as established fact. An answer choice that states the "process should be used in certain situations, if…" is much more likely to be correct than one that states the "process should be discontinued completely." The first is a calm rational statement and doesn't even make a definitive, uncompromising stance, using a hedge word *if* to provide wiggle room, whereas the second choice is far more extreme.

11

⌀ BENCHMARK

As you read through the answer choices and you come across one that seems to answer the question well, mentally select that answer choice. This is not your final answer, but it's the one that will help you evaluate the other answer choices. The one that you selected is your benchmark or standard for judging each of the other answer choices. Every other answer choice must be compared to your benchmark. That choice is correct until proven otherwise by another answer choice beating it. If you find a better answer, then that one becomes your new benchmark. Once you've decided that no other choice answers the question as well as your benchmark, you have your final answer.

⌀ PREDICT THE ANSWER

Before you even start looking at the answer choices, it is often best to try to predict the answer. When you come up with the answer on your own, it is easier to avoid distractions and traps because you will know exactly what to look for. The right answer choice is unlikely to be word-for-word what you came up with, but it should be a close match. Even if you are confident that you have the right answer, you should still take the time to read each option before moving on.

General Strategies

⌀ TOUGH QUESTIONS

If you are stumped on a problem or it appears too hard or too difficult, don't waste time. Move on! Remember though, if you can quickly check for obviously incorrect answer choices, your chances of guessing correctly are greatly improved. Before you completely give up, at least try to knock out a couple of possible answers. Eliminate what you can and then guess at the remaining answer choices before moving on.

⌀ CHECK YOUR WORK

Since you will probably not know every term listed and the answer to every question, it is important that you get credit for the ones that you do know. Don't miss any questions through careless mistakes. If at all possible, try to take a second to look back over your answer selection and make sure you've selected the correct answer choice and haven't made a costly careless mistake (such as marking an answer choice that you didn't mean to mark). This quick double check should more than pay for itself in caught mistakes for the time it costs.

⌀ PACE YOURSELF

It's easy to be overwhelmed when you're looking at a page full of questions; your mind is confused and full of random thoughts, and the clock is ticking down faster than you would like. Calm down and maintain the pace that you have set for yourself. Especially as you get down to the last few minutes of the test, don't let the small numbers on the clock make you panic. As long as you are on track by monitoring your pace, you are guaranteed to have time for each question.

⌀ DON'T RUSH

It is very easy to make errors when you are in a hurry. Maintaining a fast pace in answering questions is pointless if it makes you miss questions that you would have gotten right otherwise. Test writers like to include distracting information and wrong answers that seem right. Taking a little extra time to avoid careless mistakes can make all the difference in your test score. Find a pace that allows you to be confident in the answers that you select.

12

⊘ Keep Moving

Panicking will not help you pass the test, so do your best to stay calm and keep moving. Taking deep breaths and going through the answer elimination steps you practiced can help to break through a stress barrier and keep your pace.

Final Notes

The combination of a solid foundation of content knowledge and the confidence that comes from practicing your plan for applying that knowledge is the key to maximizing your performance on test day. As your foundation of content knowledge is built up and strengthened, you'll find that the strategies included in this chapter become more and more effective in helping you quickly sift through the distractions and traps of the test to isolate the correct answer.

Now that you're preparing to move forward into the test content chapters of this book, be sure to keep your goal in mind. As you read, think about how you will be able to apply this information on the test. If you've already seen sample questions for the test and you have an idea of the question format and style, try to come up with questions of your own that you can answer based on what you're reading. This will give you valuable practice applying your knowledge in the same ways you can expect to on test day.

Good luck and good studying!

Educational Vision

Selecting Appropriate Goals

CREATING A CULTURE OF LEARNING

A culture of learning is an environment with an emphasis on learning and a high expectation for academic achievement. It involves intellectual stimulation for students, staff, and leadership. Evidence of a **culture of learning** includes implementing effective classroom instructional strategies for student learning, implementing processes of continuous improvement to increase student learning and academic performance, participating in professional development for teachers and staff collectively and individually, and the acquiring and sharing of knowledge by leadership. When a culture of learning is present, school leaders seek ways to support the learning needs of all students so all can be **academically successful**. School leaders also seek ways to support the learning needs of **teachers and staff** to assist them in their professional growth.

DEVELOPING A CULTURE OF LEARNING

To develop a culture of learning on campus, a school leader must consider this culture in all decision-making. First, the school should be **designed** in a way that facilitates a culture of learning. This means that there are sufficient **learning spaces** to accommodate a variety of learning strategies, along with furniture and resources that support those learning spaces. For example, there should be a library resource center with appropriate shelving, books, and technology resources. A school leader must also hire and train **staff** in a way that supports a culture of learning. Candidates for hire that do not support a culture of learning should not be selected. The leader must also communicate **expectations** for a culture of learning to staff, students, parents, and community stakeholders to ensure that everyone is aware of the expectations. When possible, the leader can support the school's culture by encouraging **families** to develop their own culture of learning and providing the resources and support for them to do so. For example, the leader may give books to families to encourage reading in the home.

SUPPORTING A CULTURE OF LEARNING

SCHOOL VISION

The school vision serves as a guide and a foundation for all strategic planning and communicates the **purpose** and **focus** of the school to all stakeholders. One of the goals of a school leader is to create a culture of learning on campus. Including this concept in the school vision can help to communicate the importance of cultivating a culture of learning to all stakeholders. Also, the school vision will help to guide the creation of **goals** that lead to the development of this culture. A school vision that includes this focus will ensure that school goals are aligned with a culture of learning and will help to establish and maintain the culture. When the school vision clearly incorporates a culture of learning, it will be apparent to all stakeholders that this is a key part of the school's purpose and focus.

SCHOOL GOALS

School goals help to determine where to devote energy and resources. When leaders set goals, they identify the necessary **resources** for achieving them. Goals must be aligned with the **characteristics** and **outcomes** of a culture of learning to ensure that the available resources, such as staff, funds, and time, are used to develop and maintain this culture. Rather than diverting resources to various competing goals, this will maximize the use of resources and effort. When a leader uses school goals to support a culture of learning, the culture will be strengthened as school goals are attained. The various aspects of a culture of learning can be incorporated into the school

15

handwritten notes: What is our vision? student-centered? Prepared for life? real world understanding — PBL

goals. For example, school goals can include high expectations for academic performance, goals related to college and career readiness for students, and implementation of student-centered instructional strategies for teachers.

ENSURING THAT SCHOOL GOALS ARE STUDENT-CENTERED

A leader can employ several strategies to ensure that school goals are student-centered. First, goals should be designed with **student outcomes** as a focus. These can include any outcome that is measured in terms of student-related data, such as academic performance or attendance. For example, a school leader may develop a school goal of increasing the campus attendance rate to 99% for the school year. This goal is directly related to a student outcome and the strategies that would be implemented to achieve this goal would directly benefit students. Second, all school goals should directly **impact students**. When developing goals, it is appropriate to ask how accomplishing the goal would impact students, as well as how students would be affected if the goal were not accomplished. If there is no impact to students, the goal is likely not student-centered. Third, goals should be developed with the purpose of **benefitting all students**. Student-centered goals do not marginalize or omit groups of students but benefit all students. For example, a school leader might set a school goal to increase test performance in reading for all students, not just those who have demonstrated deficiencies in prior performance.

PURPOSE OF A SCHOOL VISION

The purpose of a school vision is to convey the **direction** of the school to all stakeholders. A vision is a message or statement that describes how a leader envisions the school in the future. Through the school vision, the school's **focus** and **priorities** can be conveyed to all stakeholders, including staff, students, and the community. The school vision should inspire and motivate teachers and staff to pursue the school's goals. The school vision also provides direction for the teachers and staff in decision-making processes. All **strategic planning** should be guided by the school vision so that all goals and plans are designed with the purpose of achieving this vision. An example of a school vision is as follows: Our vision at XYZ Middle School is to equip and prepare students to be college and career ready, life-long learners, and responsible global citizens who are exemplary examples of the core values of respect, integrity, and perseverance.

IDENTIFYING VISION AND GOALS BASED ON DATA AND RESEARCH
TYPES OF DATA USED TO DEVELOP A SCHOOL VISION

The majority of data that an education leader will have access to and be expected to analyze is **quantitative data**. This includes student academic performance data, attendance data, demographics, and many other key data points. Quantitative data can be analyzed using mathematical processes and can be represented in numerical form. For example, a school leader may calculate that the campus attendance rate is 96.8% annually or that 1 out of every 10 students receives special education services. Quantitative data can provide answers to "what" or "who" questions, but it cannot provide answers regarding "why" or "how." To understand why the data appears as it does, it is important for leaders to gather **qualitative data** from students, staff, and stakeholders. Qualitative data reflects opinions, perceptions, feelings, and assumptions. For example, a school leader may receive student concern about bullying on campus, or parents and community members may communicate to the school leader that the staff do not seem friendly. Quantitative and qualitative data should be used together to develop the vision for the school.

SOURCES OF DATA USED TO DEVELOP A SCHOOL VISION

There are many sources of quantitative and qualitative data that a leader can use to develop a school vision. Sources of **quantitative data** include student academic performance data, attendance data, demographics, and other key data points. **Student academic performance data** is frequently used in developing a vision. Leaders can obtain this data from historical standardized test performance data, beginning-of-the year assessments in a variety of academic areas, teacher-assigned grades for classroom performance, and benchmark assessments. **Qualitative data** can be obtained from observations of teachers and students, feedback from teachers and students, focus groups, anonymous surveys, and other information from stakeholders. This type of information tells the education leader about school culture, values, attitudes, and beliefs. It should be used as a frame for understanding the quantitative data in order to gain a complete picture of the school's status.

ALIGNING SCHOOL GOALS WITH SCHOOL VISION

The school vision describes how the leadership envisions the school in the future, and the school goals are the ways that the school will accomplish that vision. Each **school goal** should clearly demonstrate that by accomplishing the goal, the campus will be closer to realizing its **vision**. For example, a school may state in its vision that it will be a premier STEM (Science, Technology, Engineering, and Math) school. School leaders should work toward that vision by setting ambitious goals in the areas of science, technology, engineering, and math. **Aligned goals** could include the academic performance of students in these subject areas, increasing STEM course offerings, recruiting students for the STEM program, or earning awards and recognition in STEM competitions. An **unaligned goal** could be expanding the fine arts program. Aligning school goals with the school vision will ensure that all resources and energies are devoted to realizing the vision.

USING DATA FROM MULTIPLE SOURCES

It is important to use data from multiple sources to develop the school vision and goals because one source may portray a **limited** or **skewed** picture of the school. Using multiple sources can confirm the **validity** of data and provide a more complete picture of the complex dynamics of a school campus. For example, a school leader may obtain past academic data showing that fifth grade students have consistently performed at an advanced level. However, additional data may demonstrate that these students were already performing at an advanced level prior to fifth grade and were not growing academically. Additionally, using multiple sources of data can help a leader identify specific areas for **improvement** so that goals are targeted. For example, a leader of a high school may find that incoming ninth-grade students are consistently performing below standard in math. However, investigating which middle schools these students attended may reveal that the struggling students all attended the same middle school. Instead of assuming that math was an area of deficit for the ninth-grade class, this additional data could lead to a more specific goal in which resources are targeted.

INVOLVING STAKEHOLDERS IN DEVELOPING VISION

TYPES OF STAKEHOLDERS

Stakeholders include anyone who has an interest in or is vested in the school. The **primary stakeholders** in schools are the **children** because they are most directly impacted by the decisions made regarding the school, so they should be engaged in the development of the school vision. Another significant group of stakeholders includes the school's **faculty and staff** because they are also directly impacted by the decisions. Other stakeholders include parents, district personnel, school board members, community members, and community business partners. A leader can involve these stakeholders in the development of the school vision by soliciting their **opinions and feedback**. This can be done through one-on-one interviews, focus groups, and community meetings, among other methods, to obtain their perspectives. Stakeholders can be motivated to engage in the development of the school vision when the school leader communicates a desire for their involvement and demonstrates respect for their input and opinions. This requires the school

Mometrix

leader to devote time and opportunity to meet with various stakeholders and to engage in conversation regarding the school vision.

It is important to involve stakeholders in the development of the school vision to incorporate a variety of perspectives and to increase buy-in for the vision. Often, school leaders who are in the process of developing a vision for the school are new to the position, so they cannot be expected to know every aspect of the school dynamics or all the nuances of the campus. It is important to involve stakeholders in the process of developing the vision so that the leader can have as much information as possible. Also, including stakeholders in the process creates **buy-in**. If stakeholders believe that their feelings and opinions have been disregarded in the creation of the vision, they may disengage from the goals aligned to that vision or even oppose it. A leader wants all stakeholders to be **advocates** of the school vision, so stakeholders must be included in the development of the school vision.

REACHING CONSENSUS AMONG STAKEHOLDERS

When engaging stakeholders in the development of the school vision and goals, it can be a challenge to reach **consensus**, especially when viewpoints seem to conflict. It is important for a school leader to clearly communicate how consensus will be fairly achieved. Stakeholders who are aware of the process for providing input before participating will know what to expect and are more likely to be receptive to **compromise** in the event of dissension. Additionally, the leader must be **respectful** of all input and must acknowledge opinions and perspectives, even if they are not aligned with his or her own or the majority. Incorporating **voting processes**, such as an anonymous ballot or online survey, can facilitate the use of the majority's viewpoints without identifying dissenters. Finally, the school leader must convey that, although the stakeholders' input is valued and will be considered, he or she still retains the ultimate **responsibility** for decision-making.

MEETING DIVERSE NEEDS
ADDRESS EQUITY ISSUES RELATED TO RACE, DIVERSITY, AND ACCESS

When developing the school vision and goals, a school leader must ensure that all students—regardless of race, religion, academic background, or education access—will be **successful**. When collecting data to inform the development of the school vision and goals, a school leader should determine whether any groups of students have been **disenfranchised** in the past and, if so, how the school vision and goals can be designed to prevent that disenfranchisement from happening in the future. For example, a school leader may find that historically students who are of limited English proficiency (LEP) have not performed as well as their peers in math on standardized tests. This may necessitate the design of additional goals to support the improvement of LEP students in math. Equity does not mean equality. **Equity** means that some groups of students may need additional resources and support in order for them to meet performance standards. The school vision and goals must take into account the strengths and needs of all students so that all can receive an equitable education and be successful.

IDENTIFYING THE DIVERSE NEEDS OF STUDENTS

Students have diverse needs, and not all of these needs can be predicted based on the students' demographic groups. For example, not all students in poverty have the same needs, nor do all students who speak limited English. The school leader should make an effort to **identify student needs** so they can be addressed in the development of the school's vision and goals. A leader can identify these needs by speaking directly to **students**. This gives students the opportunity to articulate their own needs. Also, the leader can speak with **families** to identify additional student needs. This is particularly helpful when students are young and cannot accurately identify their own needs. Finally, the school leader can observe students in the school and identify **deficit areas** of the school program. For example, the school leader may notice that many students arrive late to

18

Copyright © Mometrix Media. You have been licensed one copy of this document for personal use only. Any other reproduction or redistribution is strictly prohibited. All rights reserved.

school and are tired and hungry when they arrive. The school leader can then use observational data to inform the development of the school goals and vision.

Implementing Vision and Goals

PLAN FOR IMPLEMENTING THE VISION AND GOALS
IMPORTANCE OF DEVELOPING AN IMPLEMENTATION PLAN

To achieve a school vision and goals, a plan must be in place. A well-constructed plan serves as a **guide** for how the goals will be accomplished. Having a plan conveys to stakeholders that the vision and goals are feasible and instills confidence in the campus administration. A plan also serves as a **framework** for directing the actions of a leadership team and campus faculty and staff. Additionally, a leader cannot be everywhere all the time, so having a plan in place ensures that **progress** can be made, even in the leader's absence. Finally, having a plan helps to keep the efforts of leadership and staff **focused**. Many aspects of a school campus can become distractions to the primary goals, and these distractions can cause leaders to divert resources and efforts to the wrong areas. A plan keeps efforts and resources focused and purposeful, which increases the plan's chance of being effective.

COMPONENTS OF AN EFFECTIVE PLAN

An effective plan should include action steps, people responsible, time frames, milestones, resources needed, and evidence of implementation. The **action steps** in a plan should clearly outline what needs to be done to accomplish the plan. These steps should be broken down so that someone who did not participate in developing the plan can understand what needs to be done. An effective plan also identifies the **people responsible** for each aspect of the plan. If no one is held accountable for the actions to accomplish the plan, they likely will not get done. The plan should also be **time bound**. This will help to identify whether the plan is on track for completion. **Milestones** serve as checkpoints that also help to determine the progress of the plan. The plan will include the **resources needed** to accomplish it so that these resources are planned for and obtained. This will prevent delay in accomplishing the plan. Finally, the **evidence of implementation** should be included in the plan so that ongoing monitoring can take place. Evidence of implementation could include documents, visible indicators, or regular meetings, depending on the aspect of the plan.

BARRIERS TO IMPLEMENTING THE VISION AND GOALS EFFECTIVELY

Both expected and unexpected barriers may arise when implementing the vision and goals. It can be **expected** that stakeholders who did not wholeheartedly agree with the creation of the vision and goals may be reluctant to implement the plan to achieve them. This can be a barrier because a lack of support for or direct opposition to the vision and goals can delay progress. Many **unexpected barriers** may also arise. These may include changes in district policy and procedure, changes in state law, shortfalls in school budgets, and staff changes, among others. For example, standardized test performance expectations or adoption of a new test can affect goals. Additionally, the loss of a teacher or the promotion of a leadership team member could also affect the successful implementation of the vision and goals. Some school districts have experienced unexpected loss of instructional time due to inclement weather conditions, creating a barrier to accomplishing school goals.

TYPES OF BARRIERS TO IMPLEMENTING VISION AND GOALS

When planning the implementation of the school vision and goals, the school leader may encounter barriers that will slow the planning process. One barrier is attempting to **analyze too much data**. Data is valuable to the planning process, but an abundance of data can become overwhelming and

19

delay progress. The school leader must identify what data is needed and what can be put aside. Another barrier is the **lack of consensus** from other stakeholders who are providing input to the development of the plan. Stakeholders such as community members, parents, and staff may have conflicting ideas and suggestions related to the development of the vision and goals. The leader must determine which feedback to incorporate in the plan, as not all ideas are sound or can be prioritized. Finally, a barrier that can be difficult to overcome is **garnering support** for the implementation of change on campus. In most instances, a school leader will be appointed in the place of a predecessor who already had a school vision and goals in place. Stakeholders may be resistant to drastic changes in the school vision and goals, so the school leader must overcome these objections to do what is best for the students.

OVERCOMING POTENTIAL BARRIERS

A leader can employ various strategies to overcome potential barriers to implementing the vision and goals effectively. To **overcome a lack of support** for the vision and goals, the leader can include as many stakeholders as possible in their development. This will increase buy-in and communicate the vision and goals often so that stakeholders are reminded of the school's focus. A leader can also include **strategies** in the action plan to address potential barriers, such as loss of staff. For example, a leader can designate teams, rather than individuals, to work on components of the plan. Therefore, if a staff member is lost, other team members can continue implementation of a goal. The leader can also consider **actions or contingency plans** to enact if barriers arise. For example, if a goal requires a designated number of new computers, a leader may consider what to do if a budget shortfall allows for the purchase of only half of the computers.

SUPPORTING THE IMPLEMENTATION BY LEADING BY EXAMPLE

Leading by example can support the implementation of the school vision and goals by inspiring others, conveying priorities, and garnering support from stakeholders. When a leader sets an **example of expected behavior**, staff and students will be inspired to participate and to follow the leader's example, **implementing** the vision and goals in the same way as their leader. This increases the effort devoted to accomplishing the vision and goals. When the leader engages in behaviors that implement the vision and goals, this conveys to stakeholders that the vision and goals are **priorities** because this is where the leader chooses to devote time. When a leader's priorities are clear to stakeholders, it is easier for the leader to encourage them to participate in those prioritized activities and to implement action plans related to those priorities. For example, if a leader makes it evident through his or her own actions that reading instruction is a priority for the campus, then stakeholders will expect and support further initiatives relating to reading instruction. In contrast, when a leader's actions do not match the goals and vision, this results in a mixed message to stakeholders.

ALIGNING HUMAN, FISCAL, AND MATERIAL RESOURCES

The strategies and initiatives for implementing the school vision and goals require **resources**, so a leader must ensure that all human, fiscal, and material resources are aligned to the vision and goals. **Aligning resources to the vision and goals** will ensure fewer barriers to implementation. In contrast, when resources are not aligned to the vision and goals, not only will leaders find it difficult to implement the mission and vision, they will also find that their efforts are diverted to the other areas that the resources have been devoted to. This results in a less significant **impact** of those resources for the benefit of students and the campus as a whole. For example, if the vision for the school is to have state-of-the-art technology for classroom instruction, the leader must ensure that there are qualified staff members who are able to utilize the technology, funds for the purchase of technology hardware and software, and additional resources such as storage and server space for the additional technology. If any aspect of the resources is **misaligned**, there is a possibility that the goal or vision will not be obtained.

Handwritten notes: ① Lead by Example; ② Allign resources, (human, material, fiscal); ③ Delegate

DELEGATING

A leader cannot do an effective job without support. In order to balance the duties and responsibilities of being a campus leader, an effective leader must identify tasks and activities that can be **delegated** to other leadership team members or administrative staff. If a leader does not delegate tasks and responsibilities, he or she may be overwhelmed and unable to meet all of the demands necessary to implement the mission and vision. When a leader designs an **action plan** for accomplishing the vision and goals, he or she must also identify the **staff members** who can complete those actions. For example, another member of the leadership team can be assigned a specific project, such as hosting the quarterly community literacy nights for the school year. Also, a clerical staff person can assist the leader in designing and formatting documents related to a project. The role of the leader is to lead and manage a team that can implement the vision, not to implement the vision independently and individually. Delegation is also important when the leader is not on campus or available. This ensures that the work of accomplishing the vision and goals will continue even in the leader's absence.

MEASURABLE EXPECTATIONS

USING DATA TO SUPPORT MEASURABLE EXPECTATIONS

Data can support the setting and tracking of measurable expectations. When a leader uses data to communicate **expectations** to faculty and staff, it increases the staff's ability to meet those expectations and helps staff to determine if they are meeting expectations. For example, a leader can set the expectation that teachers and staff maintain a 98% attendance rate at work. Setting this measurable expectation makes it easier for staff to self-regulate and also helps leaders to address failure to meet expectations. By using data, a leader can determine if expectations are being met, which can help determine whether the school is on track to **meet or exceed goals**. For example, a leader may expect 90% of students to meet performance standards in reading. If 93% of students meet performance standards, the leader will know that the expectation is being exceeded and it is likely that the school will meet their goal. In contrast, when data is not used to support expectations, it can be difficult to determine progress toward meeting expectations, identify potential areas of weakness, or address failures to meet expectations.

USING MEASURABLE EXPECTATIONS TO IDENTIFY TRENDS AND PATTERNS

The identification of trends and patterns in school performance can be valuable in forming action plans so that decision-making can be targeted and strategic. When expectations are measurable, the data that is collected and analyzed can reveal **patterns and trends**. For example, if a leader were to review student reading progress, using data from the last three assessments, it may be revealed that a particular demographic group is consistently underperforming. This trend can help the leader provide **targeted resources and interventions** to meet the reading performance expectation. Similarly, an analysis of student attendance data may reveal a pattern of poor attendance on rainy days. Identifying this pattern can help the leader to **address the barriers** that rainy days create for student attendance so that students can meet attendance expectations.

MONITORING PROGRESS TOWARD GOALS

A leader must monitor progress toward goals to increase the likelihood of meeting those goals. Leaders should check the **progress** of goals in regular intervals throughout the school year based on these measurable expectations. This allows the leader to determine if the school is **on track** to meet a goal and, if not, allows time to make changes to the action plan. For example, a leader may set an annual goal for 90% of students to meet academic performance expectations in math on standardized tests. This goal could be broken down into measurable expectations, such as performance on particular math standards, which are reviewed at regular intervals, like every three weeks. If a leader were to determine that at least 90% of students were not successful on a

21

particular math standard, this could indicate a danger of not meeting the annual goal. However, because this data was obtained before the administration of the standardized test, the leader has time to develop and implement **interventions** such as math tutorials, increasing the likelihood of meeting the goal.

SUPPORTING HIGH PERFORMANCE EXPECTATIONS

Measurable expectations support high expectations because they clearly define the expectations for students and staff, as well as the standard used to measure the expectation. A measurable expectation can lead to **higher expectations of performance** because it is clear and facilitates monitoring. When expectations are not measurable, the result is ambiguity or confusion. It can be difficult for a person to know if he or she is meeting expectations, and this ambiguity can convey that they will not be monitored. In contrast, when expectations are measurable, a leader can clearly convey how students and staff can meet those expectations and how they will be **monitored**. For example, if a leader sets a general expectation for high student performance in math, teachers may be confused about the performance indicators and subsequently have varying expectations for math performance and how students can demonstrate that performance, such as classwork, homework, and exams. In contrast, a leader could set an expectation that all students will maintain a passing grade in math classes and pass all math exams. The leader can then monitor the expectation by reviewing class and exam grades so that those who are not meeting expectations can be addressed.

DISCRIMINATING BETWEEN VISION AND GOALS THAT ARE MEASURABLE AND NON-MEASURABLE FOR ALL STUDENTS

MEASURABLE VS. NON-MEASURABLE GOALS

Measurable goals can be **quantified** and non-measurable goals **cannot be quantified**. An example of a measurable goal is: 95% of 8th grade students will earn a score of 70% or above on the math benchmark exam. This goal is **measurable** because it can be determined whether or not it was met by calculating the percentage of students who demonstrated the defined proficiency on the exam. It also identifies what **performance** is expected of the students in order to reach the goal. When goals are measurable, it is easy to determine whether or not they have been met. In contrast, a non-measurable goal may be ambiguous, and it may be difficult to determine whether or not it has been met. An example of a **non-measurable goal** is: 8th grade students will be successful on the math benchmark exam. This goal is not measurable because it does not state how students demonstrate success on the benchmark exam, nor how many students must be successful to meet the goal.

CONVERTING NON-MEASURABLE GOALS INTO MEASURABLE GOALS

Non-measurable goals can be converted into measurable goals by making them **quantifiable**. To make goals quantifiable, the leader must determine how **success** is measured for each behavior identified in the goal and how to know that success has been achieved. When a goal involves a **performance standard or assessment**, it should be clearly identified. For example, rather than using the phrase "demonstrate proficiency" in a goal, the leader should identify what constitutes proficiency, such as earning a particular score. Some goals involve behaviors that are not easily quantifiable, such as goals related to culture or attitudes. In these instances, a leader must determine how these behaviors will be measured, such as by **observations or surveys**. For example, a leader may wish all staff to be perceived as courteous. The leader can survey students and parents regarding the courtesy of staff and set a goal of an average rating of 4 out of 5 or greater in the area of courtesy. Alternatively, the leader may use observations to measure the goal, such as requiring front office personal to greet all visitors immediately upon entry 100% of the time.

INEFFECTIVENESS OF NON-MEASURABLE GOALS

Non-measurable goals can often be ineffective because they do not clearly convey how to **achieve the goal** or how one knows when the goal has been achieved. When there is no measure of what constitutes **success**, then those working toward the goal will identify their own perception of success, which may not be in line with the leader's expectations. For example, if the goal is for all 5th grade students to be successful on a test, a leader may expect students to earn scores of 90% or greater and the teacher may expect scores of 70% or greater. In order to ensure clarity of goals and to help develop strategies to reach those goals, the goals must be **measurable**. This ensures that all know the exact target that they are trying to reach and can determine if and when they have reached that target.

School Goals and Local, State, and Federal Policy

UNDERSTANDING LAWS AT VARIOUS LEVELS

RELATIONSHIP BETWEEN FEDERAL, STATE, AND LOCAL EDUCATIONAL LAWS, POLICIES, AND PRACTICES

Almost all aspects of the education process are governed by laws, policies, and practices. **Laws** governing the education process are established at the national and state level and supersede district and campus policies. **Federal laws** take precedence over state laws. **State laws** supplement and complement the federal laws. Local education agencies (LEAs) then interpret federal and state laws to create **policies** for their school districts that help schools to adhere to those laws or to clarify areas that the laws do not explicitly address. Individual campuses create **procedures** to address areas not explicitly outlined by district policy. For example, federal law states that students must be assessed by a standardized exam for grade promotion and graduation. State law dictates which tests the students take and when they are tested. School districts determine the policies for administering those tests, within the guidelines set by the state. Campuses implement district policy and may incorporate their own practices such as cell phone policies, dress code polices, or other school day aspects that are impacted by testing. Whenever there is a conflict between law and policy, law takes precedence.

AREAS OF THE EDUCATION PROCESS IMPACTED BY LAWS

Federal and state laws impact almost every aspect of the education process. Often these laws require additional policies and procedures to ensure adherence to the laws. However, there are specific areas of the education process that are highly **impacted by federal and state law**. These include educating students with disabilities, educating English language learners, standardized testing, student confidentiality, school liability, school performance expectations, technology use, school finance, and many more. School leaders must understand the laws and how these laws can influence the development and implementation of their **vision and goals**. While many school districts develop policies and practices that aid school leaders in adhering to the law, it is the school leader's responsibility to remain current on school law at both the state and federal levels.

IMPACT OF LAWS AND POLICIES ON PROFESSIONAL ETHICS

Federal and state laws dictate the requirements that educators must meet to be certified. As part of these requirements, educators must adhere to ethical codes and standards of behavior. The **ethical codes** address areas such as general conduct, conduct toward colleagues, and conduct toward students. Educators are expected to adhere to these standards of behavior; otherwise, sanctions may be placed on their educator licenses or their licenses and certifications may even be revoked. On any given school day, an education leader may make a number of decisions and must be fully aware of the legal and ethical ramifications of each one. Additionally, school leaders must understand that ethical decision-making is not only a result of personal morals and values but also of **codes and standards of behavior** that are set forth by federal and state government. The code of ethics requires that educators abide by all laws, but some decisions address "gray areas" in which there are no explicit laws, policies, or procedures. In these instances, school leaders must ensure that their decisions align with the educator code of ethics.

DEVELOPMENT OF POLICIES

Schools and school districts often develop policies as a **safeguard** for staff and students. Laws enacted at the federal and/or state level are often broad and subject to interpretation. As a result, policies are developed to **define** specific actions and behaviors that adhere to those laws, with the purpose of trying to ensure that people abide by the law by adhering to policies. Policies are meant to be a **protection** to those who adhere to them. For example, a law may broadly state that schools must administer a confidentially secure assessment of student performance in Math and Reading. The school district may then develop policies to ensure that tests are administered to students in a confidential and secure manner. A person who violates a policy does not necessarily violate a law, but this is possible. School leaders and school staff should abide by local policies as a protection, ensuring that they are adhering to state and federal laws.

RELATIONSHIP BETWEEN VISION AND GOALS WITH LEGAL RESPONSIBILITIES
ALIGNING VISION AND GOALS TO SCHOOL, LOCAL, STATE, AND FEDERAL POLICIES

The school vision and goals must be **aligned** to school, local, state, and federal policies so that they can be legally and ethically accomplished. If the school vision and goals are not aligned to these laws and policies, it is possible that working toward these goals would constitute breaking the law or violating policy. Because laws and policies supersede campus initiatives, it is important to align goals to these so that **resources** can be used efficiently. Even if the misalignment of the goal to the laws and policies does not constitute a violation of the law or policy, it could cause resources and efforts to be diverted, resulting in **loss of efficiency and impact**. For example, students with disabilities may require additional academic services, as dictated in special education law and policy. The campus leader must provide the resources necessary to meet these students' needs, so it would be efficient to align the school's other goals and resources to this requirement.

COMMUNICATING SCHOOL LAWS AND POLICIES TO THE COMMUNITY

It is important to communicate school laws and policies to the community so that they can be **informed** of the requirements and constraints that govern the school leader's actions, decision-making, and goal-setting. The community should be aware of the laws and policies that helped to shape the school leader's vision for the school. The community may be **unaware of laws and policies** that can influence the operations of the school and how these laws and policies may affect the feasibility of their ideas and suggestions. For example, the community may wish to do away with a particular extracurricular sport because of low participation and lack of performance by the athletes, but they may be unaware that certain sports must be offered on campus due to compliance to Title IX of education law. A principal could explain that the current education law requires that the particular sport be offered so that there is no perceived discrimination in sport offerings at the school.

IMPACT OF LAWS, REGULATIONS, POLICIES, AND PROCEDURES ON VISION AND GOALS

Laws, regulations, policies, and procedures should be reviewed and considered during the development and implementation of campus vision and goals. Adherence to these laws and regulations supersede campus initiatives, so it is efficient and effective to align these with the vision and goals to prevent conflict or inefficiency in use of resources. A leader can evaluate these first, and then determine how the vision and goals can be designed in a way to help the school meet or exceed these regulations. For example, if accountability standards require that schools have a passing rate of 90% or above for the state exam in reading, then the school leader should set a goal

to meet or exceed that requirement. If the school leader were to set the school goal at 85%, then meeting the school goal would still cause the school to fail according to state accountability standards. In order to be strategic, a school leader should determine what is **expected** of the school according to law and policy, and then determine how their vision and goals can **align** with those laws and policies.

Communicating and Implementing Vision and Goals

CLEAR COMMUNICATION
IMPORTANCE OF THE CLEAR COMMUNICATION OF THE VISION AND GOALS

It is important to communicate the campus vision and goals clearly so that stakeholders can **understand and support** them. If the vision and goals are unclear, stakeholders may have difficulty determining if they support the vision and goals or may be unsure of what to expect on the campus when the vision and goals are implemented. To communicate clearly, a leader should avoid **technical terms and jargon** that may not be easily understood by stakeholders. For example, a leader can communicate to stakeholders that the campus goal is to increase reading performance, rather than referring to a specific reading program or strategy that may not be familiar to them. Clear communication of campus vision and goals helps to garner **support from stakeholders** for campus initiatives. When communication is clear, the vision and goals can be easily aligned with outside support and resources from the district, community, and state and federal programs.

ENSURING CLEAR COMMUNICATION

A leader will know if the communication of vision and goals to stakeholders is clear and effective by observing the **stakeholders' behavior**. When the vision and goals are clear, stakeholders are more likely to **buy in** to the leader's vision and assist in achieving it. Stakeholders who understand the vision and goals can articulate them in their own words. They will be able to **communicate** the vision and goals to other stakeholders and to the leader. Their behavior will be **aligned** to the vision and goals as well. Also, stakeholders who understand the vision will propose ideas and actions that are aligned to the vision, avoiding those that are opposed or a distraction to the vision. When communication of the vision and goals is clear and effective, all stakeholders will **understand** the vision and goals and how they can participate in achieving them.

HIERARCHICAL COMMUNICATION

Hierarchical communication refers to communicating up and down the chain of command. Leaders **communicate up** by communicating with superiors, such as district office staff or the superintendent. Leaders **communicate down** by communicating with faculty and staff. Communicating with various members of the hierarchy often takes different communication skills. For example, communicating with a supervisor may involve responding to specific requests or demands or demonstrating alignment of campus vision and goals with the school district's vision and initiatives. Communicating up may occur via emails and memorandums, meetings, or visits on campus. In contrast, communicating with faculty and staff requires communicating in a way that inspires them to perform as a team in order to achieve the campus vision and goals. This type of communication also involves holding campus team members accountable for their performance. This communication may occur via emails or memorandums, faculty meetings, or in professional learning communities. Leaders must **recognize their audience** when communicating so that they can use the most effective communication strategy.

COMMUNICATING IMPLEMENTATION OF THE VISION AND GOALS

A leader must ensure that stakeholders are aware of how the various campus initiatives and actions align to the school vision and goals. A leader can do this by frequently and clearly **identifying this**

alignment. This can be communicated in writing or verbally. Campus plans for the implementation of the vision and goals should **identify** the planned initiatives and activities. For example, if the school's vision is to achieve excellence in literacy, the leader could indicate in the campus plan that the school will host a literacy night. At the literacy night, the leader should clearly explain to participants that it is a strategy for achieving the goal of excellence in literacy. The leader could also include the school's vision statement on the agenda for the literacy night. A leader cannot assume that all stakeholders understand the connection between the day-to-day campus activities and the vision and goals. Therefore, the leader needs to **verbally explain the connection** at every opportunity.

COMMUNICATING THE VISION AND GOALS THROUGH OTHERS

A school leader can utilize other people to help communicate the vision and goals. Members of the leadership team can help. Often, these **other school leaders** come into contact with staff and parents more frequently than the principal and therefore have more opportunities to convey the vision and goals. Additionally, parents can be instrumental. **Parent leaders**, such as those who lead parent organizations or are influential in the community, can help to spread the word about the school vision and goals. Also, in diverse communities, **staff members** who speak multiple languages may be utilized to communicate the school vision and goals to parents and community members of a variety of backgrounds. When **stakeholders** hear the vision and goals from people other than the leader, they will perceive that the vision and goals are supported and are more likely to support them as well. In order for this type of communication to be effective, the school leader must ensure that all have a sound understanding of the school vision and goals before sharing them with others.

VERBAL AND NONVERBAL COMMUNICATION

Leaders can clearly communicate the campus vision and goals to stakeholders using verbal, written, and nonverbal communication. Leaders can **communicate verbally** by formally hosting meetings and events that help to share the vision and goals for the campus. Leaders can host community meetings and invite parents, community members, and other stakeholders to attend. These meetings are opportunities for the leader to clarify and elaborate on the vision and goals. Leaders can also hold staff meetings and student assemblies with those on campus. Additionally, the vision and goals should be verbalized at every opportunity. A leader can use **written communication** to communicate the vision and goals, such as in formal reports, emails, and memorandums. For example, some leaders incorporate the school's vision in the footer of formal written documents so that it is always visible. All written communication should align to the vision and reinforce the goals for the campus. Finally, the leader's behavior can serve as **nonverbal communication** of the vision and goals. For example, if the vision of the school is to cultivate students who are life-long learners, then the leader can model this behavior by reading, participating in training, and taking classes.

ASPECTS OF CLEAR COMMUNICATION
TIMELY COMMUNICATION

Timely communication requires proper planning. The **calendar of events** for the school year should be outlined in advance. The leader needs to identify the types of communication to share at various **periods** throughout the year, such as the beginning of the school year, school holidays, testing periods, and others. A leader must also provide **advance notice** so that staff and families can properly prepare and plan for school events and activities. Leaders can provide this advance notice using calendars, announcements, flyers, and phone calls. Communicating in **multiple ways** ensures that the communication is received in a timely manner. There can be an abundance of information about events, activities, and other aspects of the school that needs to be shared with staff, families, and students, so the leader should delegate the aggregation and dissemination of this

information to other staff as necessary. The leader can set expectations for how these staff members communicate to families and students. For example, if a school department hosts an event, the event should be placed on the school calendar, and parents should be informed with sufficient time to prepare for and support the event.

TWO-WAY COMMUNICATION

The act of communication involves a sender and a receiver. If communication is sent but not received, it is not effective. A leader can increase the possibility of effective communication by using a **variety of mediums**. These may include phone calls, meetings, emails, memorandums, and formal letters or documents. Additionally, a leader can survey stakeholders to determine the **preferred mode of communication**. For communication to be deemed effective, leaders must confirm that it has been received. Leaders can request a response or feedback on the communication so that it is acknowledged and the leader can be sure that the message was received in the intended way. Effective communication also means that the leader can be the **receiver** of communication, not just the sender. Leaders should be open to taking phone calls, responding to emails, or participating in meetings that allow others to communicate with them. When the leader acts as the receiver, he or she should acknowledge that the message was received so the sender is aware that the communication was effective.

HANDLING MISCOMMUNICATION

If the leader becomes aware of a miscommunication, he or she should act immediately to correct it. Failing to correct a miscommunication can lead to confusion, conflict, and lack of engagement in and support of the school program. First, the leader should **identify the miscommunication**. Then the leader should make an effort to **correct** it by acknowledging that the message was not sent properly and providing the correct message. For example, a school leader could notify parents that the school's art program would not be part of the vision for the upcoming school year, and the parents might infer that the art program would be eliminated. The school leader should inform parents that the art program will not be eliminated and then explain how it would be affected in the upcoming school year. The school leader should also assume **responsibility** for the initial ineffective communication.

CULTURE OF LEARNING

It is the leader's goal to develop a culture of learning on campus. The leader must incorporate this goal into the school vision and goals. As a result, when there is **evidence of a culture of learning** on campus, this is also evidence that the leader's vision and goals are being implemented. In a culture of learning, both adults and students work toward **learning goals** and are self-motivated to achieve these goals. They also have access to the necessary **resources** to support and drive engagement in the learning process. Evidence of the culture of learning includes **students and staff** who are goal-oriented and self-motivated to learn and engage in the learning process, who have motivation to perform at the highest levels academically, and who perform skilled use of available resources to engage in the learning process. When these are present, it will be evident that the vision and goals can be accomplished.

SUPPORTING A CULTURE OF LEARNING BY COMMUNICATING THE VISION AND GOALS TO STAKEHOLDERS

When the vision and goals are communicated effectively to stakeholders, they can in turn support the culture of learning. When stakeholders know and understand the vision, they can identify how to **support** it and help to **develop the culture of learning**. For example, if a business stakeholder in the community becomes aware of the school's vision to implement technology in the classroom to develop a culture of learning, he or she may decide to donate computers for a computer lab. Had

the stakeholder not known that the school could benefit from the donation, he or she may not have taken that action. All stakeholders may not be in a position to give to the school, but they can support the culture of learning through their **participation** in school and community events and by **advocating** for the school and its needs to school and government representatives. Communicating the vision and goals to stakeholders increases the number of people who can offer their support in implementation.

Roles, Delegation, and Accountability

MODELS OF LEADERSHIP
IMPACT OF A LEADER'S PERSONAL VALUES AND BELIEFS ON THE EFFECTIVENESS OF LEADERSHIP

A leader's personal values and beliefs shape his or her behavior, as well as expectations from staff and students. One's personal beliefs will dictate what is **prioritized** as a leader and as a campus team. If the leader's values and beliefs reflect positive attributes, these can have a positive impact on the effectiveness of leadership. In contrast, beliefs and values that are contrary to district and community norms can make it difficult to lead effectively. Additionally, if **staff members** have values and beliefs that are contrary to the leader's, they may find it difficult to follow the leader. For example, if the leader values reading and believes that everyone should be an avid reader, he or she would likely emphasize and prioritize reading initiatives and be effective in promoting reading on campus. On the other hand, if a leader did not personally value a characteristic such as punctuality in staff and students, that leader may have difficult effectively enforcing promptness among staff and students on campus. The leader's values and beliefs are often demonstrated in the school mission and vision, as well as through the leader's words and actions.

ACTING AS A ROLE MODEL

People observe the leader's behavior for **alignment** between his or her words and actions. This alignment is necessary for a leader to be viewed as genuine and authentic. The leader serves as a **role model** for both staff and students. For **staff**, the leader should exemplify the mission and vision of the school through behavior and words. The leader should also set the example in adhering to campus and district policy, like those described in the employee handbook. Additionally, the leader should set the example for **campus culture**, such as how staff members treat one another and students. For **students**, the leader is a role model in dress, conduct, speech, and other areas. Many people in the community may look up to the leader as well as an example to follow. As a role model, the leader's behavior can influence the behavior of others as he or she comes into contact with them.

SERVANT LEADER

A servant leader is a person who leads by **serving others first**. A servant leader identifies the team's needs by assessing the team or listening to team members and then meets those needs. Meeting the team's needs helps to equip them to get their job done effectively and efficiently. A servant leader shares power through **empowering** others to be effective and by providing them with the tools and resources to be effective. This is in contrast to a leader who exerts authority over others in a "top-down" approach. A servant leader is often found **participating** in the work with the team, both to support the team and to experience the team members' jobs. A faculty with a servant leader is more likely to feel more confident in their ability to do their job because their leader has empowered and equipped them and does not micromanage their work. Servant leaders are often described as caring, compassionate, thoughtful, and humble.

28

TRANSACTIONAL AND TRANSFORMATIONAL LEADERSHIP STYLES

Transactional and transformational leadership styles are very different and produce different results from team members. **Transactional leaders** are most concerned about how to effectively implement and perform under the current rules, policies, and procedures, whereas transformational leaders are focused on change and improvement. Transactional leaders emphasize compliance and monitor progress toward goals using systems of rewards and punishment. These leaders can be task-oriented or focused on results only. These types of leaders can become micromanagers. In contrast, **transformational leaders** focus on the staff behaviors that lead to success. They focus on organizational values and implementation of the mission and vision in order to meet goals. These types of leaders focus on growing staff members in order to meet goals and solicit staff buy-in in the decision-making process. There are pros and cons of each leadership style and many leaders alternate between these leadership styles or blend them together in order to lead effectively.

SHARED LEADERSHIP

Shared leadership is the **delegation** of authority and responsibility to other team members. This type of leadership is the opposite of **authoritarian leadership** or micromanaging. Instead, a leader will appoint people with particular leadership responsibilities and grant them the authority to fulfill those responsibilities. For example, the school leader may ask a skilled teacher to lead a curriculum revision process and supervise a group of other teachers on the task. When sharing leadership, responsibility can be delegated to any staff persons who are capable of fulfilling the role. It is not dependent on job titles. Shared leadership also involves including team members in the leader's **decision-making processes**. This means that the school leader may solicit opinions, ideas, and feedback from staff members before making a decision. This can be accomplished through focus groups, appointing advisors, or taking votes during meetings.

USING A VARIETY OF ROLES TO ACCOMPLISH VISION
CAMPUS ROLES THAT CAN HELP ACCOMPLISH THE VISION

Many roles are performed on campus to ensure that day-to-day activities are carried out. Each of these roles can contribute to accomplishing the **school vision**. Some of the roles include the administrative team, school counselors, teacher leaders, and support staff. The **administrative team** is essential in accomplishing the vision because projects and assignments that directly impact the vision and school goals can be delegated to them. These administrators have the authority and training to support the leader in leading the campus to success. **School counselors** can help accomplish the vision by supporting the psychosocial needs of students so that they can be their best, academically and socially. School counselors are often part of the team that handles student scheduling and post-graduation plans, so they can help students meet the expectations associated with campus goals. **Teacher leaders** can also help to accomplish the vision by leading, encouraging, and supporting their fellow teachers. Finally, **support staff** can help accomplish the vision by ensuring that plan logistics are appropriate, communication is timely and effective, and staff and stakeholders feel supported and equipped to implement the vision.

DISTRIBUTING RESPONSIBILITY AND THE ROLE OF SHARED VISION
HELPING GOAL IMPLEMENTATION WITH A SHARED VISION

A vision can be shared in two ways. In the **development** of a vision, the leader can solicit the **opinions and feedback** of stakeholders so that a variety of perspectives, opinions, and beliefs can be incorporated into the vision. When the vision is developed in this manner, participants can see their contribution to the vision by the way that it is articulated and implemented. A vision is also shared when a leader effectively **communicates** the vision, the rationale for the vision, and the plans for implementing the vision to stakeholders. When a vision is shared, this can assist with **goal implementation** because of buy-in from stakeholders. People are more willing to agree with and participate in plans that they helped to develop. Additionally, having a shared vision means that stakeholders will understand it well enough to work toward goal implementation, even without direct supervision from the leader. They will be able to take action to advance toward the campus goals.

IMPORTANCE OF DELEGATING TASKS AND RESPONSIBILITIES

Leading a campus is a great responsibility that cannot be done alone. To lead effectively, a leader must **delegate** tasks and responsibilities. Delegation is important because a leader does not have the time or resources to perform all responsibilities alone. Most initiatives require a **team** of people to get the job done in a timely and efficient manner. Delegation is also important because a leader will not have all of the **skills** necessary to perform every task. For example, a project may require computer networking expertise, which the leader may not have. In order for projects to be completely effective, tasks and responsibilities should be delegated according to **skillsets**. Delegation is also important because there are tasks and responsibilities that only the leader can perform, so his or her time should **prioritize** these types of activities. Other activities that can be accomplished by other team members should be delegated whenever possible. Delegation also ensures that the campus will run efficiently in the **absence** of the leader, such as during a meeting or other event.

RELATIONSHIP BETWEEN DELEGATION AND ACCOUNTABILITY

For delegation to be effective, a leader must hold team members **accountable**. A leader cannot delegate tasks and responsibilities without checking on the progress, or he or she may discover too late that the job was not done or did not meet expectations. Instead, a leader can incorporate accountability into delegation. This can be done by setting regular **check-in dates** with team members to meet about task progress, providing the leader with an opportunity to give feedback. The leader can also set certain **milestones** that must be accomplished to demonstrate progress. The leader should emphasize to the team member that **completion** of the project is his or her responsibility and that completion is a reflection of job performance. When a leader includes accountability through regular check-ins, pre-established milestones, and communication of responsibility, the team member will be clear about expectations and able to perform the delegated task, and the leader will be reassured that the job is being completed to satisfaction.

RELATIONSHIP BETWEEN DELEGATION AND AUTHORITY

For effective delegation of tasks and responsibilities, those responsible must have the appropriate **authority** to accomplish the tasks. Often, the projects that need to be delegated are not ones that can be done independently. They require the **coordination** of other people and resources. It may be necessary for the school leader to expressly communicate to the person to whom the task is delegated as well as those assisting that the project leader has the authority to implement the project. This will help those leading the project to have **confidence** in their ability to get the job done. For example, if a project requires the scheduling of a community meeting, the project leader would need the authority to secure the venue, make purchases, and gather volunteers for the event. Providing team members with authority enables them to accomplish their delegated tasks with little to no dependence on the school leader. In contrast, when a project leader does not have the appropriate authority to get the project done, the project could be delayed or remain incomplete, waiting on assistance from the school leader.

MONITORING AND COMMUNICATING ABOUT PROGRESS TOWARD THE GOAL
EFFECTIVELY MONITORING GOAL PROGRESS

A leader effectively monitors goal progress by implementing clear checkpoints and milestones in goal activities. Each goal should be broken down into smaller goals, or **milestones**, that can be reviewed in regular intervals. This allows the leader to analyze progress toward the goal in a timely manner so that, if progress is insufficient, there is time to intervene and make changes to the action steps. For example, if the campus goal is to achieve a 90% passing rate on reading assessments for third-grade students, the campus leader would want established milestones to monitor reading progress throughout the school year. The leader may review reading data every three weeks to determine if third-grade students are reaching and maintaining a 90% passing rate in reading. If not, the leader could implement additional strategies to increase the support for reading instruction. **Checkpoints** for goals are often aligned with grading periods, as identified on the school academic calendar.

EFFECTIVELY COMMUNICATING GOAL PROGRESS

Goal progress should be communicated effectively and in a timely manner, especially to those who are instrumental in achieving the goal. First, the school leader should **monitor goal progress** closely so that it can be communicated in a timely manner. Communicating goal progress is pointless if it is done with no time left to make adjustments. The school leader should **communicate progress consistently**, whether positive or negative. Communicating **positive goal progress** is encouraging to others and reassures them that their actions are appropriate. This can serve as positive reinforcement that may even increase staff performance. In contrast, communicating **negative goal progress** is necessary so that corrections can be made. When communicating goal progress, conducting **in-person** conversations or meetings is beneficial because it allows for two-way communication. During these conversations, the school leader may discover unexpected barriers and challenges that need to be addressed.

Revising Goals

ADJUSTING VISION, GOALS, IMPLEMENTATION, AND COMMUNICATION STRATEGIES
CONTINUOUS IMPROVEMENT

The process of continuous improvement is the ongoing act of assessing performance and adjusting efforts to improve that performance. With a process of **continuous improvement**, parts of the work process can be addressed before they begin to fail. Low-performing processes are improved as well as performance that is considered acceptable. All aspects of the work process are examined to determine where improvements can be made to reach **excellence**. To implement a process of continuous improvement, **procedures of evaluation** must be developed and implemented at regular checkpoints. Based on these evaluations, the leadership team can identify areas of improvement and initiate **interventions and actions** based on these areas. In schools, the regular evaluation of process toward the campus vision and goals can be developed into a process of continuous improvement. However, campus leaders must focus on both the strengths and weaknesses of the campus in this process. Deficient areas can be improved to perform to standard and areas performing at standard can be innovated for improvement.

EFFECTIVELY MONITORING PROGRESS

A leader can effectively monitor progress by planning regular checkpoints, analyzing data, and actively engaging in the work. The leader must plan in advance when to check progress on the projects and tasks that are being implemented on campus. This monitoring should include the projects that the leader is working on as well as those that have been delegated to others. These

31

checkpoints should occur with enough frequency that adjustments can be made in a timely manner. The leader must also **analyze data** on a regular basis. All goals should have measurable metrics, which means that data points can demonstrate whether the goal is on track to be achieved. Therefore, a leader must be skilled at analyzing data and making decisions based on it. Finally, a leader can effectively monitor progress by viewing the work and **engaging** in it firsthand. For example, if a campus goal is to reduce the number of students who are tardy, the school leader may engage in morning duty to monitor the arrival and attendance tracking of students. This engagement can add context to the data and help the leader to identify areas of improvement.

FACILITATING SELF-DIRECTED CHANGE AND IMPROVEMENT ON CAMPUS

Self-directed change and improvement can help achieve the campus vision and goals. Staff members who can make changes and improvement to their practice on their own do not require as much **intervention** of campus leaders and coaches as other staff members, freeing those resources to be utilized in other areas. To succeed on their own, staff members must be fully aware of the **campus visions and goals** and the **expectations** placed on them in pursuit of those goals. A leader can facilitate self-directed change and improvement by providing **adequate staff resources**, such as instructional resources and professional development opportunities. The leader must also provide staff members with **access to data** for monitoring progress and performance. Finally, the leader must develop a **culture and climate of self-improvement** in which staff are comfortable revealing weaknesses and taking risks to improve their practice.

HELPING WITH ADJUSTMENT OF THE VISION AND GOALS BY SELF-REFLECTION

Self-reflection is the process of examining one's self in relation to a desired expectation of performance. This process can help with **adjusting the vision and goals** when it is completed by those responsible for carrying out tasks and projects related to the vision and goals. Self-reflection can help to determine whether the goals should be **revised** or if they or the people striving toward the goals need **improvement**. For example, if a campus goal is to improve reading instruction, reading teachers could engage in self-reflection to determine if they are implementing the action plan with fidelity and are teaching to their best ability. If not, the teachers would engage in **self-directed change** to meet the goal. In contrast, if the reading teachers were faithfully implementing the action plan and performing to the best of their ability, this could indicate that the goal itself and its associated strategies may require revision to meet the students' needs. When all staff members engage in self-reflection, it becomes easier for the campus as a whole to make changes and improve.

SYSTEMATICALLY REVIEWING AND REVISING GOALS

Goals are not concrete and should be reviewed and revised periodically. A leader can examine goals to determine whether a campus is likely to **achieve or exceed** them. A leader can also determine whether goals are in complete **alignment** with the vision of the schools. Just as a leader regularly monitors the activities implemented for the completion of the goal, the leader will need to examine the goals themselves. Since a goal is measurable, the leader can determine if the **current data** shows that the campus is on track for meeting it. The leader may observe unexpected **barriers** to achieving the goal that require a revision or the setting of an additional goal. For example, if the school sets a goal for reading performance, the leader may notice that students receiving special education services are not performing as well as students who do not receive these services, and that their reading performance is contributing to a low overall reading performance goal. The leader may then create a new goal that specifically addresses the needs of this student population with its own set of strategies and interventions.

DETERMINING IF COMMUNICATION STRATEGIES NEED TO BE ADJUSTED

Communication of the vision and goals to all stakeholders is critical to the successful achievement of the vision and goals. The leader will know that communication strategies need to be adjusted if

32

staff members have difficulty **articulating** or **implementing** the goals and vision. All staff members should be able to discuss the campus goals and vision among themselves and with other stakeholders. If they are unable to do this, it is possible that communication was not **effective** initially or that subsequent communication of changes and adjustments to the vision and goals was ineffective. Another indication that communication strategies need adjustment is difficulty for staff members in **implementing the action plans** related to the vision and goals. If they are unclear about what is expected of them or what steps they need to take to meet expectations, these aspects of the action plan may not have been conveyed clearly. Communicating effectively removes **barriers to implementation**.

GATHERING DATA AND IDENTIFYING STRONG AND WEAK AREAS
IDENTIFYING STRENGTHS AND WEAKNESSES OF CAMPUS PERFORMANCE

The school leader can use quantitative, anecdotal, and observational data to identify the strengths and weaknesses of campus performance. This involves regular reporting of **student performance data** and other data points related to key areas such as attendance and discipline. This data is usually analyzed in relation to goal setting and review, so leaders can actively identify the **strengths and weaknesses** of the campus when this data is reviewed. Also, other team members or district office personnel might convey areas of strength or weakness to the leaders based on their campus experiences. These people may share how a particular teacher or department is performing or provide feedback regarding a system or process on campus. Also, a leader may make **observations on campus** to help identify areas of strength or needed improvement. For example, a leader may participate in lunch duty in the cafeteria and observe processes that need to be improved. A leader should refer to **multiple sources of data and evidence** to develop a holistic view of the strengths and weaknesses of campus performance.

ADDRESSING IDENTIFIED STRENGTHS ON CAMPUS

A leader should address identified strengths on campus by using them as opportunities for praise and reinforcement, as well as leverage for improvement. Effective leaders encourage staff by praising and celebrating **achievements** and recognizing **strengths**. This motivates staff members to continue the effective performance. For strengths to remain as strengths, a leader must recognize them and **reinforce** the actions and attitudes that led to their achievement. The leader can also use these strengths as **leverage** for making improvements. For example, if the third-grade reading teachers have consistently achieved high performance in reading, this can be recognized and praised. Then the strategies that these teachers implement in the third-grade classroom can be analyzed for application to the other grade levels. Reinforcing and praising strengths builds confidence in team members, helping them to address needed improvements on campus. Similarly, the skills that are effective in building the strengths can also be applied to areas of weakness.

ADDRESSING IDENTIFIED WEAKNESSES ON CAMPUS

Weaknesses identified on campus must be addressed to improve them. However, this should be done strategically to avoid demoralizing team members. If a leader identifies multiple weaknesses, they can be **prioritized** rather than attempting to address all of the weaknesses at once. Attempting to address all at one time can be overwhelming to team members. When developing plans to address weaknesses, the leader needs to identify how the **strengths** of the campus and the individual team members can be used to improve the areas of weakness. For example, a campus may be having difficulty with classroom management, but certain teachers may be effective classroom managers. These teachers can be used to develop a campus-wide strategy for addressing this area of weakness. Similarly, the campus may demonstrate weakness in math performance, but strength in reading performance. The campus leader can identify the strategies that make reading performance effective and implement them in math instruction.

USING SCHOOL ACCOUNTABILITY MEASURES TO IDENTIFY STRENGTHS AND WEAKNESSES

The purpose of school accountability measures is to ensure that all students are learning and performing according to predetermined standards. These **measures of accountability** are standardized, and the state and federal governments provide **assessments** of schools based on these accountability standards. School leaders can use these school reports to identify areas of strength and weakness in the school programming as measured by performance on state-mandated assessments. For example, the school leader may review the school's accountability ratings and find that the third-grade class did not perform according to expectations in reading. Based on that information, the leader can identify which teachers taught third-grade reading, what curriculum was used, and other factors that may have impacted students' scores. That information can then be used to determine what aspects of the third-grade reading program are strong and which are weak and need improvement. School accountability measures are a critical means of determining a school's strengths and weaknesses.

IMPLEMENTING CHANGE

PROFESSIONAL DEVELOPMENT

To implement change, identifying areas for improvement is not enough. Staff members need to know what they can do to improve their practice. As a result, **professional development** can help a leader implement change. When leaders participate in professional development themselves, they can learn how to be better leaders and how to implement new or better instructional practices on campus. When teachers and other staff participate in professional development, they can also learn how to grow as professionals and implement **improved instructional strategies** in the classroom. Leaders should tailor professional development to meet the needs of the staff and to address campus weaknesses. Leaders should also offer opportunities for **staff members** to participate in individualized and group professional development, organized by content area, grade level, or shared strengths or weaknesses. Also, leaders should implement professional development in innovative ways, such as coaching, modeling, book talks, and other professional development strategies.

STUDYING RESEARCH-BASED AND PROVEN BEST PRACTICES

Areas of deficit or weakness on campus often result from a lack of knowledge rather than a lack of capability. Leaders and team members must continually learn about their practice and how they can improve and should search for successful strategies that can be implemented on their campus. To address weak areas, it is better to implement strategies that are backed by **research** and have been **proven** to obtain good results. This can save the campus the time, effort, and resources that could be wasted if untested, unproven strategies are implemented unsuccessfully. When a leader is looking for strategies to foster change on campus, using research-based, proven best practices is beneficial because there will be **clear direction** for successfully implementing the strategy as well as an idea of the expected results. When untested strategies are implemented, the outcome is less sure. Untested strategies also often take more research and a process of trial and error to implement, also known as a learning curve, both of which can delay the implementation of change.

ENLISTING SUPPORT FOR CHANGE ON CAMPUS

A leader cannot bring about campus change alone. To make changes happen, the leader must enlist support. Fostering change as a **change agent** requires leaders to be strategic in how they communicate the change and how they garner supporters for it. First, the leader needs to **communicate** the change effectively. Many people are unwilling to support changes because they fear the unknown. The leader should not only communicate what is to be changed, but also how it will affect the various staff members and how they are aligned to the vision and goals. Next, the leader needs to gather other leaders within the team and **persuade** them to support the change.

34

Leaders on campus may carry official titles of leadership or simply have influence over other staff members. Enlisting the support of these people will positively affect the perceptions of the remaining staff. Lastly, the leader needs to be a constant **advocate** of change and **participate** in it. Staff members will watch the leader to see if the desire for change is authentic and long-lasting. They will be more likely to support it when they observe that the leader is serious about change.

ANTICIPATING AND PREPARING FOR WHEN TO IMPLEMENT CHANGE

When implementing change, a school leader should anticipate and prepare for **varying levels of support**, as well as direct **opposition** to the change. Some team members will be as **enthusiastic** about the change as the leader. The leader should be prepared to leverage these team members by encouraging them, providing them with resources necessary to implement the changes, and using them to influence the other team members. Some team members will be **indecisive** about the change and not quite ready to support it. The leader should be prepared to spend more time and resources on this group to help encourage them to support the change. This group may require additional communication strategies and support to bring them on board. The school leader should also anticipate a third group of staff members who are **opposed** to the change and may even be vocal in their opposition. The school leader should be prepared to defend the change and offer rebuttals to arguments against it, both publicly and privately. The majority of the leader's focus should be on the first two groups; however, the oppositional group can be detrimental to the progress of the first two groups if it is not addressed appropriately.

MODELING OPENNESS TO CHANGE

The leader is a model on campus and team members will imitate his or her attitudes. If a leader would like the staff to be open to proposed change, he or she must also be a **model of openness to change**. There are many ways to accomplish a goal, and just because something is working does not mean that it cannot be improved. Changes may be proposed by team members other than the leader, from the school district, or even from the state. In these instances, the leader should model openness to change. The leader can be **receptive** to the proposed change and **optimistic** as to how the change can positively affect the campus. The leader can also demonstrate a **positive attitude** during the change, should it be implemented. The leader can expect a similar response from staff if change is proposed on campus, so leadership should model the qualities and attitudes they desire from staff. In contrast, if the leader is not open to change, staff will likely imitate that attitude and be opposed to changes proposed by the leader.

Trends in Education

CURRENT TRENDS IN EDUCATION

TECHNOLOGY

ONE-TO-ONE TECHNOLOGY MODEL

The one-to-one technology model is the practice of providing a **device or access to technology** to each student on campus. As technology use has increased in schools, access to technology has been a focal point to aid in student performance and growth. In many instances, school leaders calculate the **ratio** of computers or devices to students. For example, the school may purchase enough computers to ensure that there is one computer for every 10 students. When there are not enough devices on campus for every student, computer and internet access may be limited due to the need to share technology on campus. This may be done by equipping classrooms with a limited number of computers, making laptop carts available, or creating computer labs, all of which must be shared by teachers and students. With the one-to-one technology model, the ratio of technology to students is **one device for each student**. This allows **maximum access to technology** on campus. These devices are usually personal laptop computers or tablets. In some instances, the students are

entrusted with the technology and are permitted to take the devices home for technology access outside of school hours.

BRING-YOUR-OWN-DEVICE TECHNOLOGY MODEL

The bring-your-own-device technology model describes the practice of allowing students to bring their own **technology devices** to school for use in classroom instruction. Many families provide their children with computers, tablets, and phones that can access the internet. When this model is implemented, students can bring these devices to school and use them to participate in computer-based or web-based activities. The bring-your-own-device model is **beneficial** because it saves schools from purchasing the number of devices necessary for every student to have access. The **downside** of this model is that the school is not responsible for the care or repair of students' devices, not all students have a device, and there is often difficulty in designing lessons compatible with various types of technology. For example, there are different specifications for playing videos on tablets, laptops, and phones, which can be challenging to a teacher attempting to incorporate videos into the lesson. Also, this model has **limited efficacy** in impoverished communities, in which the majority of students do not have access to these devices.

VIRTUAL SCHOOL MODEL

The virtual school model is the practice of providing **online courses** to students, using a web-based platform or other computer-based program rather than physically attending a class. A student has access to instructional content online and participates in activities and tests to assess learning. In some virtual school models, students have **virtual access to a teacher**. In other models, the computer program is **automated** and student progress may be self-paced. Virtual school has been used in all grade levels as a supplement to traditional instruction or as a replacement. Virtual school can also be utilized for students who are home schooled. When used as a supplement to traditional classes, students may use virtual school to make up failed courses, participate in tutorials or interventions, or to access courses that are not offered on campus. The virtual school model requires that students have access to a technology device and internet service. Many **businesses** also develop platforms and coursework for virtual schools. Most commonly, courses focus on the core content areas of reading, math, social studies, and science, but many learning platforms offer electives and tutorial programs.

BLENDED LEARNING

Blended learning is the process of incorporating **technology use** into **traditional classroom instruction**. In the blended learning model, teachers identify places in the lesson that can be **supplemented** with technology or in which technology can be used to drive the lesson. In this model, the teacher may use the technology in the lesson, but the focus is on students utilizing technology in the classroom. For example, a teacher may deliver content on a topic and then assess students' understanding with an online assessment tool. In the blended learning model, technology can be used to deliver content, such as accessing information through reading and videos or by creating slideshows or other presentations. Technology can be used to **assess** student learning as well. Blended learning models are often paired with **project-based learning models**. This allows students the freedom and opportunity to use the technology with limited guidance by the teacher to meet lesson objectives. In the blended learning model, technology use is **flexible**, so it may vary by content area or lesson as teachers still implement traditional instructional strategies.

SCHOOL DISCIPLINE
ROLE OF MEDITATION IN SCHOOLS

Meditation is the act of engaging in quiet and silent thought or reflection. This practice has been used in schools as a strategy for **redirecting poor student behavior**. When a student breaks a school rule or disrupts class, rather than discipline with in-school suspension, out-of-school

36

suspension, or other traditional consequences, the student is instructed to **meditate**. When students are given the opportunity to meditate, they are placed in a quiet environment where they can focus on calming down, breathing, and thinking about appropriate behaviors to display. Schools that have implemented meditation as a discipline strategy have seen a decrease in suspension rates and fewer discipline referrals from teachers. The practice of meditation is thought to alleviate **emotional issues** such as anxiety, anger, depression, and frustration, which could be sources of student misbehavior.

CHALLENGES OF PROMOTING SCHOOL SAFETY

It is a school leader's primary responsibility to keep students safe while at school. This responsibility can be challenging for a variety of reasons. Recent acts of school violence have caused educators and government officials to revisit laws, policies, and procedures relating to school safety. In some schools, **metal detectors** are used to promote school safety, but some deem that practice to be controversial. As schools are built or remodeled, **school designs** include limited entrances and exits to the school building and compartmentalized front office areas that can prevent unauthorized people from gaining entrance into the school. Other strategies include staffing **uniformed police officers** on campus during school hours, implementing **standardized dress**, and limiting **backpacks and other large bags** on campuses. Additionally, many schools practice **drills** for emergencies, such as having an intruder on campus. Promoting school safety is challenging because even the best preventative measures cannot guarantee that nothing will threaten the safety of students and staff.

CURRICULAR PROGRAMMING
ACCELERATED LEARNING

Accelerated learning is the practice of delivering content to students at an **accelerated pace**. For example, a traditional high school course that is delivered during an 18-week semester may be condensed into six or nine weeks. The purpose of accelerated learning is to provide students with **additional learning opportunities**. For example, if a student is already proficient in math, it can be reasoned that he or she should not have to sit through an 18-week course. Accelerated learning is also useful for students who have previously taken a course but were unsuccessful. These accelerated classes may be offered during summer breaks or built into the school's instructional program. Accelerated programs are often facilitated with **technology-based programs**, which can personalize and deliver content based on a student's needs. For example, a student enrolled in an accelerated course may take a pre-assessment online and then be assigned coursework based on assessment performance. A student would not have to complete coursework in areas of the course in which mastery is demonstrated.

SCHOOL-WITHIN-A-SCHOOL MODEL

A school-within-a-school model describes the creation of a specialized school program to be operated on the **same campus** as the traditional school program. The students participating in the specialized program are still students of the school, but may have limited or no interaction with the rest of the student body. For example, a high school may implement an engineering-based program on campus to which students must apply and be accepted. Students participating in this program will attend school on campus, but their classes, course pathways, and other activities are **separate** from the remainder of the student body. A school may have several schools within the school or just one. Each of these schools may be designated with its own budget, programming, and administration. In most models, the schools are still identified as one school for state and federal accountability purposes. However, some schools and school districts have extended the model and created an entirely separate school housed on the same campus. In these instances, the school programs are separate and only share the use of the school facilities.

PROJECT-BASED LEARNING

Project-based learning is the instructional practice of assigning projects to students as a means of driving instruction. In **project-based learning**, students are presented with a problem that must be solved. They are usually assigned to **groups or teams** for completion of the project. To solve this problem, students have to learn content, usually from more than one content area, and demonstrate **mastery of a variety of objectives and skills**. The teacher who has assigned the project delivers certain content to students and often provides access to designated resources. Students are responsible for extending their learning and conducting research, using the available resources and the internet. The project is generally complex and can take as little as a few days to complete, or an entire school semester. With more complex project assignments, teachers expect students to demonstrate mastery of a greater number of learning objectives. Therefore, there may be multiple performance expectations for the project, such as papers, presentations, and more. Some schools integrate project-based learning into the curriculum, while other schools have designed their entire curriculum around project-based learning.

FLIPPED CLASSROOM MODEL

A flipped classroom model describes the instructional practice of changing the **delivery** of instructional content and the opportunities for **guided practice** within the lesson cycle. In a traditional classroom, a teacher delivers the content and may provide limited guided practice on an in-class assignment. The student may be assigned extended practice independently within the class or in the form of homework. In a flipped classroom model, the student is provided with the instructional content **electronically**, typically in the form of a recorded lecture or presentation video to watch outside of the classroom. In the classroom, the time that would have been dedicated to delivering content is used to support the student in **guided practice**. This allows the students more time and access to the teacher during the aspect of the lesson in which they are likely to need the teacher's guidance the most. This practice is considered a flipped classroom because in essence the lesson is done at home and the homework is done at school. Many schools have incorporated flipped lessons into their curriculum sparingly, while other schools have transformed their entire curricular program using the flipped classroom.

CHARTER SCHOOLS

A charter school is a specialized public school that operates according to a **charter** with a local or national organization. The charter may dictate how the school operates and whom it serves. Charter schools are **publicly funded**, which means they have to meet state and/or federal accountability standards. However, unlike traditional public schools, charter schools do not obtain funding from **local taxes**. Attending a charter school is free to students and their parents, but there may be an application or entrance requirements. Charter schools provide communities with additional options for educating their children. Some charter schools specialize in serving at-risk youth, a particular gender, certain career paths, or other niche areas. Proponents of charter schools view these schools as an additional option for students, especially if the community schools are not meeting their needs. However, opponents of charter schools believe that these schools take funding, enrollment, and support away from neighborhood schools.

MIDDLE COLLEGES

Middle colleges are **alternative high school programs** that are operated on community campuses. The purpose of a middle college is to provide an alternative environment for high school students and facilitate **independent student learning**. Students who attend middle colleges are given freedoms and liberty similar to college students and may even have a shorter school day or flexible school schedule. The school is operated by school district staff and students take their traditional high school courses, but they are also given the opportunity to take **college-level courses** taught by **community college professors**. Middle colleges often appeal to students who do not fit in with

38

the environment or culture at their traditional school or who seek to earn college course credits while still in high school. Some middle colleges are designed and funded as charter schools while others are developed and operated as part of the traditional public-school system.

PERSONALIZED LEARNING

Personalized learning is the instructional strategy of tailoring academic content and instruction to students based on their individual needs. **Personalization** can be achieved based on a student's learning styles, personality, interests, career goals, and academic progress. Providing personalized learning can be complex, so much is implemented with **computer programs**. Before personalization can occur, a student must be **assessed** on content relative to the type of personalization. For example, if learning will be personalized based on a student's learning style, he or she may take a learning style inventory. Based on the inventory results, a personal learning plan will be developed. The purpose of personalized learning is to address the **individual needs** of the student, with the goal of helping him or her achieve **academic growth and success**. Instruction may be differentiated based on the content the student receives, how the content is delivered, how the student is expected to engage with the content, the pace of progress through the content, and how students demonstrate mastery of the content. Personalized learning often accompanies **technology implementation models** such as one-to-one technology.

FLEXIBLE SCHOOL DAY

In a traditional school day, students report to school at a certain time in the morning, remain at school for nearly seven hours, and are then dismissed in the afternoon. A **flexible school day** modifies this traditional schedule to **accommodate** students and their families. There are many variations of the flexible school day, which may include attending a four-hour block of school at some scheduled time throughout the day, attending school in the evenings, or attending school at unscheduled times and accumulating hours over the course of a school week. A flexible school day is especially beneficial to students who are at risk of dropping out or have dropped out of school in the past. These students may have personal obligations that make it difficult to attend school on a traditional schedule, such as working full-time or caring for a child. Implementing a flexible school day is beneficial to the school and to students because students can attend school in a way that meets their individual needs and the school can help students complete their academic expectations for accountability purposes.

COLLEGE AND CAREER READINESS

DUAL-CREDIT ENROLLMENT

Dual-credit enrollment is a curricular program designed to give students the opportunity to earn **college credits** while they are still in high school. The program is called **dual-credit** because students enroll in high school and college at the same time. To participate, students must meet entry requirements for the **local community college**. This usually involves earning a specific score on an exam for math and reading. Once admitted to the college program, students take core courses that earn high school and college credits **simultaneously**. For example, a student may take a Freshman English 1301 course at the college level, which will also earn credit for the high school English year four requirement. The number of college credits that students may earn depends on the school-college partnership and availability of courses, but many schools offer the opportunity to earn an **associate's degree** while students are still in high school. This saves students and their families money in college tuition and also increases the likelihood that students will persist in college and earn degrees. These college classes can be taught on the high school campus by a qualified teacher or a visiting professor, or the students may travel to the local community college for part of the school day.

ADVANCE PLACEMENT COURSES

Advanced placement courses are college-level courses that are taught to high school students. **Advanced placement (AP) courses** contain the content of college-level courses and are taught with college-level rigor by teachers who meet certain qualifications. These courses are usually core content courses such as reading, math, science, or social studies. Students remain on the high school campus to take these courses and receive **high school credit** for successful course completion. However, students also have an opportunity to take an exam at the end of each course that can qualify them to earn **college credit**. If the student achieves an acceptable test score, he or she will earn college credit for that course, which is transferrable to most colleges or universities. Students may participate in a combination of AP and dual-credit courses to increase the number of college credits they can earn while still in high school. This saves students and their families money in college tuition and also increases the likelihood that they will persist in college and earn degrees.

INTERNATIONAL BACCALAUREATE PROGRAMS

An **International Baccalaureate (IB) program** is a rigorous school curricular program that has been implemented in schools across the world. In order to participate in this program and to be recognized as an IB school, schools must meet certain program requirements and be monitored and evaluated regularly. The authorization process can take two to three years. As an IB school, schools receive **professional development** and participate in the **international network** of IB schools. Additionally, students who attend IB schools often demonstrate higher levels of academic success when compared to schools without IB programs. This is due to the **specialized curriculum** offered as well as the **higher level of rigor** in IB schools. Students also have the opportunity to become more culturally aware and sensitive due to their acquisition of a **second language** as part of the program and their exposure to other students around the world.

ROLE OF CAREER PATHWAYS IN SCHOOLS

Career pathways are specific tracks that students can participate in to prepare them for specific career fields or jobs. These tracks or pathways include **coursework** that is relevant to a student's chosen field. For example, if a student is interested in a career pathway for law and public office, his or her pathway may include more reading, writing, and social studies courses than students in other career pathways, as well as more elective courses related to the skills necessary to be successful in that career. **All school levels** can implement career pathways. In elementary schools, the delineation between the various pathways may not be as defined as in high schools, but it can lay the foundation for future studies. For example, a student in a fine arts career pathway from elementary school to high school would likely have an advantage over students who did not participate in a career pathway but are interested in fine arts due to the general exposure to and participation in fine arts related coursework. Some state accountability systems require high school students to identify career pathways as part of **graduation requirements**.

ACCOUNTABILITY

STUDENT GROWTH

Student growth has become a focus in school accountability. In years past, **student performance** has been the sole focus. As a result, educators primarily focused on students who were likely to perform well on high-stakes tests. As a result, students who were not likely to pass these tests were **underserved**, along with students who would likely pass the test regardless of teacher intervention and support. In contrast, a focus on **student growth** and accountability for such growth means that educators must serve all students. Even if a student does not pass a state-mandated test, growth in performance must be demonstrated. This growth is often measured against a prediction of how the student is expected to perform, based on assessment data from previous years. To ensure that schools are adequately educating all students, **accountability standards** incorporate measures of student growth in addition to measuring student performance.

40

STUDENT PERFORMANCE

Student performance in school accountability describes how students perform on **state-mandated assessments**. A certain percentage of students must pass these tests for a school to be deemed acceptable. This performance is evaluated in each **core content area**, depending on the accountability system, but most frequently in reading and math. The performance standards and content areas evaluated can vary based on grade level and can also change with federal or state legislature. A school that performs well in one subject and not in another is still a failing school. Additionally, to ensure that all students are performing well and not just certain groups of students, school performance is evaluated for particular **subgroups** of students, based on demographics. These demographics may include race or ethnicity, socioeconomic status, special education status, limited English proficiency status, and more.

CURRENT FEDERAL LEGISLATION

The most recent legislation related to public school accountability is the **Every Student Succeeds Act (ESSA)**, which was enacted in 2015 during President Obama's administration. This legislation replaced the **No Child Left Behind (NCLB) Act** of 2002, enacted during President Bush's administration. ESSA provides more flexibility to states by allowing individual states to provide plans for addressing **key educational goals** such as closing the achievement gap, ensuring and increasing equity in schools, improving the quality of instruction in schools, and improving growth and performance outcomes for all students. However, the basis of the law remains the same as that of NCLB. All students should have **full educational opportunity**. Consequently, there is a remaining focus on serving low-income students, students with special needs, and other students who have traditionally been marginalized in the public school system.

CONSEQUENCES FOR SCHOOLS THAT DO NOT MEET ACCOUNTABILITY STANDARDS

Schools that do not meet accountability standards may be subject to local, state, or federal **sanctions**. For a first-time failure, consequences may not be severe. The school will likely have to provide **notice** to parents and the community that accountability standards were not met. The school may then have to develop a **formal plan** that outlines changes to help meet accountability standards the following year. Many school districts have strategies and supports in place for schools that do not meet accountability standards. Additionally, the state and federal government provide **resources** for these schools. The goal is not to punish school staff but to provide the resources and supports necessary to increase the likelihood of student success. This may include training and professional development, consulting staff, curriculum, and more. However, schools that **consistently fail to meet accountability standards** may experience more severe consequences. These may include changing or removing staff, changing the school leader, implementing specialized or stringent school programming, or even closing the school.

DECREASING STUDENT DROPOUT RATES

A school's dropout rate is measured for school accountability. Additionally, dropouts miss their educational opportunity. Consequently, many school leaders are developing creative ways to **decrease dropout rates**. To encourage students to remain in school, leaders are implementing more engaging **curricular programs** and featuring **career pathways** and opportunities to earn **college credit**. Other strategies include providing mentoring programs, offering a variety of extracurricular activities besides sports, and providing counseling and other mental health services. Also, some schools offer **accelerated school programming** to potential or recovered dropouts in an effort to help them to graduate more quickly. To encourage dropouts to return to school, schools are providing assistance, support, and resources to **families**. This type of support often requires partnership with other **organizations** within the community. School leaders and other school staff often visit homes in the community to persuade students who have dropped out to return to school.

School Culture, Equity, and Cultural Responsiveness

High Standards and Achievement Gaps

COMMITMENT TO HIGH STANDARDS FOR ALL STUDENTS

EQUITY VS. EQUALITY

All students are expected to meet the standards outlined by the state and federal governments. School leaders are responsible for providing students with the instruction, resources, and support necessary to meet these standards. **Equality** refers to providing all students with the same resources and support, regardless of their needs. **Equity** refers to providing students with the resources and support that meet their individual needs. An example of equality would be that all students receive ninety minutes of reading instruction each day. An example of equity would be that students who have shown deficiencies in reading receive an extra thirty minutes of reading instruction each day. When leaders implement equity in schools, this may mean that some students receive more **resources and support** than others, or different support and resources. Leaders must be aware of what students need so that the right resources and support can be used to support these students. This need may be due to a lack of educational opportunity, physical or intellectual disabilities, or other circumstances. All students need resources and support to enrich their education, but practicing equity means that students will receive appropriate resources based on their identified needs.

CREATING A CULTURE OF HIGH EXPECTATIONS

A culture of high expectations means that staff and students strive toward high goals and excellence. A leader can create a **culture of high expectations** by setting campus goals **above minimum standards**. For example, if the required student attendance rate is 90%, the leader can set a goal for a 95% attendance rate for the campus. The leader can also **reward** student and staff performance that exceeds expectations. For example, the leader may publicly celebrate students who achieve Honor Roll. Another strategy for creating a culture of high expectations is to provide **models of excellence** for students and staff. These models can be effective programs on other campuses, role models in the community, or exemplary staff and students on campus. To create a culture of high expectations, a leader must also **address performance that does not meet expectations** in an effective manner. It must be clear to staff and students that performing below expectations is not acceptable. The leader must also **provide the resources necessary** for staff and students to meet the high expectations that have been set.

EVIDENCE OF A CULTURE OF HIGH EXPECTATIONS ON SCHOOL CAMPUSES

It is evident that a school has a culture of high expectations by what is seen and heard on campus. The culture of high expectations is evidenced by the **campus appearance**, including its cleanliness, organization, and posted materials. Bulletin boards and other visual aids in the hallways and in classrooms should demonstrate high expectations for academic achievement, character, and behavior. For example, a school may post college pennants and posters in the hallways to demonstrate an expectation that students are college-ready. Also, the **instruction** that is observed in the classroom should be evidence of high expectations for students and their ability to perform academically. The culture of high expectations is also evidenced by how **students and staff speak**. When there are high expectations, teachers and students speak positively about learning and meeting goals. There is little to no negative talk in regard to learning and performance. Instead, there is problem-solving, brainstorming, and action-planning to meet academic goals. A culture of high expectations on campus is evidenced by the **performance**, which is indicated by goal attainment and student performance data.

EVIDENCE OF A CULTURE OF HIGH EXPECTATIONS IN CLASSROOMS

Within the classroom, a culture of high expectations is evident by the **appearance** of the classroom and the **behavior** of teacher and students. First, the classroom will be neat, organized, and conducive to learning. Posted materials will be academically relevant, positive, and encouraging. In a classroom with a culture of high expectations, the teacher begins class on time and is prepared for the lesson. Materials and technology are ready for the start of class and there is a clear objective for the day's lesson. The teacher makes an effort to engage all students and uses a variety of instructional strategies to do so. In this classroom, students are eager to participate and remain engaged in the lesson throughout its entirety. Students demonstrate engagement in and mastery of the content by engaging in discussion with the teacher and their peers. There are few, if any, behavioral problems in this type of classroom, and if they do arise the teacher addresses them quickly and appropriately. There is evidence in the classroom of a good relationship and rapport between the teacher and the students, and no students are allowed to disengage from the lesson.

IDENTIFYING ACHIEVEMENT GAPS
ACHIEVEMENT GAPS

The term "achievement gap" refers to the disparity in educational performance of students of low socioeconomic status, minority students, and female students. **Educational performance** is measured by many indicators such as course grades, pass/fail rates and promotion, standardized test performance, course selection, graduation rates, college enrollment rates, and many other indicators. The achievement gap exists as a national phenomenon but is also observed at the state level, district level, and even within campuses. The achievement gap was identified over fifty years ago and continues today. There is an abundance of research regarding why it exists and how to address it at all educational levels, but so far there has not been any success in eliminating it. As a result, leaders should be prepared to **identify and address** achievement gaps on their campuses.

PERFORMANCE INDICATORS

The best way to determine the existence of an achievement gap on campus is to analyze **student performance indicators**. Leaders can use a variety of performance indicators to identify if an achievement gap exists on their campus and, if so, for whom. Leaders can analyze performance data for **standardized tests** administered over the past 2–3 years to identify any disparities. The data should be compared based on socioeconomic status, race and ethnicity, gender, special education status, limited English proficiency status, and any other subgroups that are relevant to the campus. If an achievement gap exists, students in a particular **subgroup** will consistently perform at a lower rate when compared to the other groups of students. This method of analysis should be repeated for other performance indicators such as grades, pass/fail rates, promotion and retention, graduation, and any others that are relevant to the campus goals.

COMPARING PERFORMANCE WITH OUTSIDE STANDARDS

A school leader may evaluate data on campus and determine that all students, regardless of demographics, are performing academically at **comparable rates**. This is often the case in schools with little to no diversity. However, a lack of evidence of an achievement gap within a campus does not mean that students are not affected by it. The school leader should **compare** the performance of students on his or her campus to other schools in the surrounding area, both within and outside of the school district. The leader may then find that his or her students are not performing at the same level as students in other schools. For example, a school leader may find that the majority of

students on his or her campus are demonstrating a proficiency of 76% in math, while students in other schools are demonstrating a proficiency of 88%. Consequently, the school leader may realize that students at his or her school need to improve in math to remain on pace with their academic peers.

PLANNING TO REDUCE GAPS
REDUCING THE ACHIEVEMENT GAP

To reduce the achievement gap on campus, leaders should **assess** the needs of the underperforming groups of students and **align resources and support** in an equitable manner. Leaders can provide **targeted interventions** to these students based on their identified needs. For example, the leader may schedule math and reading tutorials for a particular subgroup of students who have demonstrated deficiencies in that area. A leader should also set **campus goals** that specifically address the performance of underperforming groups of students. This will ensure that there is an action plan for addressing the needs of these students, as well as specific resources dedicated to their performance. Finally, a leader should **track data** for the performance indicators that show the achievement gap. This data should be collected and analyzed at regular intervals so that additional interventions, resources, and support can be implemented, if necessary. In order to reduce the achievement gap, the leader should target these students with resources and support and monitor their progress on a regular basis.

ADDRESSING THE ACHIEVEMENT GAP
GOAL-SETTING

Goal-setting can help to address the achievement gap because it focuses attention on the groups of students who need extra support and helps to target resources in those areas. Areas in which school leaders create goals receive **attention and targeted resources**. When goals are developed that specifically address areas of the school programming with evidence of an achievement gap, the school leader can turn the focus of students, staff, and the community to these areas. Additionally, when goals are created, there is a **determination** to accomplish those goals, so if a goal is related to the achievement gap, it is more likely that the gap will be addressed. For example, if the school leader has seen evidence in the data that Hispanic students with limited English proficiency are lagging behind their peers in reading performance, the school leader can develop a school goal that specifically addresses the reading performance of Hispanic students with limited English proficiency. As a result, there would be increased focus on all Hispanic students with limited English proficiency, including the dedication of time, effort, and resources.

DATA MONITORING

Data monitoring can be used to address the achievement gap because it can help to **identify** areas of the school program where the gap exists and to **monitor changes** in the achievement gap on campus. First, data should be used to identify where an achievement gap is present. The achievement gap is typically present in **reading and math content areas**, but can vary among other subject areas, as well as by groups of students. For example, a school leader may find that there is a gap in math performance between African American students and their peers, but that the gap is largest among African American males. Additionally, the data can show the school leader where the gap may be **narrowing** due to the instructional strategies and changes in school programming, or where the gap has **shifted** to another group of students. Therefore, data monitoring is key in identifying the achievement gap, determining the efficacy of strategies implemented to address the achievement gap, and assessing changes in the achievement gap among other student populations.

Professional Development

RECRUITING AND EVALUATING STAFF MEMBERS
RECRUITING TEACHERS AND OTHER STAFF MEMBERS

A leader should be strategic in recruiting new teachers and staff members. To determine whether candidates will be a good fit on the campus, the leader should examine them in relation to the school culture, vision, and goals. A leader should first use the **school culture** as criteria for recruitment. For example, if the school culture is one of innovation and creativity, the leader will want to recruit candidates who have demonstrated creativity in the past and are comfortable taking the risks necessary to try new things. Also, the leader will want to recruit candidates with the necessary skills to aid in implementing the **school vision and goals**. For example, if the school vision is to become an exemplary campus in the integration of technology into the learning process, the leader should recruit candidates who are skilled with technology and are comfortable utilizing it. Using such criteria when recruiting teachers and other candidates will ensure that they will be a good fit on campus and contribute to the school's success.

INCLUDING OTHER TEAM MEMBERS IN THE RECRUITMENT PROCESS

Including other team members in the recruitment process is beneficial for several reasons. First, having more than one person participating in this process reduces the potential for demonstrating **bias** during the recruitment and hiring process. Other team members may notice aspects of potential candidates that the leader missed, which can help to provide a **well-rounded view** of each candidate. Also, other team members may have different perspectives regarding the **needs and dynamics of the campus**, which can help to determine whether potential candidates are a good fit for open positions. Lastly, **staff morale and campus culture** can benefit from allowing team members to participate in the process of selecting their future coworkers. Some schools allow students to participate in the recruitment and selection process of teaching candidates because they are the ones who will ultimately be affected.

EVALUATING STAFF MEMBERS

For a campus to reach its goals and achieve its vision, all staff members must perform to expectations. It is essential that staff members be **evaluated** to ensure that all are performing to expectations. Evaluations of staff members provide an opportunity for leaders to identify areas of **strength and weakness** among the staff and to provide constructive **feedback** to staff members so that they can grow professionally. Leaders can use these evaluations to determine what additional **support and resources** are needed to support or improve the staff member performance. For example, a leader may discover through evaluation that the science department demonstrates deficiencies in providing hands-on instruction to students. The leader can then identify professional development and coaching to assist the science teachers in improving this area. Evaluations are also used to determine whether staff members will have continued employment on campus. Staff members who consistently perform below expectations may have to be removed from their position and assigned to a different position or campus.

EVALUATING TEACHERS

State law requires that teachers be evaluated with a **standardized evaluation system**. The state may recommend a certain teacher evaluation system, but school districts can often choose which system to implement. Whether the school district adopts the recommended evaluation tool or develops its own, the standards for evaluation must meet or exceed the expectations outlined by the state. For teachers to be evaluated, the **evaluators** (usually campus administrators such as principals and assistant principals) must be trained in using the tool. Additionally, **teachers** must be trained on the tool that will be used to evaluate them. Evaluation often includes regular

45

observations by the evaluator, collection of artifacts or data related to their practice, and conferences with the evaluator to discuss feedback. Teacher evaluation is usually based on **performance** in relation to the standards outlined in the evaluation tool, as well as **growth or progress**. Teacher performance standards are often related to instructional practice and strategies, professionalism, growth and professional development, and student performance. The evaluation process occurs throughout the school year and teachers receive a final evaluation rating at the conclusion of the school year.

OBSERVE STAFF PERFORMANCE IN VARIED SCENARIOS

OBSERVING STAFF PERFORMANCE

Leaders should use as many opportunities as possible to **observe staff performance** so they will have a well-rounded view of the performance. The opportunities may include various days of the week or times of day, as well as varied circumstances. Teachers can be observed while engaging in their instructional practice in the **classroom**. They can also be observed while they are engaged in collaboration as they participate in **professional learning communities**. Additionally, teachers can be observed while they are fulfilling **duty assignments** such as arrival, dismissal, cafeteria, or hall duty. Other staff members can also be observed at different times, whether performing normal duties or engaging in special events such as community events, student events, or district events. A leader should be intentional and deliberate about seeking out different opportunities to observe staff at a variety of times, in a variety of circumstances, to obtain a fair and holistic view of staff performance.

OBSERVING STAFF IN A VARIETY OF SCENARIOS AT DIFFERENT TIMES

It is important to observe staff in a variety of scenarios and at different times to get an accurate impression of staff performance. If a leader observes a staff member infrequently or always at the same time, this may lead to an inaccurate perception of that person's performance. For teachers, **class dynamics** may vary throughout the day. When a leader does not vary the time of day for observing a teacher, he or she will not know how that teacher responds to varied classroom dynamics or how instruction is practiced in all of the assigned courses. For example, a teacher may have a small class in the afternoon with fewer challenges than other classes. If a leader observes the teacher only during that class, he or she may not see all of the **instructional and classroom management skills** that the teacher demonstrates throughout the school day. If a leader consistently observes a teacher at the same time, it can also lead to predictability. A staff person could prepare for observation, so that it is not an authentic reflection of that person's regular work performance.

IMPROVING STAFF PERFORMANCE

Conducting observations can help to improve staff performance by providing opportunity for **feedback and growth**. Observations allow a leader to see a staff member in action. When a leader observes a teacher or other staff member, he or she will note **strengths and weaknesses** in that employee's performance in relation to campus and district expectations. The leader can specifically reference what was observed as evidence of those strengths and weaknesses. This data will then help the leader to provide feedback regarding performance. The leader can also provide suggestions for improvement or give access to professional development and resources that will help the staff member to improve. Observations can also illustrate staff members' strengths so that they can build on them and continue to grow in those areas. Feedback and recommendations can also be used immediately to improve performance.

CALIBRATION AMONG STAFF EVALUATORS

One campus may include multiple people who evaluate the performance of teachers and staff. The process of **calibration** is the training of all evaluators to maintain and look for the same **standards**

of performance. When a team is not calibrated, different evaluators may have different perceptions of excellence, which can lead to confusion and inconsistency in staff performance. To calibrate staff evaluators, the team of evaluators should observe a staff person **together** at the same time. They each conduct an observation as if they were conducting it alone. After the observation is complete, the team of evaluators meets to discuss what they observed and how they would evaluate the staff person. The leader helps the team identify where their evaluations are **aligned or misaligned** in regard to the performance expectations. For example, a leader may believe that the observed teacher did a poor job implementing collaborative learning, while another evaluator believes that the teacher implemented collaborative learning in an acceptable manner. The leader would then refer to the performance standards and discuss the observed evidence to reach a consensus. This process would be repeated until all evaluators are able to assess staff members in like manner.

DEVELOPING PROCESSES TO SUPPORT TEACHERS' GROWTH
SUPPORTING TEACHERS' GROWTH WITH EVALUATIONS

Teacher evaluations support their growth because evaluations help to identify **areas of needed improvement** and hold teachers accountable for addressing those areas. Evaluations are based on a set of **performance standards** and will reveal if a teacher is not adequately meeting any of those standards. A teacher who needs to improve will know exactly where to focus improvement efforts, based on the evaluation results. The evaluation will also help the leader know how to best support the teacher in **growing professionally**. Additionally, evaluations hold teachers **accountable** for improving their practice. The accountability comes from the process of conducting evaluations, including timelines and deadlines, self-reflection, and conversations with the evaluator regarding areas of growth. When professional growth or efforts to achieve growth are not observed in the teacher, the teacher is at risk for receiving a negative evaluation at the end of the school year. A negative evaluation could result in outcomes such as probation or termination. The process of evaluating teachers ensures that they are growing professionally to become the best teachers they can be.

SELECTING PROFESSIONAL DEVELOPMENT FOR STAFF MEMBERS

A leader needs to be deliberate in selecting professional development for staff members so that it is purposeful in helping staff achieve the campus goals and vision. One strategy a leader can use includes analyzing how the professional development **aligns** with the campus vision and goals. For example, if the campus goal is to increase reading performance, then selecting a professional development session on implementing effective reading instructional practices would be appropriate. Another strategy that a leader can use to select professional development is to **identify weak areas** of staff based on observations and evaluations. A leader may observe that several teachers are having difficulty implementing effective classroom management strategies, so that leader may seek out professional development that addresses classroom management. Also, a leader must ensure that staff members participate in professional development that is **mandated by the district or the state**, such as something related to special populations of students or law and policy.

SUPPORTING TEACHERS' GROWTH WITH COACHING

A coach is a professional who helps a teacher to develop the skills necessary to work effectively. A coach is a staff person who does not supervise or evaluate the person being coached. This helps to foster a **relationship of trust** between the coach and the teacher. A coach will identify a teacher's areas of **strengths and weakness** based on a predetermined rubric or set of expectations. Then the coach will provide one-on-one support to help the teacher **improve targeted areas**. The coach may provide books and resources or recommend professional development sessions. The coach may

also **model** effective teaching, **observe** the teacher in practice to provide real-time feedback, **assist** in the lesson planning process, and **guide** the teacher in self-reflection and critical analysis processes. A coach provides **individualized, targeted support** to teachers, which helps them to grow, usually in a shorter period of time than other forms of professional development support.

UTILIZING HIGH-PERFORMING TEACHERS TO SUPPORT THE GROWTH OF OTHER TEACHERS

High-performing teachers on campus can support the growth of other teachers by becoming leaders, serving as models, and coaching. High-performing teachers may exceed performance expectations in many areas or only a few, but their strengths can be **leveraged** to benefit the other teachers on campus. A leader may utilize high-performing teachers as leaders on campus in several ways. These teachers may be promoted to **lead departments** or be tasked with **leading collaborative meetings**, such as professional learning communities. Leaders may also direct these teachers to lead **on-campus professional development sessions** relating to their areas of strength. These teachers can also serve as **models** to the other teachers. Teachers who need to improve in certain areas may be asked to observe a high-performing teacher to see how a particular skill or strategy is implemented in the classroom. A high-performing teacher can also have a coaching role for other teachers to provide one-one-one support in certain performance areas.

RECOMMENDS APPROPRIATE TEACHING AND LEARNING PRACTICES

IMPORTANCE OF THE PRINCIPAL AS AN INSTRUCTIONAL LEADER

The principal should act as the instructional leader on campus. This is important because it helps the leader to focus on instruction on campus, helps to support teachers, and establishes credibility with the faculty. When a principal is an instructional leader, **instruction** is prioritized. This impacts all school operations, including scheduling, alignment of resources, and support. Also, instructional leaders are able to support teachers in improving their skills related to **teaching and learning**. A principal who is experienced in and familiar with instruction will be a better evaluator of instruction and can offer expertise in improving instructional practice. Also, acting as an instructional leader gives **validity** to the principal's feedback relating to instruction. Teachers will be more receptive to feedback and advice regarding their instructional practice if the leader has demonstrated that he or she prioritizes instruction and has knowledge and expertise in that area. The principal should be prepared and willing to take the lead instructionally on campus in a variety of forms, such as providing feedback, demonstrating or modeling expectations, and collaborating and problem-solving with teaching staff.

IMPORTANCE OF THE SCHOOL LEADER'S PARTICIPATION IN PROFESSIONAL DEVELOPMENT

A principal should participate in professional development for his or her own growth and development and to demonstrate solidarity with staff members. When possible, a leader should participate in **professional development** with the staff so that he or she can learn as well. Leader participation in professional development helps to identify the actions and behaviors he or she can expect from **staff** that also participate in the session. For example, if teachers participated in a professional development session regarding collaborative learning strategies, the leader would need to know what effective implementation of those strategies would look like in the classroom and how to support teachers as they implement them. Also, when the leader participates in professional development with staff, this demonstrates to the team that the leader values the opportunity for professional development and views it as a **priority**. This will increase **buy-in** from the staff and help them to be more receptive of the information and training that they receive at the professional development session.

Curriculum and Instruction

Teaching Resources, Time, and Procedures

COLLABORATIVE TEACHING AND LEARNING

Collaborative teaching involves two or more teachers engaging in instruction together. Collaborative teaching can take many forms, such as team teaching, co-teaching, and others. For example, one teacher may act as a **lead teacher** and present instruction to students while the other teacher acts as a **support**, helping to manage student behavior and reinforce concepts with struggling students. In another model, a teacher may present **new instruction** to students while another teacher in the room provides **remedial or intervention instruction** to a small group of students. Other team-teaching models involve students being divided into **groups** and receiving new instruction from a teacher within their groups. In a team-teaching model in which both teachers act as lead teachers, there are often **student rotations** or **instructional stations** involved. Collaborative teaching requires **co-planning** on the part of the team teachers and a good **working relationship** between them. Collaborative teaching allows for more flexibility within the classroom and exposes students to differentiated instruction and a variety of teaching styles.

STRUCTURE OF PROFESSIONAL LEARNING COMMUNITIES

Professional learning communities can be structured in a variety of ways to support collaboration among educators on campus. Most often, these **professional learning communities** are organized in a way that allows staff with shared roles or responsibilities to collaborate together under the leadership of one person who is designated to **lead** the community and is often trained to do so. For example, a professional learning community structured by **grade level** may consist of all eighth-grade teachers. In contrast, a community structured by **content area** may consist of all math teachers on campus. The campus leader may determine which structure best meets the needs of the teachers and students. Professional learning communities are usually **goal-driven**, which encourages participants to collaborate in order to achieve the established goals. Professional learning communities are often guided by the following questions: What do we want students to learn? How do we know if they learned it? What do we do if they did not learn it? What do we do if they did learn it? While participation in professional learning communities may be voluntary on some campuses, for many schools it is mandatory for teachers to participate.

PURPOSE OF PROFESSIONAL LEARNING COMMUNITIES

The purpose of professional learning communities, also referred to as **PLCs**, is to improve the educational performance and achievement of students through **educator collaboration**. PLCs are structured ways to facilitate **sharing knowledge** and **improving skills** among educators through data analysis, action research, exchange of expertise, and professional dialogue. In PLCs, teachers may discuss their practice and seek ways to improve. For example, teachers participating in a PLC may share lesson plans with committee members for feedback. Teachers may also share student work with committee members to calibrate grading practices or solicit ways to improve the quality of students' work. For example, a teacher may present a sample of student writing to committee members to get feedback on suggested focus areas for subsequent instruction. Teachers may also discuss student performance data in PLCs. This data may include summative assessment within the classroom or formative assessment, such as benchmark data or standardized testing data. Teachers may also use PLCs to discuss professional literature.

49

BENEFITS OF COLLABORATIVE TEACHING AND LEARNING

There are many benefits of collaborative teaching and learning. When teachers collaborate, they are able to **share ideas**. This fosters innovation and growth on campus. Collaboration also helps to **solve problems** more quickly. When a teacher has an issue, other teachers can provide resources, suggestions, or advice to help address the issue so the teacher does not have to research solutions independently and attempt to solve the problem through trial and error. For example, if a teacher has difficulty reaching a particular student, collaborating with other teachers who have that student in class and have been successful can help to identify ways that the teacher can reach the student. Also, collaboration among teachers builds **community** and fortifies the **school culture**. When teachers work and plan together, they build relationships with one another that can foster feelings of belonging and support. Teachers who are collaborative know that they can celebrate successes with their team members and that if they have a problem or challenge, they have a team of supporters. When teachers have these types of relationships and feel **supported**, it is easier to retain them in the classroom and encourage them to grow professionally.

SUPPORTING COLLABORATIVE TEACHING AND LEARNING ON CAMPUS

A school leader is instrumental in ensuring that teachers are able to collaborate on campus. First, the school leader must plan a **school schedule** that allows for collaboration. This could mean that there are designated times for professional learning communities or that teachers who need to plan together have planning periods scheduled at the same time. For example, if the school leader expects all teachers in a certain grade level to collaborate, then the instructional schedule must accommodate a shared planning time for those teachers. The school leader also needs to **train staff** how to participate in a collaborative learning environment in line with the campus vision and goals. This requires the leader to set clear expectations for the operation and outcomes of collaborative planning, such as those outlined in professional learning communities. Also, the leader must designate teachers or leadership team members to **lead collaborative planning** so that there is organization and accountability. Finally, the leader can support collaborative teaching and learning by **participating** in collaborative meetings when possible and **modeling** collaboration in other areas.

COLLABORATIVE LEARNING

Collaborative learning is an instructional strategy in which students are organized into **groups** for learning. These learning groups allow students to support each other and dialogue about the instruction and content. Collaborative learning reinforces **listening and speaking skills** in addition to the presented content. Teachers may employ several different strategies to organize students into collaborative groups. These include ability grouping (or homogenous grouping), heterogeneous grouping, and flexible grouping. In **homogenous grouping**, a teacher may organize students into groups based on proficiency with a certain skill so that targeted support and activities can be provided to groups based on their collective need. In **heterogeneous grouping**, students with different strengths or skills may be grouped together to balance out the group's deficits. Students may remain in these designated groups for a certain period of time, such as a grading period. **Flexible groups** are dynamic and take on different forms based on the instructional goals set by the teacher. These groups may have different sizes and composition based on needs.

APPROPRIATING RESOURCES FOR EFFECTIVE INSTRUCTION

SUPPORTING INSTRUCTION THROUGH APPROPRIATE PHYSICAL RESOURCES

Effective instruction requires appropriate physical resources. The leader can support instruction on campus by providing adequate physical resources for instructional staff. **Physical resources** include all of the tangible items needed to deliver instruction, such as furniture, books, and supplies. For example, **classroom spaces** must be able to accommodate teachers and learners, so there must be an adequate number of desks or tables and chairs, as well as physical square footage of the instructional space. Also, teachers need access to **instructional supplies** and appropriate **technology** for instruction. Other physical resources include curriculum, textbooks, computer labs, and other instructional resources. Leaders can identify necessary physical resources based on the school's **vision and goals**. For example, if the campus is striving to excel in STEM instruction, the leader needs to equip the school with science materials, computers, and other physical resources required for effective STEM instruction. Also, the leader may seek feedback from instructional staff regarding the necessary resources to be effective in the classroom. For example, a teacher may need additional bookshelves to accommodate leveled books within the classroom.

SUPPORTING INSTRUCTION THROUGH THE APPROPRIATE HUMAN RESOURCES

Effective instruction requires the appropriate staff in place to deliver and support the instructional program. **Human resources** that are part of the instructional program include teachers, librarians, aides, and many others. A leader must ensure that the right number of people with the appropriate skills and qualifications are placed in the appropriate **instructional positions**. For example, it is the leader's responsibility to ensure that all classes are assigned a highly-qualified teacher for the start of the school year. This may mean that the leader actively recruits and screens teaching candidates to have a fully-staffed campus throughout the school year. Additionally, a leader must respond to needs for **additional staffing** or **changes in staffing** throughout the school year. For example, if students demonstrate deficits in math, the leader may identify math tutors to provide additional instruction. Also, a leader may notice that students with special needs require more support within the classroom and can implement a co-teaching model to support instruction. The leader can also seek **feedback** from staff to determine where additional instructional staff may be needed or where staff changes need to be made.

IMPORTANCE OF RESOURCES FOR EFFECTIVE INSTRUCTION

A leader must ensure that the appropriate resources are provided to instructional staff in order to support **effective instruction** on campus. A **lack of resources** on campus can make it difficult for teachers to teach and for students to learn. For example, if a teacher is assigned 22 students in her classroom, but there are only 20 desks, the teacher will have difficulty arranging her classroom in a way that is conducive to learning. Also, if a classroom does not have a highly-qualified teacher assigned to it, students will lose out on quality instructional time. In contrast, when teachers and other instructional staff are provided with the **physical and human resources** needed for effective instruction, both they and the students benefit. For example, if the school's vision is to cultivate reading skills in students, teachers would benefit from books, bookshelves, online reading programs, a library, and a librarian in order to achieve that vision. As a leader may not be able to provide all of the desired resources for instructional staff, he or she must decide which resources can be provided based on the school budget.

OVERCOMING BUDGETARY CHALLENGES WHEN PROVIDING INSTRUCTIONAL RESOURCES TO TEACHERS

At times, the school budget will not be sufficient to provide the desired instructional resources for teachers. In these instances, a school leader may need to seek additional ways to provide these resources. One way to overcome this challenge is to seek **funding from outside the school**. This may mean applying for **grants** or seeking **donations** from various businesses and organizations. The funds acquired can be used to purchase the desired resources. An additional strategy is to ask the **manufacturers** to donate the resources to the school. The school may volunteer to be a pilot school for the implementation of new resources. Also, parent organizations can conduct **fundraisers** to supplement the school budget and secure the needed resources. For example, the PTO may conduct a fundraiser to purchase supplies for the art program. The school leader should also determine whether the next school year's budget should accommodate the resources for the subsequent school year.

TIME MANAGEMENT

USING PLANNING TIME TO SUPPORT EFFECTIVE INSTRUCTION

Teachers have planning time scheduled into their instructional day. This **planning time** is determined when the master class schedule is designed for the campus, so leaders must consider in advance how much time is allotted to teachers for planning. A leader should encourage teachers to use this time to **support effective instruction**. For example, teachers can assess the quality of student work, prepare feedback for students, and determine which skills or content may need to be retaught. Planning time can be used to examine **resources** and determine how they can be incorporated into instruction or to identify differentiated instructional strategies for reaching diverse learners. Teachers may also choose to **collaborate** with other teachers in the planning and delivery of lessons. Leaders should ensure that teachers have adequate planning time and access to resources to support their efforts during planning time. Additionally, leaders should be considerate of teachers' planning time by avoiding scheduling meetings, conferences, duty, or other assignments during this time whenever possible.

IMPACT OF TIME MANAGEMENT ON INSTRUCTION

Instruction on a school campus is delivered according to a strict **schedule**. Specific times are allotted for various aspects of the instructional program. A school leader's ability to **manage** his or her own time as well as to occupy the time of other **campus staff** can affect instruction. For example, the leader's timeliness in approving decisions relating to instruction can impact the timeline of projects. The timeframe in which the school leader obtains **resources** for the instructional program can also impact instruction. For example, if the campus would like to integrate technology into the curriculum, the leader's ability to secure computers for the students and teachers affects when instruction could begin. Additionally, the leader's daily decision-making regarding use of time can impact **instruction**, such as scheduling of meetings, school assemblies and activities, and conferences with staff. The leader must manage his or her time in planning, decision-making, and other duties throughout the school day to support the instructional program.

PRESERVING INSTRUCTIONAL TIME

Preserving instructional time means reducing the number of distractions and interruptions to the instructional program, specifically the time students spend in the classroom. **Interruptions** to instructional time may include announcements, school assemblies, meetings, or any other activities or events that distract from the instructional routine. For example, a campus leader may desire to host a school-wide event such as a pep rally during the school day. The leader would need to consider the impact on the instructional day from hosting such an event. He or she may decide to adjust the day's schedule by taking a few minutes from each class, rather than having students miss a large portion of instructional time from one class, to accommodate the event at the end of the day. A leader may also decide that a pep rally does not warrant the interruption of instructional time and instead may postpone the event. Leaders who **preserve instructional time** use school-wide public announcements sparingly, adjust schedules for school assemblies to reduce the impact on instructional time, and try to schedule other meetings and events outside of the instructional day when possible.

Curriculum and Instruction

RIGOR AND RELEVANCE

RIGOR

Rigor in academic instruction refers to **challenging curriculum and instruction**. Rigorous instruction challenges students not only academically, but also intellectually, and even personally. Rigorous instruction is often complex and challenges students to think deeply and critically. Through rigorous instruction, students are able to develop the **soft skills** necessary for success in college, career, and adulthood, such as problem-solving, critical thinking, inferring, studying, time management, self-discipline, working in teams, and many others. Rigor does not mean something is excessively hard or difficult. However, rigor does involve stimulating, engaging instruction. Rigorous instruction often requires students to make connections **across academic content areas** and apply concepts to the **real world**. For example, if a high school English teacher wanted to assign a rigorous assignment based on a reading of *To Kill a Mockingbird*, he or she could assign a project in which students discuss the impact of the political setting in the United States at the time of the story on the plot. In contrast, a non-rigorous assignment could be a worksheet of multiple-choice questions.

ENSURING RIGOR IN THE INSTRUCTIONAL PROGRAM

A school leader must ensure that all students have access to a rigorous instructional program. First, a leader must evaluate the curriculum for **alignment to state standards**. This ensures that all curriculum is designed to instruct students based on the expectations set by the state. This prevents the lowering of standards in the classroom, which could lead to students falling behind. Next, a leader must determine that curriculum is taught in a **rigorous manner**. This includes creating lessons that require students to think critically. A leader may encourage instructional strategies such as differentiated instruction, project-based learning, and collaborative learning to help foster rigorous instruction in the classroom. Finally, the school leader must ensure that **assessment** of instruction is rigorous. This may mean encouraging the use of projects and other creative means that allow students to demonstrate mastery of standards and objectives. A rigorous instructional program avoids reliance on worksheets and other assessment activities that do not align with a rigorous instructional program.

HOW CAMPUS GOALS CAN SUPPORT RIGOROUS INSTRUCTION

Rigorous instruction is challenging yet feasible for students. Campus goals can support rigorous instruction by motivating instructional staff to have **high expectations** for teaching and learning. When a goal is set high, it challenges instructional staff to work harder and with greater urgency, which requires utilizing **rigorous instruction**. For example, if a campus has had prior reading performance of 65%, a campus goal of 70% would not require significant change from the prior year's strategies and practice. However, setting a reading performance goal of 80% for the school year would encourage teachers to provide rigorous instruction to students to meet the higher performance expectation. Low expectations in goal setting will result in low expectations in instruction and high expectations in goal setting will result in high expectations in instruction. Similarly, when campus goals include all populations and sub-populations of students, rigorous instruction is supported. This ensures that low-performing students and high-performing students receive instruction at their appropriate level of rigor.

BENEFITS OF CROSS-CURRICULAR INSTRUCTION

Cross-curricular instruction is the deliberate making of connections between **various content areas** so that students may apply their knowledge in more than one content area at a time. For example, students may examine the historical setting of a story in a reading class, utilize math

53

strategies in a science class, or discuss geometric principles in an art class. Cross-curricular instruction is beneficial for students because it demonstrates the **relevance** of their content knowledge. When students understand that the instruction is not isolated to one particular area, but has applicability in other areas, students find the knowledge to be more **meaningful**. Additionally, utilizing concepts and skills in different contexts helps students to **master and retain** those skills. Cross-curricular instruction also aids students in their critical thinking skills such as inferring, drawing conclusions, predicting, and so forth. Cross-curricular instruction benefits teachers as well as students because it facilitates **collaboration** among colleagues. Teachers can plan together when lessons align across content areas and even team-teach lessons.

SUPPORTING CROSS-CURRICULAR INSTRUCTION

Leaders can support cross-curricular instruction by facilitating collaboration and providing resources for teachers. Cross-curricular instruction can be done independently but is more effective when teachers can **collaborate in lesson planning**. Leaders can provide time during the school day or at other times for teachers of different content areas to collaborate and examine the curriculum for opportunities for cross-curricular instruction. Also, leaders can support cross-curricular instruction by providing the appropriate resources. Teachers may have ideas that require books, supplies, or other materials to facilitate these lessons. Additionally, teachers may need **training or professional development resources** to help them present cross-curricular lessons effectively. Leaders can cultivate an environment where cross-curricular instruction is supported, encouraged, and praised.

ALIGNMENT OF CURRICULUM AND INSTRUCTION TO ASSESSMENT

Curriculum and instruction must be aligned to assessment because what is taught must be measured and what is measured must be taught. If instruction is not aligned to the assessment, there will likely be no **measurement** of how well students mastered what was taught. Additionally, if instruction is not aligned to the assessment, students will likely be assessed on concepts and material they have **not been taught**. Neither scenario is fair or beneficial to students. In the case of district- or campus-created assessments, the **assessment** is often created first because this defines what students should know at the conclusion of the given time period. Then, based on the assessment's expectations, teachers can plan the order and pacing of the concepts and skills to teach. On state-mandated tests, students are expected to have mastered all skills and objectives provided by the state, but no one is aware of the test content until its administration.

RELATIONSHIP BETWEEN RIGOR AND DIFFERENTIATED INSTRUCTION

Rigorous instruction is challenging to students, but not impossible. However, classrooms are diverse and not all students perform at the same academic levels. As a result, teachers must provide an appropriate level of rigorous instruction to students based on their **current performance**. When teachers **differentiate instruction** for students, they cater to the individual needs of students, such as identifying the appropriate level of rigor for particular students or groups. For example, an eighth-grade math teacher would not give the same assignment to a struggling student as he or she would to a student who is performing above grade level. Each student needs a **unique level of rigorous instruction**. The teacher may identify that adding and subtracting fractions is a rigorous activity for the struggling student whereas the high-performing student may be able to solve algebraic equations that include fractions.

RELEVANCE IN INSTRUCTION

Relevance in instruction refers to how content is related to other content and to the real world, as experienced by the students in the classroom. When instruction is **not relevant**, students may have difficulty making connections to the instruction, identifying or connecting any background knowledge they may have, or retaining the information. In contrast, when instruction is **relevant**, students understand how the content connects to what they already know, what they are learning in other areas, and to the world around them. For example, a math teacher may explain to students how using an algebraic function can help them calculate their weekly paycheck on a job. An English teacher may compare a plot from classic literature to a modern-day movie or story to help students to make connections. Teachers make instruction relevant by demonstrating how the new content **connects** with old content, with the content they are learning in other courses, and with the real world as they experience it.

SUPPORTING STUDENT ENGAGEMENT AND PERFORMANCE WITH RELEVANCE IN INSTRUCTION

When instruction is relevant to students, they are more likely to engage in it and demonstrate better academic performance. Students are better able to **engage in relevant instruction** because they understand how the new content **relates** to what they already know, which can build their interest and provide them with a way to contribute to the lesson. For example, if the students are reading a story in which a character spends a day at the beach, a student who has never been to the beach may have difficulty engaging in the lesson, whereas a student who has visited the beach is more eager to share experiences and connections to the lesson. Similarly, when students are taught **abstract concepts**, they may have difficulty grasping and retaining them if they are not relevant. In contrast, when students understand how concepts are applied in the **real world**, they are more likely to retain them. For example, students may learn about chemical reactions in a science course, but if they are shown how these chemical reactions occur in everyday life, such as cooking, they will have a deeper understanding of the concept and be more likely to retain it.

SCHOOL-WIDE PRACTICES AND FOCUS ON STANDARDS-BASED INSTRUCTION

DIFFERENTIATED INSTRUCTION

Differentiated instruction refers to providing **customized or tailored instruction** to students to meet their diverse learning needs. These learning needs can be determined by previous academic performance, special needs such as a physical or learning disability, learning style, or other means. Based on the identified needs, teachers can **differentiate** the content, process, or product of the instruction. When teachers differentiate **content**, they provide different content to students, such as a math teacher instructing one group of students on fractions and another group on algebraic equations. When teachers differentiate by **process**, a teacher provides different modes of instruction, such as video or media, field experiences, exploratory discovery, or other means. When a teacher differentiates by **product**, she provides different ways for students to demonstrate mastery of the content such as through writing, performance, or projects, among others. Teachers may differentiate instruction in all of these areas or in selected areas, based on the needs of the students.

USING DATA TO SUPPORT DIFFERENTIATED INSTRUCTION

Instruction is differentiated based on **students' needs**. Data can be used to identify these needs, especially in the area of academic performance. **Historical student performance data** as well as current **formative and summative assessments** can help to determine the type of instruction a student may need. For example, the data may show that a certain group of students has deficits in reading. These students may benefit from not only reading a text, but additional methods of instructional delivery, as well as specific instruction that helps to build their reading skills. Data may inform campus leaders on what **courses** to offer. For example, if historical data demonstrates that many students have achieved advanced performance on state assessments, the leader may consider offering advanced classes in certain academic areas such as Advanced Placement, Gifted and Talented, Honors, and others. Other data that can be used to identify ways of differentiating instruction for students includes learning styles inventories, personality assessments, and

observational data. These types of data can help teachers determine how to tailor instruction in a way that will support student learning and increase their academic performance.

MONITORING CURRICULAR PROGRAMS TO ENSURE STUDENT NEEDS AND CONTENT STANDARDS ARE MET

MONITORING CURRICULAR PROGRAMS TO ENSURE THEY ARE MEETING STUDENT NEEDS

The school leader must monitor curricular programs to ensure that student needs are being met. If curricular programs do not meet student needs, students will not be successful and campus goals will not be met. The curricular program must meet the **academic and social needs** of students. For example, if a population of students on campus is consistently exceeding the performance standards on assessments, they need a curricular program that extends their learning and supports their academic growth. If the entire curricular program is centered on remediation, that group of students will not have their needs met. Campus leaders examine student needs and design the curricular program based on those needs. Such decisions may include which classes to offer, the uses of self-contained instruction or content-specific instruction, the offering of the arts and other ancillary instruction, the integration of tutorials and remediation into the school day, and many others.

MONITORING CURRICULAR PROGRAMS TO ENSURE THAT THEY MEET CONTENT STANDARDS

The school leader must monitor curricular programs to ensure that they meet content standards. **Content standards** are determined by the state and are the basis for the design of **state testing**. Therefore, when curricular programs are not aligned to the content standards, students will not be prepared for state testing. If students are not prepared for state testing, they will not perform well and campus goals will not be met. Campus leaders must be mindful of how students will be assessed so that the curricular programs support instruction to adequately prepare students for those assessments. Additionally, ensuring that the campus curricular program meets content standards aids in **vertical and horizontal alignment** of instruction and curriculum both on campus and within the district. Vertical and horizontal alignment helps with collaborative planning among colleagues and ensures continuity of instruction for students, especially those with high mobility rates within the school district.

EFFECTIVELY MONITORING THE CURRICULAR PROGRAM

Leaders can effectively monitor the curricular program by analyzing data, conducting observations, and soliciting feedback from stakeholders. If a curricular program is **appropriate**, student performance data in regard to content standards will be reflective of that. If students are not performing well, the campus leader may need to identify whether the curricular program has **deficits** or the programming is **mismatched** with student needs. Also, the leader can identify if the curricular program is working, based on **observations of instruction** on campus. For example, if the leader observes that students are demonstrating high levels of engagement in science courses, there may be an opportunity to expand the curricular program in science. Also, the leader can solicit **feedback** from stakeholders, such as teachers, students, and parents. These people may identify needs or strengths of the curricular program for the leader to address. For example, Language Arts teachers may identify a need to separate reading and writing instruction in the curricular program to provide students with more time for instruction in these areas.

Assessment and Accountability

ONGOING ANALYSES FOR QUALITY OF TEACHING AND LEARNING
EVALUATING THE QUALITY OF TEACHING ON CAMPUS

The quality of teaching on campus can be evaluated through observations and data. A school leader should spend time in the classrooms to **observe** teaching in action. A school leader will recognize effective and ineffective teaching practices. It is important to observe teaching to evaluate quality so that if corrections are necessary, these can be made in time to affect student performance. After teaching has been completed, the school leader can analyze **student performance data** to evaluate the quality of the teaching. If teaching is of good quality, the majority of students should be able to grasp the concepts and demonstrate mastery on assessments. If many students are unable to master these concepts and objectives, teaching efficacy needs to be evaluated. School leaders can use both formative and summative assessments as indicators of teaching quality.

EVALUATING THE QUALITY OF LEARNING ON CAMPUS

Student learning can be evaluated in a number of ways. A school leader can determine the quality of learning on campus through observations, feedback from students, and student performance data. When the school leader **observes classroom instruction**, he or she has the opportunity to observe students in the learning process. If students are excited about the content, are engaging significantly in the process, and are successful when checked for understanding, there is likely a high quality of learning. Also, a school leader may solicit **feedback from students** regarding their learning. This can be in the form of surveys, focus groups, or individual interviews. The students can be asked about the learning environment, the relevance of content, and the rigor of the instruction, among other quality indicators. Finally, a school leader needs to **analyze student performance data** to determine the quality of learning. If students are not meeting expectations on assessments, the quality of learning can likely be improved.

IMPROVING TEACHING ALREADY DEEMED EFFECTIVE

Even if teaching is deemed effective, there are still benefits to improving. Some school leaders focus solely on improving ineffective instruction, but that narrow focus results in a missed opportunity to develop and reinforce a **culture of high expectations** on campus. Effective instruction can become highly effective with additional support and strategies. When a school leader is committed to **improving all instruction** on campus, even instruction that is considered effective, all staff are encouraged to grow professionally for the benefit of students. This fosters an environment of **continuous improvement** and also helps teachers to seek changes in the instructional program and in student diversity. This environment also encourages innovation in the classroom to find new and creative ways for instructing learners. Also, increasing the effectiveness of teaching can help high-performing students to grow and perform at even higher academic levels.

ADDRESSING INEFFECTIVE TEACHING

It is a school leader's responsibility to address ineffective teaching. First, the leader must **identify** ineffective teaching. This is done through observations of classroom instruction and review of student performance. Next, a leader must **communicate** to the teacher which aspects of the instruction are ineffective. A leader should be strategic in communicating areas of improvement to avoid discouraging the teacher and to focus the teacher's growth in the areas that will have the most impact on students. Then, the leader must provide the **resources and support** to improve the ineffective teaching. This can include professional development and instructional coaching. The leader should also continue to **monitor instruction** to determine if improvements are being made. In some instances, depending on the severity of the deficits in instruction, the school leader may decide to change staff's instructional assignments or even remove staff from their assignments. If

staff is changed or removed, the school leader must adhere to district policies regarding staff changes.

FORMATIVE AND SUMMATIVE ASSESSMENT, EFFECTIVE TEACHING, AND PROGRAM QUALITY
FORMATIVE ASSESSMENT

Formative assessment is designed to **monitor student learning**. Formative assessment is useful in providing **feedback** to students so they will know which areas they need to improve and so teachers will also know areas in which to improve their teaching. The results of formative assessment may help teachers identify **instructional areas for re-teaching** or identify **students for interventions and tutorials**. Formative assessment may include checks for understanding within the classroom, classroom activities, and other guided and independent work. Formative assessments are usually activities that are low stakes, meaning that often no grade or point value is attached. For example, a teacher may ask students to represent their understanding of a concept using a graphic organizer. A teacher may also provide feedback on a pre-writing activity before a student writes an essay. Formative assessment may occur frequently and feedback should be timely in order to be relevant.

SUMMATIVE ASSESSMENT

Summative assessment is used to evaluate student learning for **mastery**. Summative assessment usually occurs at the end of an instructional unit or a designated period of time such as a grading period or school year. These assessments are aligned to objectives or standards and are usually **high stakes**, which means they may count for a significant portion of the grade or may determine students' progress in their educational careers. A summative assessment may be a midterm or final exam, a research project, a unit test, or a standardized exam. The results of summative assessments may determine a student's grade promotion or earning of course credit. Results from summative assessment may also determine a school's performance according to accountability standards. Summative assessment results are often used by school leaders for **instructional planning** and **goal-setting** for the subsequent school year.

INDICATORS OF EFFECTIVE TEACHING

A leader can use several indicators to identify effective teaching on campus. With effective teaching, there is a clear **goal or objective** to be accomplished with the instruction. This objective is communicated to students and is evident throughout the lesson. Additionally, there is a clear **lesson cycle** throughout the instructional delivery, such as a gradual release teaching model in which students are supported throughout the learning process. When there is effective teaching, students are **engaged** in learning and demonstrate **retention** of the concepts through formative assessment. Effective instruction includes **diverse instructional strategies** to meet the needs of learners and is responsive to the results of the formative assessment conducted in the classroom. Also, effective teaching is evident in **student performance data**. Students who receive effective instruction are able to perform to standard on assessments.

ASSESSING PROGRAM QUALITY

A leader can assess program quality using data and feedback from stakeholders. **Data** that can inform a leader regarding program quality includes participation or attendance data, student performance data, and any other metrics that are collected, such as those specified by grants or state and national associations. If a program is good quality, parents and community members will **participate** in it, which is reflected in the participation and attendance data. Also, **student performance** will reflect whether a program is high quality. If student performance is below standard, this may be an indicator that the school's programming may be misaligned or below standard. Other metrics dictated by **outside agencies** may include the data relating to parent and community events, awards received, college acceptance, and others. A leader can also obtain

58

feedback from **stakeholders**. Teachers, staff, students, and community members will generally be pleased with the implementation of a high-quality program. Low approval of the school's program may suggest that the leader needs to examine its appropriateness on campus or its implementation.

ALTERNATIVE ASSESSMENT METHODS

Traditional methods of assessment usually involve a standardized test with closed questions, which require students to select an answer from several choices. Educators are now trying to incorporate a greater variety of assessment methods so that students can demonstrate mastery of content and objectives in different ways. These **alternative methods** may include writing assessments, project assessments, and performance assessments. **Writing assessments** may include responding to open-ended questions or writing an essay or work of fiction. **Project assessments** typically require students to conduct extensive research and compile a final product with multiple parts or aspects. Project assessments have typically been used in science and social studies courses but are now being incorporated across the curriculum. **Performance assessments** require the student to perform in front of peers or the teacher. These may include a speech, skit, dance, or some other physical demonstration of their learning. Many of these alternative assessments are also facilitated using technology applications.

COMMUNICATING PROGRESS TOWARD GOALS

COMMUNICATING WITH STAFF

It is important for a school leader to communicate with staff about progress toward goals to maintain or increase **momentum**, as well as to celebrate **successes**. A leader can communicate with staff about progress toward goals through the **normal channels**: emails, employee newsletters, or staff meetings. Incorporating goal progress within these forms of communication helps the staff to view goal progress as something that is as important as the other topics that are being communicated. Also, it does not require staff to utilize a new or foreign form of communication to determine progress toward goals. However, a leader may want to publicize progress in more **public or visible ways**. These may include public announcements, posters or charts in hallways and meeting rooms, or special charts and graphs that can be shared with staff. Reaching goals or goal milestones can also be celebrated with awards, certificates, or other means.

COMMUNICATING WITH PARENTS AND COMMUNITY

A leader should communicate with parents and community about goal progress often and in a variety of ways. This can include **community meetings** in which stakeholders are invited to hear about school performance in a variety of areas, with a focus on goals. Additionally, the leader can provide a **newsletter or bulletin** to update the community on school performance, upcoming events, and ways to get involved with the school to help achieve the goals. Many schools feature phone systems that can **mass call** the homes of students, which can be used to communicate announcements regarding school goals and progress toward them. Similarly, school leaders can mail **letters** to parents with updates regarding the school goals. Progress toward school goals can also be communicated in other **meetings** that involve parents and community members, such as committee meetings, parent teacher organization meetings, and advisory board meetings.

COMMUNICATING WITH STUDENTS

Teachers can communicate with students about the school's goals and how their individual efforts and performance contribute toward achieving them. For goals that are related to student academic performance, teachers can help students take ownership of their own performance by setting **individual goals** and tracking their progress toward them. Students can be provided with **data trackers** to track their own progress toward their individual goals. Teachers can speak with students individually about the support they need to accomplish their goals. Teachers can also set **class goals** that align with campus goals and encourage students to reach them. For example, if the

59

school has a goal of 90% proficiency in math performance, a math teacher can help students set individual goals in math. This ensures that students understand how their behaviors affect their class and school and demonstrates how they can contribute to the school's success while achieving their own success.

IMPORTANCE OF FACILITATING TWO-WAY COMMUNICATION

Two-way communication on progress toward goals is important because it provides stakeholders with the opportunity to convey to the leader why **goals** may or may not be achieved. When a leader facilitates two-way communication, he or she can receive **feedback** on the efficacy of existing strategies, ideas for additional strategies, or requests for additional resources or support. For example, if the campus has a goal to increase student proficiency in technology and the leader has purchased certain technology hardware to accomplish this goal, teachers may provide feedback that the chosen hardware has not been effective in exposing students to technology and that another type of hardware may be necessary. Additionally, two-way communication may reveal unexpected **barriers** to achieving goals. For example, a teacher may inform the leader that the technology goal may be difficult to achieve because the school technology infrastructure cannot support the increased internet usage on campus. A leader can benefit from two-way communication about progress toward goals by receiving additional information that can lead to **refining or revising goals**, or that assures the leader that the right actions have been **implemented**.

Managing the Organization, Operations, and Resources

Managing Operational Systems

TYPES OF ORGANIZATIONAL SYSTEMS

ORGANIZATIONAL SYSTEMS

A school organizational system refers to how a school is organized in relation to resources, personnel, time, and space to achieve student learning and success. Examples of **school organizational models** include departmental models, project-based learning models, academy models, integrative models, small community models, and the school-within-a school model, among others. The organizational system dictates the **structure** of the school and its systems, how personnel are allocated and what personnel are needed, what resources are needed, and how the physical space of the school is designed and utilized. Consequently, the organizational system in a school dictates how **instruction** is delivered and how **student learning** is achieved.

TYPES OF SCHOOL ORGANIZATIONAL SYSTEMS

The different types of school organizational systems affect how instruction is delivered on campus. In the **departmental model**, the different subject or content areas are separated and distinct. Each of the subject-area departments have leaders or chairs who report to administration. In an **integrative model**, disciplines are combined or grouped together such as in the pairing of math and science classes or English and history classes. **Project-based learning models** facilitate interdisciplinary learning through student completion of large, extended projects. In **academy models**, a school may group students and classes based on college or career pathways. **Small community models** and **school-within-a-school models** are similar in that students are grouped into cohorts and remain within a small community for their instruction. Each community operates like a small school. In the school-within-a-school model, the small communities often have their own administrators. Other types of school organizational systems have developed as **technology** has become more accessible in schools, such as virtual schools and flipped classrooms.

DETERMINING THE BEST ORGANIZATIONAL SYSTEM FOR A SCHOOL

To determine the best organizational system for a school, a leader should first examine the school vision and goals. The organizational system should support the **school vision** and facilitate achievement of the **school goals**. For example, if the school is focused on reading performance and instruction, the leader may select a block scheduling structure to provide students with more instructional time in reading. A leader may also determine that, in order to provide socio-emotional support to students, dividing a large school into teams or houses would best facilitate relationship building and cultivate a small-school feel. A leader can also analyze the **school's culture** and identify the appropriate organizational system to support the ideal culture. For example, if the school vision is to create independent, life-long learners, the school organization system may involve giving students autonomy in their learning when possible. For example, the school could offer self-paced instructional programming, student course selection, and other exploratory opportunities for students.

AREAS OF ORGANIZATIONAL SYSTEMS NOT DIRECTLY RELATED TO CLASSROOM INSTRUCTION

Many organizational systems are part of the campus system but are not directly related to **instruction**. For example, the **cafeteria** represents a large system within the school. The process of feeding breakfast, lunch, and even dinner to students can be a complex organizational system. It involves providing the food, serving it, and maintaining the facilities in which it is served. This particular system may be regulated by state and federal regulations, which add additional complexities. Another organizational system is **behavior management and discipline**. There are processes in place to promote positive student behavior and deter negative behavior. This system may include the development and distribution of handbooks, training and communication regarding behavioral expectations, and imposing consequences for infractions. Other systems include student arrival and dismissal, extracurricular programming, counseling, and others. Even though these systems are not directly related to classroom instruction, they often **support** effective classroom instruction.

SYSTEMS THINKING

Systems thinking involves understanding how a system or an organization is constructed. It is an understanding of the many **parts** that make a system work, how those parts **interact** with one another, and how those parts relate to the larger context of the system. For example, the system of providing food to students in the cafeteria is one part of the larger campus system. A leader who understands systems thinking understands that how the cafeteria functions can directly or indirectly affect the way another system functions, such as the classroom. If the cafeteria is unable to serve breakfast efficiently in the morning, students may be delayed in getting to class, which in turn impacts instruction. Therefore, systems thinking helps in understanding how the organization or system as a whole can best function by improving the function of the **smaller systems** that make up the whole.

SHORT-TERM AND LONG-TERM PLANS FOR IMPROVING ORGANIZATIONAL SYSTEM

CONSIDERATIONS FOR SHORT-TERM IMPROVEMENT OF THE SCHOOL'S ORGANIZATIONAL SYSTEM

A leader should evaluate the school's organizational system for continuous, short-term improvements. Factors to consider include functionality, training, and resources. The organizational system should function smoothly and efficiently. This is indicated by **student and staff transitions** throughout the day as well as **flow of information and resources**. For example, if the school's organizational system is made up of small learning communities, it would be effective to place resources such as supplies and copiers near the learning communities. Also, the leader should ensure that staff has the appropriate **training** to support the organizational system. For example, if the organizational system is based on a project-based learning environment, staff will need appropriate, ongoing training to support this type of system. Finally, the leader should ensure that the school has the appropriate **resources**, both physical and human, to support the organizational system. This may include reassigning certain resources from one area of the school to another.

CONSIDERATIONS FOR LONG-TERM IMPROVEMENT OF A SCHOOL'S ORGANIZATIONAL SYSTEM

For long-term improvement of a school's organizational system, the leader should consider **alignment** to vision and goals, availability and allocation of resources, and spatial designs. First, the organizational system should support the **school's vision**. For example, a virtual school environment may not be appropriately aligned to a school vision that prioritizes building social and collaborative skills in students, due to its focus on individual, computerized work. Consequently, the leader needs to determine if the school's **organizational system** needs to be changed to reflect the changing needs of the students and community that the school serves. Next, the leader needs to determine the availability of both **physical and human resources** and how those are allocated to support the school's organizational system. This may require hiring additional staff, replacing or redesigning staff positions, or acquiring new resources such as technology devices. Finally, the leader needs to consider whether the layout and organization of the **physical space** in the school is conducive to the school's organizational system. To implement a school-within-a-school model, for example, the leader may need to redesign or relocate certain classrooms and offices.

PHYSICAL PLANT SAFETY AND COMPLIANCE WITH REGULATIONS
EFFECTS OF PHYSICAL PLANT SAFETY ON THE INSTRUCTIONAL PROGRAM

Failure to ensure the physical safety of the **school plant** and comply with building regulations can negatively affect the instructional program. If students and staff are in danger of being injured or hurt due to aspects of the plant that are in disrepair or do not meet codes and standards, this can **interrupt** the school day and cause the school and school district to be **liable**. For example, if the school has an elevator in use that is not up to code, there is danger of a student or staff person becoming trapped in the elevator due to malfunction. This is dangerous to the person in the elevator and would necessitate emergency personnel, causing a disruption to the instructional program. Additionally, malfunctioning equipment such as leaks, loud machinery or A/C equipment, or pest infestations are distracting to the instructional environment and may cause damage to instructional resources such as books and technology equipment. **Compliance** with regulations, such as ADA codes, is important to ensure access for all students and staff, especially those with disabilities, to all areas of the campus.

MONITORING THE PHYSICAL PLANT FOR SAFETY AND COMPLIANCE

A leader can monitor the physical plant for safety and compliance in several ways. First, a leader should have a **plant operator** who is responsible for ensuring the plant's safety and compliance. The leader should meet with the plant operator regularly to address any concerns that may arise. Second, the leader should conduct **regular walks** of the plant to inspect it for safety and compliance. During these walks, the leader should take note of plant aspects that may need repair or maintenance. Also, the leader may receive formal or informal **feedback** regarding needed repairs and maintenance from instructional staff. Finally, city or county officials will conduct regular **inspections** and provide **reports**. These reports will detail aspects of the campus that are in compliance, out of compliance, or in danger of being out of compliance with regulations. The school leader can use these reports to ensure the plant's safety and compliance.

BOND REFERENDUM

A bond referendum is a proposal to borrow funds long-term to fund **major capital improvements**. Since these capital improvements are costly, the bond allows the expenses to be spread over time so that the costs are covered by current and future taxpayers. The bond must be approved by **voters** because of the obligation that taxpayers will have in paying for the expenses incurred by the capital improvements. Funds secured through a bond referendum can be used for **construction** of new schools or district facilities, **renovation** of existing schools or district facilities, and other **updates** related to the physical aspects of the plant. Bond funds can be used to help schools update their buildings to new city or county building codes, ADA requirements, and technology requirements. Construction due to capital improvements may cause the **displacement** of students and staff from certain areas of the school plant where construction occurs or, in more substantial projects, **relocation** to another setting until construction is completed.

COMMUNICATION AND DATA SYSTEMS
PLANNING FOR CRISES

Even though crises are unpredictable, a leader can plan in advance to ensure that the school is as prepared as possible. First, the leader should have **emergency plans** in place for events such as natural disasters, fire, medical emergencies, intruders on campus, etc. These plans should be written and key emergency staff should be trained on how to implement the plans in time of crisis. Additionally, the leader can implement **drills** to practice the crisis plans. The leader can evaluate

63

staff and student performance during these drills and provide feedback to participants or revise the emergency plans based on the performance. The leader should also be familiar with **district policies** regarding emergency plans, drills, and reporting. A leader should make contact with **local emergency services** in the community to establish a relationship and ascertain important information and contacts to help in the event of an emergency or crisis.

EFFECTIVE DATA SYSTEMS

Effective data systems are important for managing the **organizational systems** on campus. Data systems relating to student and staff population data are essential to the effective planning and management of the organizational system. For example, **staffing** is often determined by the number of students enrolled in the school and the allocation of those enrollment numbers to various aspects of the instructional program, such as grade levels, special populations, magnet programming, and more. Leaders must have **accurate data** for student enrollment in order to allocate staff to the various programs on campus. This type of data also impacts class sizes and student to teacher ratios. Additionally, areas of the campus have **capacity maximums** as dictated by fire code, and these limitations must be taken into consideration when planning lunch schedules, school assemblies, and other uses of school facilities. Effective data systems are also necessary to make decisions related to **funding** and **resource acquisition and allocation**, in addition to **instructional decision-making**.

ACQUISITION AND MAINTENANCE OF EQUIPMENT AND TECHNOLOGY
DETERMINING WHAT EQUIPMENT TO ACQUIRE AND WHEN

A leader must decide if new equipment is necessary for the effective operation of the physical plant as well as the implementation of the instructional program. A leader should be aware of the **life expectancy** of the various equipment that is already on campus so that he or she can determine when new equipment may be needed. This helps in the planning of maintenance, repair, and replacement cycles. Also, the leader must determine if equipment is **mandatory** or **optional**. Equipment that must be present on campus for its operation is prioritized over equipment that can be acquired or repaired at a later date. For example, a leader may need to postpone the acquisition of new science lab equipment in order to repair air conditioning units. **School finances** must also be considered when contemplating the acquisition of new equipment. A leader may need to postpone the purchase of major equipment until a new fiscal year due to budget constraints. The school leader should also consider the **impact** of the new equipment. If the purchase of new equipment will impact the majority of the students or staff, it can be placed higher on the priority list than equipment that may impact a small group of students, such as a student organization or specialized instructional program.

ROLE OF TECHNOLOGY ON CAMPUS

Technology on campus impacts campus safety, communication, and instruction. Technology hardware and software are vital to the school. Technology can be used to assist with **campus safety**. For example, cameras are placed on campus to monitor activity. These cameras and the associated software necessary for monitoring and recording the camera feeds are important to school safety. Other technology used for safety includes intercom systems for screening of visitors, software to conduct background checks of visitors and volunteers, and automated door locking systems. Technology also aids in **effective communication** on campus. Emails, intercoms and radios, PA systems, marquees, and other forms of technology are used to communicate to staff and students. Also, technology is very useful for **instruction**. Computers, projectors, printers, and many other technological devices enhance the quality of instruction that is provided to students. Both staff and students may use these devices as part of the instructional routine.

Fiscal and Human Resources

ALLOCATING FUNDS AND BUDGETING
HOW SCHOOL FUNDING IS CALCULATED

School funding comes from a variety of sources. The **federal government** provides some funding, but this is usually not substantial and may fluctuate due to changing budget decisions at the federal level. The **state governments** also provide funding to schools based on income and/or sales taxes. The majority of school funding is gained from property taxes within the school district. Both residences and commercial properties are taxed and a portion of those taxes are allocated to school districts. Schools generally receive an allotment of funds on a **per-pupil basis**. The per-pupil allotment differs by school district but may average about $10,000 per pupil. However, certain programs warrant extra funds on top of this allotment, such as special education programs and technology programs. Schools and school districts often seek grants and donations from **foundations** to supplement their budget.

CENTRALIZED BUDGETING AND DECENTRALIZED BUDGETING

Centralized and decentralized budgeting refers to the locus of control for budgeting decisions within a school district. In a **centralized school district**, all budgetary decision-making is conducted by **district leaders** within the district office. Principals and the campuses they lead have little to no budgetary authority in a centralized district. When a district is centralized, principals must follow strict guidelines as to what can be purchased and when. The benefit of a centralized budgeting process is that budgeting decisions are controlled and quality and efficiency can be easily monitored. However, this type of system can prevent staff buy-in and cause school leaders to feel they do not have the authority to make the changes necessary for their school to be successful. In contrast, in a **decentralized district**, **principals** have the authority to make budgetary and purchasing decisions. This allows principals to determine which resources meet the needs of each individual campus and gives them the latitude and flexibility to address campus needs. The benefit of a decentralized budgeting process is the flexibility and increased buy-in of leaders. However, this type of system can be more difficult to monitor and cause more instances of mismanagement of funds.

FACTORS TO CONSIDER WHEN ALLOCATING FUNDS

A leader should consider multiple factors when allocating funds. First, the leader should refer to the school's **vision**. The allocation of funds should align with that vision. Similarly, the leader should align the allocation of funds to the school's **goals**. It is likely that the goals that are set for the school require funds and resources to accomplish them, so these funds should be allocated first. A leader should also consider whether funds are **recurring or one-time funds**. When a school receives funds that will not be renewed, a school leader must ensure that whatever is completed with those funds is sustainable for the future once those funds are gone. The school leader must also evaluate the **school program** and **organizational structure** to ensure that sufficient funds are allocated to the successful and efficient operation of the school program.

FACTORS THAT AFFECT A SCHOOL'S BUDGET EACH YEAR

A school's budget is not fixed but can vary from year to year based on a variety of factors. Funding from the federal and state government can fluctuate and impact campus budgeting. In some years, the government provides **one-time funding** that cannot be expected in subsequent years, which causes fluctuations. Additionally, the government can **change allocations** of funding for specific programs. For example, allocation of funding for Career and Technology Education may be altered, so even though the number of students participating in the program does not change, the received funds do. **Local property taxes** may change in a school district, affecting the money allocated to

65

schools. Additional factors include changes in student enrollment, changes in school programming, and other factors. Each year, a school leader must evaluate the proposed budget for the school year and make decisions based on each year's **budgetary allocations**.

STRATEGIES FOR RECRUITING HIGHLY QUALIFIED PERSONNEL

HIGHLY QUALIFIED PERSONNEL

The term "highly qualified" is used to describe the **minimum qualifications** of a teacher according to the No Child Left Behind Act, enacted in 2001. To meet staffing expectations, a leader has the responsibility of ensuring that teachers are highly qualified. This means that the teacher must hold a **bachelor's degree** and either have full **state licensure/certification** or **demonstrate knowledge of the subject** that he or she will teach. Based on this definition, states have enacted various procedures that enable teachers to demonstrate their content area knowledge, such as testing. A teacher may be highly qualified in one subject area and not in another. For example, a teacher may be deemed highly qualified to teach chemistry due to holding a bachelor's degree in science and being state certified in chemistry, but that same teacher would not be highly qualified to teach biology. Having highly qualified staff on campus ensures that teachers are knowledgeable in their assigned content areas and capable of teaching the content to students.

RECRUITMENT STRATEGIES

Leaders can employ several strategies to recruit highly qualified personnel. Leaders can participate in **recruitment fairs**. These are often hosted by the school district or by community organizations. Leaders can follow up with people from the event for interviews or may even conduct screening interviews at these fairs. Also, leaders can contact **teacher preparation programs** for referrals of recently certified teachers. These entities have lists of recent graduates along with their areas of specialization. However, these lists include people with limited or no teaching experience. It can also be helpful to post advertisements on **traditional recruitment sites**. Some sites specialize in recruiting for education. Finally, leaders can use **word of mouth advertising** to recruit highly qualified personnel. Teachers and staff on campus may have colleagues in other locations who would like to work at a new school. For example, a person may want to work at a school that is closer to home or teach a different grade level.

IMPORTANCE OF BEING FULLY STAFFED AT THE OUTSET OF THE SCHOOL YEAR

If a school leader has numerous teaching vacancies, it can be difficult to have all staff in place at the outset of the school year. However, the **beginning of the school year** is a critical time that can impact the success of the entire school year, so a leader should strive to have 100% of staff in place before school starts. First, important **training and professional development** occur prior to the start of school. A teacher who is hired later will miss these. Additionally, teaching staff begin to **bond and unite** as a team prior to the start of the year and a teacher would miss this opportunity if hired late. Also, students learn **procedures and expectations** for behavior and learning at the beginning of the school year. A teacher who is hired late may have to reset expectations for students, which could cause a difficult start for both the teacher and the students.

IMPACT OF HAVING TEMPORARY STAFF ON THE INSTRUCTIONAL PROGRAM

At times it is necessary to have temporary staff to support the instructional program. If there is a teaching vacancy or if a teacher is absent for an extended period of time, a leader may have to obtain **temporary personnel** until a permanent solution is found. Often, however, temporary staff persons are **not highly qualified** and do not have the same **training and experience** that permanent staff members do. As a result, the quality of instruction may be reduced when temporary staff persons are in the classroom. Additionally, with temporary staff persons, there may be a need for increased monitoring and support from other permanent staff persons, such as clerks and administrators, to ensure the effective and efficient progress of the instructional program. This

66

can produce further strain on staff and the instructional program. To ensure that the instructional program is excelling and that students are receiving high quality instruction, the school leader should minimize the need for temporary staff.

IMPACT OF SCHOOL CULTURE ON TEACHER RECRUITMENT

School culture is determined by the leader and the staff of the campus. The school culture can create a welcoming environment for new teachers or it can repel them. When the school culture is **positive**, focused on students, and driven by excellence, teachers will want to be part of that culture. They will be motivated by the positive culture and will recruit others to join the team. Additionally, when the culture is positive, students thrive, which can make the teacher's job easier and more enjoyable. On the other hand, if the school culture is **negative**, teachers and staff will likely have negative attitudes as well. Teachers will seek a way out of that school environment rather than encouraging others to join the team. This negative culture can negatively affect student academic performance and behavior. If a potential teacher candidate observes a negative school culture, he or she may be unwilling to work at that campus.

IMPACT OF LEADERSHIP STYLE ON TEACHER RECRUITMENT

The leadership style of the school leader and other leaders on campus can positively or negatively impact **teacher recruitment**. A leadership style that is perceived as **negative** can deter teachers from wanting to work at that leader's campus. During the recruitment process, a candidate may observe how the school leader speaks to him or her, the way the leader treats staff and students, and other indicators of leadership style. For example, if a leader is perceived as being overly demanding, negative, or micromanaging, a teaching candidate will not want to work for him or her. In contrast, if a leader is **fair, supportive, and warm**, a teaching candidate will be attracted to the position. Effective leaders attract effective teachers. Teachers will seek to work on campuses where they will thrive and grow, and the school leader is an indication of whether the campus will meet a teacher's professional needs.

SEEKING COMMUNITY-BASED AND OTHER ADDITIONAL RESOURCES NEEDED FOR ACCOMPLISHING GOALS

SEEKING ADDITIONAL RESOURCES FOR ACCOMPLISHING GOALS

A school leader may seek additional resources for accomplishing goals because there may not be sufficient school funding to accomplish everything that needs to be accomplished. When planning school budgets, leaders have to determine how to **allocate funds**. Often budgets have **shortfalls**, especially for initiatives that are lower on the priority list. As a result, a leader may have to seek funding and resources from **outside of school** to accomplish these goals. These additional resources may be in the form of grants, donations, volunteers, etc. For example, if a school leader wanted to establish a garden on campus, rather than using school funds for the gardening supplies and staff to tend the garden, the leader may solicit donations of gardening tools and volunteers to work in the garden. These types of resources can be very beneficial to the instructional program and alleviate some of the constraints of the school budget.

The leader has the primary role in ensuring that **sufficient resources** are available to accomplish the set goals. First, the leader should properly allocate the funds and resources allotted by the **school district** to meet goals. If there is a shortfall in resources, the leader is responsible for advocating on behalf of the school to solicit **additional resources**. This may include petitioning for additional resources from the school district or seeking resources from community organizations and businesses. A leader may apply for grants to support the school program; seek donations of funds, resources, or equipment; or gather volunteers for staffing support. For example, if the school cannot afford to purchase new computers, a leader may ask a business organization to donate used computers to the school. The leader should take initiative in securing the resources necessary to accomplish the goals that he or she set for the school.

POTENTIAL COMMUNITY-BASED RESOURCES

There are many community-based resources that are likely available to schools. For many communities, **local churches** offer a variety of resources that can support the school, such as volunteers, food and clothing for students and families in need, and much more. Also, many cities have **local community programs** to support the physical and mental health needs of the community and to provide nutritional support to families in need. There may be programs related to local transportation, arts, sciences, sports, clubs, and others that are available in the community. A school leader should be aware of all of the **organizations** in the surrounding community and communicate with these organizations to determine how they can partner to support students and their families. Often, these community-based resources can support students' **non-instructional needs** so that they can participate in the school program. These needs may include counseling, health-related needs, food and housing needs, and others.

Safety

PHYSICAL AND EMOTIONALLY SAFE ENVIRONMENTS AND POLICY FOR STUDENTS AND STAFF

PHYSICALLY SAFE ENVIRONMENT

A physically safe environment is free from seen and unseen dangers that would pose a threat to the physical safety of anyone exposed to the environment. A **physically safe environment** is in good repair, accessible to all, and accommodating to its designated purpose. For example, a physically safe classroom would be free from damaged walls, ceilings, or floors; broken or damaged furniture; leaky pipes or plumbing; and electrical hazards. Additionally, a physically safe environment includes **well-controlled people** so that no one is physically harmed by the presence of others. This includes adhering to **capacity limitations** and monitoring the **conduct** of those present in the environment. For example, a school cafeteria should not exceed the posted maximum capacity of people, even for special events, and people should be able to move safely and freely in the cafeteria in accordance with its purpose.

EMOTIONALLY SAFE ENVIRONMENT

An emotionally safe environment is an environment in which all people are able to **learn**. This type of environment is free from all obstacles, emotions, and conflicts due to **preventative strategies** and **quick resolutions**. When an environment is not emotionally safe, children can feel fear, anxiety, and a host of other emotions. In an **emotionally safe environment**, both adults and children feel comfortable participating in the learning environment and interacting with one another. There is an absence of peer-to-peer and peer-to-adult conflict as well as bullying. **Procedures and systems**, such as counseling, mentoring, and other interventions, are in place to ensure the emotional safety of students on campus. There is an emphasis on **communicating** one's needs to foster active participation and engagement in the learning process. Additionally, the **physical arrangement** of the environment is designed to contribute to emotional safety, such as including windows and natural lighting, inspirational and positive posters and bulletin boards, and aesthetically pleasing furniture and decoration.

ENSURING THE SCHOOL PHYSICAL PLANT, EQUIPMENT, AND SUPPORT SYSTEMS OPERATE SAFELY, EFFICIENTLY, AND EFFECTIVELY

A leader must ensure that the school's physical plant, equipment, and support systems operate safely, efficiently, and effectively. The first step is to identify the appropriate staff to **manage** the physical plant. This person has the primary responsibility to ensure the safe functioning of everything on campus, so the leader must have the right person in place and must monitor his or her performance. Also, the leader must provide the plant manager with **competent staff** to support plant maintenance. In partnership with the manager, the leader can develop systems of **monitoring and inspection** to ensure that all aspects of the plant are running efficiently and safely. The school leader should also solicit **feedback** from other staff members who use certain aspects of the school plant. For example, if the school has a swimming pool, the leader should get feedback from the swimming coach or athletic director regarding the pool facilities. This feedback can help to identify areas of improvement, repair, or replacement needs.

ROLES THAT LOCAL, STATE, AND FEDERAL LAWS AND POLICIES PLAY IN MAINTAINING A SAFE ENVIRONMENT

Local, state, and federal laws and policies help school leaders maintain a safe environment for students and staff. These regulations and policies, when adhered to, create a minimum level of safety. For example, **federal laws** regarding aspects of school safety such as asbestos management, ADA compliance, internet safety, and others are interpreted into school policies. **School districts** may have additional safety requirements, such as the presence of police officers on campus, campus visitor policies, volunteer policies, and others. **Local laws and policies** may include fire codes and occupation limits, as well as other mandates for building safety that are not particular to schools but are implemented in all public places in the area. Each of these regulations and policies is meant to **enhance the safety** of the school, so the school leader should prioritize adherence to these regulations and policies. Failure to comply with local, state, and federal laws and policies can result in sanctions, fines, or other repercussions.

MAINTAINING A PHYSICALLY SAFE ENVIRONMENT FOR STUDENTS

A leader should take proactive steps to maintain a physically safe environment for students. First, the school leader should conduct regular **inspection and maintenance** of all parts of the building to ensure that no aspects of the physical building pose hazards to students. Next, the school leader should **monitor flows of traffic** within the school building to maintain safety. For example, a leader may notice that a school banner obstructs visibility in a hallway, causing students to bump into one another during transitions between classes. To promote safety, the leader should relocate the banner to a different area of the school. The leader should also ensure that common assembly areas such as hallways, courtyards, auditoriums, and others are monitored by school staff to prevent or identify **conflict between students** that could lead to physical harm.

MAINTAINING AN EMOTIONALLY SAFE ENVIRONMENT FOR STAFF

Like the students, staff members need an emotionally safe environment. A leader can establish and maintain an **emotionally safe environment** through leadership style, communication, awareness, and support. When a leader has a **caring and empathetic demeanor**, employees will feel emotionally safe. In contrast, **high-strung, micromanaging leaders** can create fear and anxiety in staff. Also, leaders need to maintain **open lines of communication** with staff members. This allows them to communicate their needs so the leader can address them when possible. A leader should be able to recognize and be aware of aspects of the environment that **endanger emotional safety** for staff and should be able to address those concerns. For example, a lax discipline policy can create a challenging environment for teachers and staff. A leader can take steps to remedy this and create a safer environment. Finally, a leader should provide **avenues of emotional support** for staff. This may include staff counseling, referrals, or other accommodations and support that can help staff members feel emotionally safe.

69

NORMATIVE BEHAVIOR EXPECTATIONS FOR STAFF AND STUDENTS

ROLE OF STUDENT BEHAVIOR IN MAINTAINING A SAFE ENVIRONMENT

Student behavior must be regulated and controlled for a safe school environment. Students who are unsupervised or do not adhere to established rules and procedures pose a **threat** to the safety of the school and to themselves. As a result, **student behavior management** is necessary to maintain a safe environment. School staff and ultimately the school leader are responsible for the safety of students the entire time they are at school. Unsupervised students may lead to an unsafe environment since they are less prone to follow rules when supervision is absent. All students should be accounted for at all times and actively monitored. Additionally, students who misbehave can cause disruption, conflict, destruction of property, and a host of other actions that threaten the safety of the school environment. As a result, negative student behavior must be addressed quickly and effectively to maintain a safe environment.

BEHAVIOR MANAGEMENT AND DISCIPLINE STRATEGIES TO USE TO MANAGE STUDENT BEHAVIOR

A leader may use a variety of behavior management and discipline strategies, as well as instructing staff to use them, to properly manage student behavior. These different techniques and strategies almost all have certain characteristics in common. Effective **behavior management** requires active **supervision**. It is not enough for adults to be present wherever students are. They must survey students, anticipate student behaviors, and be prepared to intervene when necessary. Also, most strategies require that adults set clear **expectations** for student behavior. This can be done through establishing rules, behavior contracts, or other ways to articulate expectations. Finally, there must be clear **consequences**, applied fairly and equitably, for behavioral infractions. Many behavior management strategies encourage building relationships and rapport with students, incorporating positive consequences for appropriate student behavior, and addressing student behaviors without overly emotional responses such as yelling, sarcasm, or unprofessional language.

STUDENT BEHAVIOR MANAGEMENT AND STUDENT SUCCESS

Student behavior management and student success are related because poor student behavior detracts from the learning environment. If a student is behaving in a disruptive or disengaged way in the classroom, he or she cannot **learn effectively**. If the poorly-behaved student misses the instructional content, he or she will be less likely to succeed academically in that class. Poor student behavior can also negatively impact the **academic success of other students** in the room. For example, speaking out of turn, interrupting, and bothering others detracts from the learning environment. Finally, some behavioral consequences require the misbehaving student to be **removed** from the classroom. In these instances, the student often loses out on instructional opportunities, which can negatively impact academic success. Consequently, when student behavior is appropriately managed, the learning environment is preserved and all students have an opportunity to learn in a safe environment.

IMPORTANCE OF FAIRNESS AND EQUITY IN APPLYING STUDENT BEHAVIOR MANAGEMENT PRINCIPLES

Student behavior management strategies and discipline must be applied in a fair and equitable manner to be effective and maintain a positive school environment. **Fairness** involves **communicating expectations** prior to applying discipline. If expectations are unknown or unclear, students can be frustrated and deem it unfair to be held responsible. Fairness also means that the adults **adhere** to the expectations and consequences that have been communicated to students and parents. For example, a behavior strategy may be to give a student a warning before applying consequences. A teacher may give students multiple warnings on one day and never give consequences for a particular behavior, but on another day, the teacher may immediately give a consequence for the same behavior without a warning. This type of inconsistent behavior from the teacher would be deemed unfair. Also, staff must practice **equity** in discipline. Adherence to written policies and procedures can ensure that all students are disciplined in an equitable manner, regardless of race, gender, or academic and behavioral history.

EMERGENCY SITUATIONS AND SUPPORT

ROLE OF PROCEDURES IN EMERGENCY SITUATIONS

Procedures are necessary in emergency situations to ensure the safety of everyone affected. In emergency situations, emotions can cloud thinking and judgment. Additionally, people who are not familiar with a particular emergency situation may not know what to do in these instances. Having a **procedure** in place ensures that the right actions are taken in the event of an emergency, regardless of the emotional state or expertise of those involved. For example, if a person has a health emergency on campus, procedures should be in place for addressing the situation, including calling an ambulance, providing emergency aid, and maintaining the safety and order of the staff and students not immediately involved in the situation. These procedures should be taught to all **staff** on campus and be available in **written form** so they are accessible in the event of emergency. Having written procedures in place and abiding by them in the event of an emergency can also serve as legal protection for the school leader and staff.

KEY EMERGENCY SUPPORT PERSONNEL INSIDE AND OUTSIDE OF THE SCHOOL

The school leader should identify key emergency support personnel **on campus** to prepare them for emergencies. These key staff members should know their **roles** in each emergency instance and be trained on how to fulfill those roles in the event of an emergency. These staff members may include the school nurse, counselor, police officer or security personnel, administrators or other school leaders, clerks, and others, depending on the nature of the emergency. For example, a different team of personnel may be needed to respond to a health emergency than a natural disaster emergency. Emergency support personnel **outside of the school** may include key district staff members and personnel at various emergency response organizations, such as the fire department.

DOCUMENTATION AND COMMUNICATION IN EMERGENCY SITUATIONS

Emergency preparedness means that the school leader and staff have identified **potential types of emergencies** and planned the **procedures, staff, and resources** needed to address each type. Emergencies may include health emergencies, fire, natural disaster, intruders on campus, and many others. For each of these potential emergencies, a **written plan of procedures** should be created, detailing how everyone on campus should behave in the event of such an emergency. **Key personnel** with specific roles and responsibilities should be identified in the written plan. Everyone should be trained prior to the emergency to follow the written procedures. For many emergencies, **practice drills** can be conducted, such as fire drills or school lockdowns. Also, **resources** should be acquired, stored in designated locations, and inspected periodically. These resources may include printed copies of emergency procedures, fire extinguishers, automatic defibrillators, first aid kits, and other resources.

Welfare of Staff and Students

PROMOTION OF COUNSELING AND HEALTH REFERRAL SYSTEMS

KEY STAFF THAT CAN PROMOTE THE WELFARE OF STAFF AND STUDENTS

The key staff member responsible for promoting the welfare of staff and students is the **school leader**. The school leader creates a **school culture** in which students and staff feel safe, as well as **structures and systems** to provide support and intervention for students and staff in need. The school leader also sets the **example** for treatment of students and staff, such as displaying understanding, empathy, and compassion. The school leader should also identify other key staff who can promote the welfare of staff and students. Each member of the **leadership team**, such as assistant principals or deans, should take the lead in promoting the welfare of all and lead by example. The school leader should also enlist the support of counselors, nurses, and others who can be proactive in identifying and responding to the needs of students and staff. Additionally, teachers play a key role in identifying the needs of students and promoting their welfare within the classroom.

PROMOTING COUNSELING AND WELLNESS

A leader should promote counseling and wellness to encourage staff and students to take advantage of these supports for their own welfare. A leader can do this by making **counseling and wellness programs** visible to all. This may mean having signs and displays around the school that promote these programs. Also, the leader can communicate the **availability of these resources** using common means of communication, such as emails, news bulletins, school public announcements, and announcements in staff meetings. The staff members who lead counseling and wellness programs can be included in other school projects and programs, such as in behavior intervention meetings or academic interventions, so that they are viewed as an **integral part of the campus team**. A school leader can also consider hosting **mental health and wellness fairs** for school members and the community to raise awareness about potential health concerns and to promote available services.

INDICATORS THAT STAFF MAY NEED COUNSELING AND HEALTH REFERRALS

A leader can watch for several indicators to determine that staff members may need a recommendation to **counseling and health services**. Teachers and staff who need help may be **frequently absent** without a reasonable excuse. These absences may be jokingly referred to as "mental health days" but are often indicators that a staff person is stressed or overwhelmed. Another indicator of a need for counseling and health services are **overly emotional responses** to everyday stimuli. These responses may include yelling, crying, or bursts of anger. The school leader can also look for **changes in staff behavior**. For example, if a staff member who is usually outgoing, energetic, and talkative becomes withdrawn and disengaged, this may indicate a need for additional support. Staff who are unable to do their jobs satisfactorily, especially if they have a history of satisfactory performance, may need support from counseling and health services. The school leader should keep communication open so that staff are comfortable communicating that they need help.

INDICATORS THAT STUDENTS MAY NEED COUNSELING AND HEALTH REFERRALS

A leader can watch for several indicators to determine that students may need a recommendation to **counseling and health services**. A student may begin to act out and display **negative behaviors** in the classroom with other students or with adults on campus. This can be an indicator if the student does not usually display poor behavior at school. Additionally, a student who is usually engaged in classroom activities and with peers but becomes **withdrawn and disengaged** may also need help. These indicators can also lead to poor academic performance, indicated by falling grades. Students in need of support may also demonstrate **emotional responses** in school such as angry outbursts, crying, yelling, or even physical altercations with other students. In some instances, a **parent** may communicate with a staff member that the child is having difficulty at home as well. A school leader should ensure that **systems** are in place on campus to allow students to express their needs so that they can be referred for services. This may include having walk-in counseling hours or open-door policies with key staff members.

Making Reports to Child Protective Services

Child Protective Services is a service provided by state agencies to protect the welfare of children. This agency investigates allegations of **child abuse or neglect** and provides services to children should such allegations be proven valid. There will be instances in which the school leader or a school staff member has reason to believe that a child is being neglected or abused. Whenever there is suspicion of abuse or neglect, it is each staff person's responsibility, including the school leader's, to submit a **formal report** to Child Protective Services for investigation. For example, if a teacher reports to the school leader that one of her students has confided that his mother is hitting him with various objects and shows the teacher bruises, both the teacher and the leader should file a report. There can be legal ramifications for staff members who fail to report suspected child abuse or neglect.

Being Proactive in Promoting the Wellness of Staff and Students

Being proactive in promoting the wellness of staff and students means that the leader is actively looking for ways to **maintain the wellness** of all before problems arise. This is important because **prevention** is often more effective and less costly than trying to address a problem after it has already occurred. For example, taking steps to prevent teen suicide is a better course of action than addressing a grieving student body after a teen has committed suicide. Similarly, it is more effective to help an unwell teacher obtain needed help than to lose the teacher for the remainder of the school year due to a health crisis. The school leader should **proactively** promote wellness and identify potential wellness needs among students and staff so that mental health crises can be prevented or at least detected early in an effort to prevent tragedies that directly affect the student body and staff. Being proactive demonstrates to all that the leader is concerned about the wellness of staff and students and is willing to take the needed steps to address their health concerns.

Helping Staff and Students Deal with Grief on Campus

At times the student body and staff members will experience the loss of a peer or colleague. In these instances, the school leader will need to implement strategies to address the **grief** that students and staff experience. The first step that the leader must take is to **acknowledge** the loss. The leader should not operate with a "business-as-usual" attitude. Many schools have access to grief counselors who can be present on campus to assist students or staff who need assistance in dealing with their emotions. The school leader should also demonstrate **understanding and compassion** during this time and recognize that grief may cause students or staff to behave out of character, such as missing school, expressing outbursts of emotion like sadness or anger in school, or being disengaged from academic activities. It is important to **listen** to the needs of the students and staff during this time. The leader may provide opportunities for students and staff to express their feelings or to honor the one who has died.

Preventing Teen Suicide

The school leader can take steps to aid in the prevention of teen suicide or self-harm. Although many factors and influences outside of the school can lead a young person to commit suicide, the school and its staff can serve as a resource and support to students who experience suicidal thoughts. First, the leader should create a **school culture** in which students feel comfortable turning to teachers and staff for support. When this type of culture is present, a student is more likely to share thoughts of self-harm with a staff member, which can aid in prevention. The school should also have **counseling staff and resources** available for students who are experiencing emotional issues. Many schools discuss this topic with the student body and provide telephone hotline numbers for support 24 hours a day. Also, if an adult becomes aware that a student is contemplating suicide or self-harm, he or she has a duty to report it to the proper authorities.

Role Social Media Plays in Student Wellness and Mental Health

Social media has a large influence on students' wellness and mental health. Students who engage in social media often experience **negative emotions** as a result. Some students develop feelings of **inadequacy or low self-esteem** when they compare themselves to others online. This is the result of unrealistic beauty expectations and exaggerated portrayals of others' lives. Additionally, students may be exposed to **cyberbullying** via social media. This type of bullying can involve name-calling, threats, shaming, spreading rumors, and other negative behaviors that can negatively impact a student's well-being. Cyberbullying can lead to bullying and other conflict on campus as well. Finally, engaging in social media can be addictive for some youth. They may spend excessive amounts of time on social media or engage in risky behaviors in an attempt to gain social media attention. For example, a student may post provocative pictures of him or herself in an effort to attract attention. This can have negative consequences for the student's mental health and overall wellness.

Leader's Own Physical and Mental Wellness

In addition to ensuring the wellness of students and staff, the school leader should take steps to ensure his or her own **physical and mental wellness**. A leader cannot fulfill job responsibilities properly if he or she is not well. Also, the school leader should set an **example** for staff and students by prioritizing personal health needs. This is primarily accomplished by being proactive instead of waiting until a health problem arises to address it. First, the leader should **delegate responsibilities** and **accept assistance** whenever possible to keep stress levels low. The leader should also get regular **checkups** to quickly identify potential health problems. **Eating and sleeping** properly are also key components of maintaining physical and emotional health. Finally, the school leader should take advantage of the **resources and supports** that are offered on campus and through the school district. These may include counseling, use of workout facilities, support groups, nurse hotlines, and many other resources designed to support the physical and mental health of staff.

Resources for Promoting Wellness

Utilizing Community Services for Staff and Student Welfare

It is important for a school leader to utilize community services for staff and student welfare because school funds and resources are often insufficient to provide abundant resources for staff and students. Even if a school has sufficient budgetary resources, there is no need to spend funds on resources that may be available as a **free community service**. Also, utilizing community services may expand the number and type of resources that are available, which means more support and help for members of the school community. Most school services only provide services directly to students, whereas community services often have programs, resources, and support for the **entire family**, which can be more impactful to students and their families in many instances. Finally, utilizing community services builds **partnerships and relationships** between the school and the community, which can have long-range benefits for both parties. For example, schools and community organizations can partner in community events, student recruitment, and applications for grant funding.

Identifying Community Resources for Promoting Wellness

A leader can identify community resources for promoting wellness in a variety of ways. Often, these organizations desire to partner with the school and will visit or call the school to inform campus leadership of their services and identify ways that they can serve the school community. Sometimes school district offices maintain **directories** of community organizations and programs that support students and their families within the school district. The school leader can also do a basic internet search to identify nearby resources. **Local resources** include branches of city, county, or state

organizations and are easily identified online. Finally, the school leader can make an effort to venture into the community and make **connections** with the leaders of area organizations to determine how the school and the organizations can collaborate.

Disciplinary Policy

DISCIPLINE POLICY AND CONFLICT RESOLUTION

DISCIPLINE

Discipline is training students to abide by a specific **code of behavior**. When discipline is present, **rules** are typically stated and taught, and **expectations for behavior** are defined in a variety of contexts and situations. In addition to the rules that are outlined as part of the discipline policy, there are **consequences** associated with failing to abide by the stated rules and expectations for behavior. Many people associate discipline with administering consequences for failing to follow rules. However, the essence of discipline is the practice of **training or teaching behavior**. In schools, rules are often set by the school district and written in a student code of conduct for district-wide discipline. Schools may also have campus-wide expectations for behavior as part of their discipline, as well as sets of rules for individual classrooms. When discipline is effective, students are fully aware of behavior expectations and the consequences associated with not meeting those expectations.

PROMOTING CONFLICT RESOLUTION

Conflict resolution is the practice of resolving conflicts or disagreements, such as verbal or physical altercations, between students to prevent further disruption. To promote conflict resolution, staff members must be vigilant in **identifying potential conflicts** among the student body. **Early intervention** is essential in resolving conflicts effectively. Staff members also want to **build relationships** with students and create an environment in which students feel comfortable reporting conflicts to adults. Both people experiencing the conflict should feel that there is an adult on campus who is willing and able to help them resolve the conflict. There should be **structures or systems** in place to practice conflict resolution, which can include identifying mediators, locating neutral spaces for conversations between the conflicted parties, including parents and guardians, and support services to meet students' mental health needs. Additionally, the campus culture should utilize and promote **conflict resolution**, rather than simply administering consequences. This can be done by promoting conversations between students and adults and among peers regarding various aspects of their school experiences.

APPLYING DISCIPLINE POLICY IN A FAIR AND EQUITABLE MANNER

The school discipline policy must be applied to students in a fair and equitable manner. Many studies have shown that male students, especially minority males, are disciplined more often and more severely than their peers. **Unfair discipline** can lead to increased misbehavior from students who receive the discipline at a higher rate than others, as well as by students who witness the inequitable discipline. The student who is disciplined more frequently may believe that he or she will receive consequences regardless of behavior, so he or she may choose to misbehave and earn the consequences. Students who witness this may believe they will not be punished for their behavior, so they can behave however they like. Rules should be enforced **consistently**. For example, if a school rule states that students should not chew gum, this rule should be enforced at all times and with all students, not just when it is convenient for the teacher or other staff member. Additionally, applying discipline in an unfair or inequitable manner can **damage relationships** with students and parents and can negatively influence the school culture.

COMMUNICATING THE SCHOOL'S DISCIPLINE POLICY TO STUDENTS, STAFF, AND PARENTS

The school's discipline policy should be communicated to students, staff, and parents. Students must understand **behavioral expectations** if they are to meet them. It cannot be assumed that all students and their families hold the same expectations for behavior. As a result, the school's discipline policy must be **clearly communicated**. This can be done with a printed **handbook** for student behavior, as well as through **verbal communication**. When the discipline policy is not communicated clearly, this can lead to confusion and anger when consequences are administered. Emotional reactions from students and their parents or guardians can be expected when consequences are administered, especially for severe consequences. Ambiguity around rules and consequences makes it difficult to administer discipline and can lead to the nullification of warranted consequences due to ineffective communication of the discipline policy.

BULLYING

Bullying occurs when one uses strength or other means of influence to **intimidate** another person. Bullying can be verbal, social, or physical and involves an imbalance of power. To prevent bullying, a school leader must employ several strategies. First, students and staff must be aware of what bullying is and is not. This will help to **identify** bullying quickly if it occurs. Also, the leader should create an environment in which bullying is **not acceptable or tolerated**. This will encourage those who are being bullied and those who observe bullying to report it so that it can be stopped. The school leader and the staff should also **model healthy, respectful relationships** with one another. The leader should not be a bully to staff, nor should staff bully students, as this would set an inappropriate model for students on campus. Additionally, acts of bullying should be addressed **swiftly and effectively**. This may include disciplinary consequences or other interventions such as peer mediation, counseling, or other strategies.

MILD AND NORMAL DISCIPLINARY PROBLEMS

COMMON DISCIPLINARY PROBLEMS

Many disciplinary issues among students are common and can be prepared for with effective **classroom management strategies**. One category of common discipline problems is **disengagement**. Students who disengage are not usually disruptive of others in the instructional setting but are not receiving instruction. These students may put their heads down and sleep or participate in off-task activities such as drawing, reading, writing, or daydreaming. Another category of discipline problems is **disruptive**. These behaviors indicate that the misbehaving student is not participating in instruction and is also preventing others from participating. These behaviors include excessive talking, standing or walking around at inappropriate times, calling out, touching or hitting others, making disruptive noises, and many others. These types of behavior are often addressed by the teacher when they occur and do not require serious disciplinary consequences unless the behaviors are repeated and the student does not respond to redirection.

USING RESTORATIVE JUSTICE IN SCHOOLS

Restorative justice is a practice in which students who have harmed their school community or an individual through their misbehavior are required to **repair the harm**. The first step is to facilitate a **conversation** regarding the offender's behavior. This is usually led by an adult in the school. The offender has the opportunity to provide his or her side of the story and give input on the consequences. Traditional consequences usually include detention, suspension, and expulsion, among others, whereas restorative justice provides an opportunity for a holistic approach to **correcting the misbehavior**, i.e., "righting a wrong" or "making it right" and preventing it from recurring in the future. There are **no predefined consequences**, as these might vary significantly, based on the individual incident. For example, if a student has a temper tantrum, flips a desk in a classroom, and overturns a supply table, a community of adults and peers may determine that the

76

student must clean the classroom during lunch for a week in addition to offering a public apology to the teacher and classmates.

CLASSROOM MANAGEMENT

Classroom management refers to the strategies that teachers use to maintain order in the classroom and establish an environment conducive to learning. Classroom management is effective in preventing and addressing **minor disciplinary problems**. A teacher who demonstrates effective classroom management considers student behavior and management in all aspects of the instructional process, including lesson planning, lesson delivery, room arrangement, procedures, and more. For example, a teacher may use **diverse instructional practices** to engage students and prevent disengagement or off-task behavior during a lesson. A teacher may also design a lesson so that students can get out of their seats and **move** to different areas of the classroom at various points. Classroom management also involves having clear **expectations** for student behavior, established **procedures** for all instructional activities, and strategies for effective **redirection** of students who misbehave. Teachers with effective classroom management also build **rapport** with students and utilize **parental communication** to preserve the learning environment.

DIFFERENT DISCIPLINE APPROACHES

School discipline approaches range from lax to very stringent. A **lax approach** does not mean that school discipline does not exist; it means that discipline is often determined on an individual basis, reflective of the circumstances and individuals involved. This may include practices such as teen or peer courts and restorative justice models. Some discipline approaches combine **individualized disciplinary strategies** with **set disciplinary policies**. These approaches may offer flexibility in disciplinary options for relatively minor offenses and more defined options for more severe offenses. The most **stringent discipline approaches** have strict, pre-determined consequences for student misbehaviors. The most common example of this type of discipline approach is a zero-tolerance policy. In **zero-tolerance policies**, the consequences associated with particular behavioral infractions are administered without regard to the individual offender, context, or other variables within the situation. Many schools implement discipline approaches that fall within the midrange of this continuum, but a school leader should determine the best discipline approach for the campus based on student needs.

ROLE OF PARENTAL COMMUNICATION IN ADDRESSING DISCIPLINE PROBLEMS

Parental communication is an asset when addressing student discipline problems. It is important that parents are aware of their children's behavior while at school. This awareness, fostered through consistent and effective communication between the school and the parent, can help build a **positive relationship and rapport**. Additionally, the parent can support the school in disciplinary efforts and vice versa to establish **consistency** in behavioral expectations of the student. Finally, communication provides parents with the opportunity to **intervene** in a child's misbehavior before those behaviors escalate to more severe behaviors or have a negative impact on the student's academic progress. Failure to communicate with a parent regarding a child's behavior can cause **negative consequences** for the school, such as complaints about how the discipline was handled by school administration or contesting of assigned consequences. Parents or guardians should always be part of the disciplinary process.

SEVERE DISCIPLINARY PROBLEMS
ROLE OF SPECIAL EDUCATION STATUS IN ADDRESSING DISCIPLINARY PROBLEMS

When a student who is identified as receiving special education services displays behavioral issues, it is important to take certain steps to meet the child's needs. Some students with this identification already have **behavioral plans** in place. Teachers and school leaders must abide by these plans, which may include specific strategies for correcting a student's behavior or predetermined disciplinary consequences decided by the special education committee, which may or may not be aligned to the general student code of conduct. If a student who receives special education services commits a **severe disciplinary infraction** that could warrant consequences such as suspension or expulsion, a special meeting must be held by the special education committee to determine if the behavior was a manifestation of the student's identified disability. If it is concluded by the committee that the behavior is a manifestation of the student's identified disability, that student would likely not be subject to the traditional disciplinary consequences outlined by the student code of conduct. On the other hand, if the committee determines that the student's behavior is not associated with the disability, the student would likely be subject to the outlined disciplinary consequences.

ROLE OF DISCIPLINARY ALTERNATIVE EDUCATION PROGRAMS

Suspension and expulsion are consequences for severe student behavioral infractions. **Suspensions** typically last one to three days, but for some offenses, students are removed from the traditional education setting for longer periods of time. The public school system provides a means of education for all students, even those who have been removed from their traditional school due to extended suspension or expulsion. Students in these situations may receive their education through an **alternative education program**. In these programs, students may be assigned to attend the program for a certain number of days, usually for no longer than a school year. School districts may establish alternative education programs within the district or work with a program operating in that region. Additionally, students who commit crimes punishable by law may attend a school operated by the local **juvenile justice department**. Like other alternative education programs, the assigned duration that a student must attend varies based on the offense, as deemed by the courts.

ROLE OF LAW ENFORCEMENT IN SCHOOL DISCIPLINE

Some student behavioral infractions are not only violations of school codes of conduct, but also of the law. Consequently, **law enforcement** has the right and responsibility to administer **legal consequences** in addition to local disciplinary consequences. For example, if students engage in a physical altercation on campus, they are subject to local disciplinary consequences which may include suspension, but they are also subject to the law, which may warrant a citation. Many school districts and school leaders have opted to maintain a **police presence** on campus at all times. A school district may have its own police department dedicated to its schools. This police presence is established for the safety of everyone on campus, but if students break the law, the police exercise their authority by addressing the infraction. The involvement of law enforcement is discretionary, at times, depending on the offense. Law enforcement is not a replacement for school discipline, but a supplement.

Collaborating and Communicating with Stakeholders

Using Community Resources

COLLABORATE WITH STAKEHOLDERS TO USE RESOURCES

ENGAGING COMMUNITY STAKEHOLDERS

A school leader can take several steps to engage **community stakeholders** in order to utilize community resources and build partnerships. First, the leader should **communicate** effectively with stakeholders. Stakeholders are more likely to engage when they are aware of the activities happening at the school, the vision and goals for the school, and the accomplishments of the students and staff. When stakeholders are aware of these things, they are able to identify where they can support the school. Next, the school leader should invite stakeholders to **visit** the school and **participate** in school activities. This may include activities such as Career Day, awards assemblies, graduation, fairs, and more. Finally, the school leader should engage in **activities hosted by community stakeholders**. This will demonstrate that the school leader is supportive of their endeavors and is open to learning about the stakeholders' roles in the community. As the leader builds relationships with these stakeholders, he or she can identify individualized ways to further engage community stakeholders.

SUPPORTING SCHOOL PROGRAMS WITH COMMUNITY RESOURCES

Almost all aspects of the school program can be supported with community resources. **Local community organizations** can prove to be valuable in a broad range of areas that benefit the school, its staff, and the students. These may include transportation, training, academic support, extracurricular activities, fundraising, clubs, sponsorships, internships for students, physical resources such as equipment, services, and much more. For example, community volunteers help to **maintain school safety** with services such as greeting visitors, monitoring halls, or assisting with arrival and dismissal. Some community organizations may be able to provide **school supplies** for students or classroom supplies for teachers, which can support the instructional program. Other organizations may have access to men and women who can serve as **mentors** to at-risk youth on campus. It is up to the school leader to identify community resources near the school and determine if and how those resources can benefit the school community.

BENEFITS OF COMMUNITY PARTNERSHIPS

Community partnerships are beneficial to the school and the community. Establishing **community partnerships** is a way of providing **resources** to students and their families, usually at little or no cost to them. This can be invaluable to low-income families who otherwise would not be able to afford the services. Additionally, establishing community partnerships creates **sustainability and stability** within the community. When the school and its families patronize the organizations in the community and utilize their services, this helps to ensure that the organization will remain operable in the community. Frequently, services disappear from communities because they are underutilized, especially in impoverished communities. Finally, community partnerships established by the school leader help to **align** the school vision and goals with those of the community to garner more support and resources to accomplish the vision and goals.

VARIETY OF SERVICES

SERVICES PROVIDED FOR STUDENTS THROUGH COMMUNITY RESOURCES

Many community resources used to support schools are targeted toward students in need. Some community resources target **academic needs**. These include providing tutorial services, free or low-cost school supplies, free books, internships, training programs, and more. Other community resources target **physical health needs**. These resources may include free or low-cost immunizations, free or low-cost dental services, free or low-cost medical checkups, and more. These types of resources may also address other physical needs of students, such as food, clothing, toiletries, or haircuts and grooming. Additionally, some community resources cater to the **psychosocial needs** of students. These resources may include mentoring, counseling, therapy, peer mediation, and many others. Some organizations provide specific services while others offer a variety of services. School leaders need to coordinate access to and delivery of these services to best meet students' needs.

SERVICES PROVIDED FOR STAFF THROUGH COMMUNITY RESOURCES

Even though staff members of the school do not necessarily reside in the community associated with the school, some community organizations extend benefits and resources to **staff** because of their service to the community. These resources may include **memberships or discounts** to local businesses for purchasing food or supplies for the classroom, access to free **training or resources** that can aid in their professional development, or **partnerships** with local businesses to supplement instruction in the classroom. Many organizations in the community are willing to donate time, money, or resources and supplies for special events or activities hosted at the school. Consequently, the school leader and staff members should keep community stakeholders informed about school events to help determine how these community partners can support the school.

SERVICES PROVIDED FOR PARENTS THROUGH COMMUNITY RESOURCES

As residents of the community, parents often have access to certain resources. At times, these resources can be delivered through the school to increase the likelihood of **parental engagement** in these resources. These services may include English as a Second Language (ESL) classes for non-native English speakers, GED or adult high school programs, technology courses, individual and family counseling, and much more. Additionally, some community services assist adults with acquiring housing or meeting household expenses such as rent, utilities, and food. Other services may include childcare, parenting classes, and other supports for the adults and their families. For many of these community organizations, the rationale for providing support to parents is that the children will benefit, which in turn **positively affects their school life** in areas such as attendance and academic performance.

VALUE OF PARTNERING WITH COMMUNITY AND RECREATIONAL CENTERS

Partnering with community and recreational centers is often an opportunity to provide students and their families with **resources** they may not normally have access to or take advantage of. Often, community members are unaware of services that these organizations provide at little to no cost, such as childcare, use of gym facilities, access to technology, and more. Similarly, these organizations can help to **expand the school program**. For example, an organization may partner with the school to provide childcare on campus for students whose parents cannot pick them up at school dismissal time. Similarly, a community center may provide GED preparation to adults and can offer these services on the school campus to parents. These partnerships are **mutually beneficial** and often involve sharing services and facilities.

80

Collaboration to Benefit Both School and Community
Memorandum of Understanding

A memorandum of understanding is a contract between two parties, outlining the details of an agreement in which no money is exchanged. It is an agreement of **services to be provided**. For example, an organization may offer to provide tutorial services for students in reading and math after school on campus at no cost to the school. The school and the organization would draft a **memorandum of understanding** that outlines the tutorial services to be provided and the school leader's promise to provide a location on campus for the services. Both parties would sign the document and receive an original copy. The verbiage of the memorandum of understanding can be the same as in a traditional contract, but often the language is simpler as the sole purpose of the document is to state the exchange of services with no monetary compensation. The purpose of the memorandum of understanding is to **document** the services that are to be provided. This type of documentation can be helpful for both parties in providing evidence that the services were agreed upon and delivered.

Long-Term Benefits of Collaborating with Community Members

Collaborating with members of the community can have long-term benefits for the school and the surrounding community. When there is collaboration and partnership between the community and the school, there can be an **alignment of vision and goals**. This fosters long-term, mutually beneficial **partnerships**. For example, community organizations and the school may identify a need for increased technology education within the community. They can collaborate to add technology programs in the school, programs for adults within the community, and an increase in internet access for community members. Also, community programs can be integrated into the school program and even housed on the school campus. For example, a GED program may be based on a school campus to increase accessibility to parents and encourage parental engagement at the school. Community support can sustain or boost student enrollment in school and participation in special school programs.

Connection Between the School and Local Employment Trends

The school provides education and training that make students **employable** in the community workforce. As a result, the school can supplement or adjust programming to respond to **community needs**, such as training students in particular fields that are experiencing an employment shortage within the community. For example, the school leader and community members may identify a need for more healthcare workers in their community. They can tailor a school program to offer healthcare courses and training that could lead to certifications and degrees in the healthcare field. These students could then enter the local workforce with the skills to fill the needs of local employers. Many schools, especially secondary schools, partner with **local community colleges and community organizations** to identify employment trends to support the local community as well as to increase the likelihood that graduates can obtain employment.

Connection Between the School and Local Education Trends

It is beneficial to the school community, the community at large, and postsecondary education institutions to **align education expectations** between public school and college. Schools and students benefit when there is communication between area colleges and the school for the purpose of understanding the local education trends and needs. For example, the local community college can communicate to school leaders that recently enrolled freshmen have significant deficits in math skills. This information can prompt a school leader to analyze and revise the current math program and make the needed adjustments to ensure that students are graduating with the knowledge and skills needed to be successful in college. Similarly, communication between postsecondary institutions and school leaders can help to identify the **soft skills** that students need to be successful in college, as well as **trends in degree programs and career paths**. This type of communication can also lead to the institution of **higher education programming** on school campuses, such as dual-credit enrollment or training and certification programs.

BENEFIT OF MAINTAINING A SAFE SCHOOL FOR THE COMMUNITY

The first priority of a school leader is maintaining school safety. This benefits not only the students and staff, but also the community as a whole. When issues and conflicts identified at the school are resolved promptly, this can prevent **escalation** of those issues outside the school, which can ultimately prevent violence or other altercations in the community. Also, a safe school in the community becomes **a safe haven or refuge** for unsafe communities and neighborhoods. Community members are willing to engage in school events when they know that the school is safe and organized. Additionally, community members and organizations are willing to support and invest in schools that are safe and well-run. In contrast, when a school is not safe, this can lead to decreased enrollment and a lack of parental and community support.

BUILDING RELATIONSHIPS WITH BUSINESS, RELIGIOUS, POLITICAL, AND SERVICE ORGANIZATIONS

BUILDING RELATIONSHIPS WITH VARIOUS COMMUNITY ORGANIZATIONS

A school leader can build relationships with various community organizations through effective communication and active participation in community events. First, the school leader should effectively **communicate** to community leaders that he or she desires to partner and build a relationship. This communication can involve sharing the school vision and goals and learning about the vision and goals of the community organizations. This can lead to a discussion of how the school and community organizations can organize **mutually beneficial plans and activities**. Collaborating will help to establish relationships. Then, the school leader should be an **active participant in community events** so that he or she will be visible and recognizable, as well as to show support for the community. This participation may include attending events at other schools in the community, attending church services in the community, or participating in other community-sponsored events. Supporting the activities of community organizations demonstrates investment in the community and helps to build relationships.

INFORMATION SOURCES TO LEARN ABOUT COMMUNITY DYNAMICS

It is important for a leader to understand the dynamics of the community to meet the community's needs and to establish productive relationships. These **dynamics** can be revealed in a variety of ways. Often, **community leaders and parents** in the community are willing to discuss the community's makeup and dynamics. The school leader can search for **publications**, such as community newspapers or bulletins, to stay up to date on community affairs. These newspapers often highlight community leaders, organizations, community needs, and upcoming community events. Additionally, the school leader can attend **community meetings** such as town hall meetings to learn about the concerns of the community. It is also important to learn who the **government officials** in the area are, as well as candidates running for office in upcoming elections.

Communication with Family and the Public

COMMUNICATING WITH FAMILIES AND THE PUBLIC
COMMUNICATING WITH FAMILIES AND THE PUBLIC

A school leader should take advantage of multiple ways of communicating with families and the public. Communication can be facilitated through **technology**. Methods include emails, electronic newsletters, websites, social media, mass automated phone calls, and other forms of technology that can be used to share messages with large groups of people. The school leader can also communicate in ways that require **little or no technology**. This includes making personal phone calls, hosting community meetings, making public announcements at community events, mailing letters, and other methods. When hosting community meetings, the leader should ensure that these meetings are held at a **variety of times** that are convenient for parents and the community, such as early morning, late evening, or weekends. A leader can use a variety of ways to communicate and must identify the **most preferred and effective means of communication** for the school community. Additionally, the school leader can use **multiple modes of communication** to share the same message and reach as many people as possible.

OVERCOMING LANGUAGE BARRIERS IN COMMUNICATION

In diverse communities, school leaders often encounter language barriers when attempting to communicate with parents of students or other community members. It is helpful when a leader is fluent in more than one language, but often a variety of languages are spoken in these communities. To **overcome language barriers**, a leader should be proactive in devising communication strategies. First, the leader should be **aware of all languages** that are spoken in the school community. Then, the leader should attempt to have school employees who are fluent in the languages spoken on campus so they can **translate** when needed. Additionally, **school communications** can be translated into a variety of languages. Translators or translation machines can be available at community meetings, including sign language when appropriate. Many businesses offer translation services for documents, as well as for meetings and conferences held in real time.

EFFECTIVELY COMMUNICATING WITH THE MEDIA

There are times that the school leader will need to communicate effectively with the **media**, for both positive and negative reasons. The school leader should first follow the protocols and procedures outlined by the school district when communicating with the media, especially in situations in which the media attention is negative for the school or district. Some school districts **centralize media communication** and do not permit school leaders or other staff to communicate with the media without express approval. When communicating with the media, school leaders should speak truthfully, communicate in alignment with the school and district vision and goals, and communicate according to instructions from the school district staff. A school leader can utilize media outlets to **positively highlight the school**, such as broadcasting upcoming events or spotlighting student and staff accomplishments.

FORMAL VS. INFORMAL COMMUNICATION

Formal communication is usually prepared in advance. The school leader knows what is to be communicated and how. **Formal communication** is typically **structured and controlled** and is delivered in a formal way, such as in a presentation to the community or a speech at an event. Formal communication also involves **prepared print communication** such as a letter, email, or bulletin to the public. In contrast, **informal communication** is often **impromptu**. This often involves conversation with an individual or group, an unexpected phone call, or a text message. In informal communication, the topic may be unexpected or vary within the course of communication. Informal communication can occur before or after a formal meeting or event, as a result of an unexpected phone call, or in any variety of circumstances in which the school leader was not prepared for the communication or conversation.

PRECAUTIONS WHEN SPEAKING INFORMALLY WITH STAKEHOLDERS

School leaders should take precautions when speaking informally with stakeholders to **protect** themselves, the school, and the school district. **Informal conversation** can be used negatively by people who do not have the best interest of the school or school leader in mind or who are seeking personal gain. As a result, a leader should take care to be professional even in informal speech and to speak in accordance with the school and district vision and goals. For example, a school leader may make a joke during an informal conversation after a parent meeting that the parent does not believe to be in good taste. That parent can then make a formal complaint to the school district regarding the leader's professionalism. Regardless of the leader's perception of his or her relationship with the stakeholder, it is imperative to remember one's position as school leader when engaging in informal conversation. The leader should view all communication, formal or informal, as a **reflection** of the position of school leader and of the school and school district.

BEST PRACTICES FOR COMMUNICATING THROUGH EMAIL

When communicating via email, a school leader should make sure that the email communicates the message in the **intended way**. In order to do this, the leader should maintain a **professional tone**. Humor and sarcasm are not often conveyed well via email and should be avoided. The school leader should also review the email for proper spelling, grammar, and word use, as errors can cause the message to be misunderstood. The leader should use features such as *Reply All* and *cc* with caution, only sending the email to those who need to be included in the conversation. Also, the school leader should confirm that any necessary attachments are included in the email, if applicable. It is also a good practice to confirm with the recipient that the email has been received. Emails with attachments or mass emails are sometimes redirected to the recipient's spam or junk mail folder and may not be received in a timely manner, if at all.

CONSIDERATIONS WHEN SCHEDULING PARENT MEETINGS

When scheduling parent meetings for large groups of parents, the school leader should consider the time of day and day of the week that these meetings are to be held. The goal of these meetings is to effectively communicate with parents in a group setting, so the school leader needs to ensure that the scheduled day and time accommodate the majority of parents for **maximum attendance**. The ideal times for these events will vary based on the needs of parents in the community. In many communities, parents work during the day, so **evening meetings** are more favorable. In some communities, certain days of the week are dedicated to religious activities, sporting events, or other engagements, and this should be taken into consideration when scheduling a parent meeting. For example, a school leader would not want to schedule a parent meeting at the elementary school on the same evening as the high school football game, as this would put the two events in competition. The school leader can talk to parents and **survey families** to identify ideal times to host meetings and should be open to hosting meetings at a variety of times, such as early in the morning or on weekends.

INVOLVING FAMILIES IN DECISION MAKING
SHARED DECISION-MAKING COMMITTEE

The purpose of the Shared Decision-Making Committee (**SDMC**) in schools is to provide a structured process for the inclusion of **stakeholders** in the school decision-making process. This committee is made up of school leadership, school staff, parents, community members, and other key stakeholders that the school leader may choose to include. The committee meets regularly to discuss **key decisions** that the school leader will make. These decisions may involve school programming, fundraising, planning for school events, and other initiatives. In these meetings, participants are informed of **key details** that should be considered in making these decisions and are given the opportunity to **voice their opinions** on the decisions as well as to provide **recommendations**. The SDMC provides recommendations to the school leader but does not have authority to dictate decisions. However, the SDMC provides an opportunity for stakeholder participation in the school process and helps to build relationships between the school leader and stakeholders.

WAYS FOR FAMILIES TO BE INVOLVED IN SCHOOL DECISION-MAKING

The school leader should provide as many opportunities as possible to **include families** in school decision-making. First, the leader should **inform families in advance** of decisions that will be made. For example, the leader may alert the parents that he or she is considering converting the school playground into a garden. This gives families an opportunity to provide feedback prior to the decision. The school leader can use surveys to gather input from families regarding the school, providing data that can be used in decision-making. Additionally, the school leader can communicate with **parent organizations** on campus or form a **parent focus group** to gather feedback and opinions on decisions to be made at the school. Also, there should always be at least one parent representative on the **Shared Decision-Making Committee**.

WAYS FOR FAMILIES TO BE INVOLVED IN THE DECISIONS MADE ABOUT THEIR CHILD'S EDUCATION

Each family should have the opportunity to be involved in decisions made about their individual child's education. These decisions may include course selection or school programming pathways, extracurricular activities like clubs and sports, opportunities for tutorials and extended learning, and many others. First, the school should provide clear and effective **communication** to the families, indicating areas of the school program in which they can help make decisions for their children. Then, the school leader can provide ways for parents to offer their **opinions**, such as through frequent parent meetings or holding one-on-one conferences. Also, phone calls and emails can be very effective in including parents in the decision-making process. Many schools send **informative letters or bulletins** home to parents to include them in the process. Some campuses have opted to staff a **parent liaison** who specializes in communicating with parents and encouraging their participation in the school decision-making process.

BENEFITS OF INVOLVING FAMILIES IN DECISION-MAKING

Involving families in decision-making is beneficial to both the families and the school. Involving families increases **buy-in** for the decisions that are made, which can lead to increased **support for school initiatives**. For example, if families help to decide which tutoring program to implement after school, they will be more likely to have their child participate in the tutorials. Involving families in decision-making also strengthens the **relationship between the school and families** and stimulates **parental engagement**. Also, when families are involved, they often share information and a **perspective** that can inform the school leader's decisions. This can help the leader make decisions that better address the needs of students and their families.

NEED FOR TWO-WAY COMMUNICATION

Two-way communication is the process of sending and receiving messages. In two-way communication, a person who receives a message has an opportunity to **respond** or send a message back to the sender. When collaborating with stakeholders and families, it is important for the school leader to provide opportunities for **two-way communication**, in contrast to only sending **one-way messages**. Two-way communication helps the leader to confirm that the message or communication was received as intended. Sometimes a message can be unclear or misinterpreted, and this confusion can be identified in two-way communication. Additionally, two-way communication allows the school leader to learn more about the opinions, needs, and concerns of key stakeholders. Finally, two-way communication promotes involvement and engagement of the stakeholders, which can foster relationships between them and the school and increase buy-in from the stakeholders in regard to the school leader's vision and goals.

ENSURING TWO-WAY COMMUNICATION

A leader can ensure two-way communication by providing many **opportunities** for stakeholders to communicate with him or her. For example, a school leader may host a community meeting and provide a time during the program for stakeholders to ask questions or voice their opinions. School leaders can also make themselves **accessible** to those seeking to communicate with them. This can be done in several ways, such as holding frequent meetings with stakeholders or choosing certain office hours with an "open-door policy." Other ways of promoting communication include sending out **surveys**, creating a **comment or feedback box** on campus, and being open to **phone calls and emails**. A school leader should be visible during parent and community events and display a willingness to engage in conversation with stakeholders, demonstrating **receptiveness** to two-way communication.

Advocacy

APPROPRIATENESS AND EFFICACY OF SYSTEM FOR PROTECTING AND ADVOCATING FOR STUDENTS

A school leader should have systems in place for the protection and advocacy of students. These systems should be based on the needs of the student population and should be responsive to the changing needs and concerns of these students. A school leader will know if these systems are **appropriate and effective** in various ways. First, there should be a **student culture of safety** in school. This culture involves students feeling free to engage in the academic program, social activities, and extracurricular activities. Also, students should have an **adequate voice**. An appropriate and effective system for protection and advocacy will allow various avenues for students to contribute their ideas and voice their concerns. Additionally, there will be evidence that students are **supported** in times of need or crisis. This means that socio-emotional needs are identified and addressed quickly so that students can engage in the school program. These systems are effective and appropriate only if they benefit all students. If some groups of students are **marginalized or neglected** on campus, the school leader must revisit the appropriateness and efficacy of the school's systems.

POTENTIAL OPPORTUNITIES TO SERVE AS AN ADVOCATE FOR STUDENTS

Advocacy for students is necessary whenever any group of students is or has the potential to be **marginalized**. These groups are commonly students of low socioeconomic status, minority status, immigrant status, or a different sexual orientation. However, any student or group of students can need advocacy at any given time. There is an opportunity to advocate for these students when their **right to an equitable education in a safe environment** is threatened. For example, a school leader may observe that an academic program offered in the district consistently leaves out students who receive special education services. The school leader may advocate for that group of students by calling for a review of the application and acceptance criteria to drive change. Opportunities for student advocacy can occur on campus, within the school district, or within the local, state, and federal political arenas.

CONFIDENTIALITY
MAINTAINING STUDENT CONFIDENTIALITY

A school leader must maintain student confidentiality according to the Family Educational Rights and Privacy Act (FERPA). This involves keeping **student information and records** confidential. However, when advocating for students, the school leader may be informed of student information by other staff members, parents, or the students themselves that should also be kept confidential. Keeping the students' confidentiality means not sharing **private information** with outside parties unnecessarily. This fosters **trust** between the school leader and the student or other stakeholders. Establishing this trust helps to create a school culture in which students and their families are willing to share sensitive information with the school staff to help **advocate** for a student. For example, a parent may inform the school leader that the family has recently become homeless. Certain documents must be completed and certain staff need to be informed of this information to advocate for the homeless student, but the school leader must ensure that the sensitive information remains as private as possible. There are circumstances in which the student's confidentiality may need to be breached, but the school leader should make an effort to maintain that confidentiality.

SITUATIONS IN WHICH STUDENT CONFIDENTIALITY MUST BE BREACHED

A school leader and other school staff must do their best to maintain the confidence of students, but under some circumstances a student's confidentiality must be **breached**. If students confide in a staff member that they are being **harmed**, pose **harm to themselves**, or pose **harm to others**, school staff members have the responsibility to act on that information for the protection of those students or others. For example, a student may confide in a teacher that he or she is contemplating suicide. The teacher would then break the student's confidentiality and inform the school leader of the student's intentions. The teacher and the school leader would then contact the student's parents and the proper authorities to obtain immediate help for the student. Other examples that warrant a breach in student confidentiality include information related to **child abuse or neglect** or **threats of violence to others**.

MOTIVATING STUDENTS
INTRINSIC MOTIVATION

Intrinsic motivation is motivation that comes from **within**. It is a person's own drive to succeed or to accomplish a goal. For students, this **intrinsic motivation** may be the result of education and career goals, family expectations, social influences, and more. Intrinsic motivation may drive students to meet or exceed academic performance expectations, participate in and excel in extracurricular activities, or choose certain education and career pathways. Intrinsic motivation is affected very little by **outside influences** because the drive comes from within. For example, a high school student may desire to become a writer and consequently excels in English Language Arts classes. This student may have an English Language Arts teacher that he or she does not get along with, but because the drive to become a writer is intrinsic, the student may still work hard and perform well in that class. Intrinsic motivation is considered more effective than extrinsic motivation. Students who excel in school, especially in the face of obstacles and challenges, are often intrinsically motivated.

EXTRINSIC MOTIVATION

Extrinsic motivation is motivation that comes from an **outside source**, such as another person, and is in the form of a reward. The reward can be **tangible**, such as money, prizes, or gifts, or it can be **intangible**, such as an experience, recognition, or approval. Teachers and other staff often use extrinsic motivation to encourage students to perform at a certain level or behave in a certain way. For example, a teacher may tell her third-grade class that all students who complete their homework will receive stickers. The students will be motivated to complete their homework and earn stickers. **Extrinsic motivation** can be effective with students, especially when they are lacking intrinsic motivation. However, extrinsic motivation is considered less effective than intrinsic motivation because in the absence of the reward, motivation significantly decreases. Additionally, if the reward loses its appeal, motivation will decrease. For example, if the third-grade teacher were to stop offering stickers for homework, the number of completed homework assignments might decline. Similarly, students may be less excited about receiving stickers for homework near the end of the school year, resulting in fewer completed homework assignments.

87

MOTIVATING STUDENTS

School staff can create **systems of rewards** to motivate students to engage in the academic program, perform at higher levels, and behave in an acceptable manner. Rewards can be given for individual and collective behaviors. Some schools have used **point systems** or **merit systems** to reward and motivate students. Students can redeem points for prizes, participation in field trips, or participation in other school activities. Some schools use stickers, tickets, or other means of reinforcing positive student behaviors, which can be redeemed as well. For example, a student may earn a ticket for participating in class discussion, which can be redeemed for a prize. This reward would encourage the student to increase participation in class discussion. Students may also be motivated by public recognition, such as receiving an award at an awards ceremony, being identified on the school website or a classroom bulletin board, or having their names announced during school announcements. Students are **motivated** when rewards systems are clear, fair, and consistent and when expectations are clearly outlined.

ASPECTS OF THE SCHOOL THAT CAN DEMOTIVATE STUDENTS

Perceived negative aspects of the school can decrease student motivation, causing them to disengage in the school program. If a student perceives school as **unsafe**, he or she may have poor school attendance or arrive late to school. If a student perceives the teacher to be **unfair or ineffective**, the student may not desire to perform well in that class, resulting in poor grades and possibly behavioral problems. When students perceive **school rules or policies** as unfair or inequitable, they may be discouraged from abiding by those policies or engaging in the programs that the policies or procedures apply to. For example, a student may desire to audition for a role in the school play. However, the student views the audition process as unfair and believes that certain students will be chosen for the roles regardless of who auditions. Consequently, that student will choose not to audition for the play or engage in the theater program. School leaders must identify aspects of the school and school program that may **demotivate** students and remedy these where possible.

Professionalism and Ethics

Personal and Professional Ethics

INTEGRITY

Integrity refers to being honest and trustworthy and exhibiting moral principles. A person with integrity is generally of good character. A school leader can demonstrate **integrity** by behaving in a **trustworthy** manner with district personnel, staff, students, parents, and community stakeholders. The school leader should behave **ethically** in regard to all aspects of the position, including finance, personnel issues, and student matters. A school leader with integrity will hold him or herself and others **accountable** for ethical behavior, will recognize when ethics have been breached, and will take appropriate action in response. A school leader will also implement systems and procedures to ensure that the **rights and confidentiality** of students and staff are maintained at all times.

WHEN A SITUATION PRESENTS A CONFLICT OF INTEREST

A conflict of interest is a situation in which the school leader can obtain personal gain or harm from a decision made as a leader. For example, a school leader may determine that the school gymnasium needs to be repainted. A family member of the leader owns a company that provides such a service and offers a bid. This would present a **conflict of interest** for the leader because he or she would potentially derive a benefit from hiring a family member's business to complete the job. Other situations that could present a conflict of interest may include hiring or terminating staff, awarding or disciplining a student who is a family member, or voting in an official capacity for colleagues or family members. A school leader should be aware of potential conflicts of interest and **alert superiors** should such a situation arise.

HOW LAWS AND REGULATIONS PROTECT PRIVACY AND CONFIDENTIALITY OF INFORMATION

Laws and regulations have been enacted to protect the privacy and confidentiality of students and staff in schools. Specifically, the **Family Educational Rights and Privacy Act (FERPA)** is a federal law that protects the privacy of **student education records**. Any school that receives funds from the United States Department of Education is subject to this law. It provides guidelines for who can access or view student records, who can alter student records, and what student information can be disseminated without student or parental consent. School leaders must abide by this law and implement policies and procedures on campus that ensure other school personnel also abide by this law. Additionally, schools have the obligation to **inform** parents and students aged 18 or older of their rights under FERPA.

SITUATIONS INVOLVING ISSUES OF ETHICS AND INTEGRITY

A school leader will find that many of the situations they encounter involve **issues of ethics and integrity**. These situations may involve students, parents, personnel, and community members. Situations regarding **students** may involve grades, retention or promotion, assigning consequences in discipline matters, awards and recognition, and others. Situations involving **parents** may be student related or involve fundraising, elections to committees, or others. Situations regarding **personnel** may involve reprimands or other discipline, promotions, pay, and others. Additionally, situations involving **community members** may involve voting and elections, awarding contracts, exchanging services, and more. The leader must also use ethics and integrity in their own **decision-making processes** in regard to budgeting, school academic and extracurricular programming, and business and community partnerships.

ELEMENTS OF A TRANSPARENT DECISION-MAKING PROCESS

Some school decisions require input from stakeholders. In these decisions, it is important to have a **transparent decision-making process** so that all stakeholders can be assured that the decision is made ethically and with integrity. First, stakeholders must be **notified in advance** of the decision to be made. They should also have **access to relevant information** for making the decision, in accordance with any privacy or confidentiality regulations. They should be notified in advance of any **public meetings** related to the decision and documented meeting minutes should be made available. Any **voting** related to the decision should also be documented for transparency. Finally, when the school leader has made a decision, it should be **shared** with stakeholders along with the rationale for it, such as community input, votes, and other information.

ENSURING EQUITABLE TREATMENT OF STUDENTS AND STAFF

The best way that the school leader can ensure equitable treatment of students and staff is to develop **policies and procedures** and adhere to them. When there are policies and procedures in place, the school leader can refer to these to determine the **best course of action** when dealing with students and staff. For example, if a student has excessive school absences, a school attendance policy should dictate when and how to address absenteeism. Similarly, if a staff member dresses unprofessionally for work, an employee handbook should outline how to address the staff member. In a situation with no guiding policy, the school leader should use **discretion** in handling the situation and subsequently develop a **guiding policy** for future incidents. This can be in the form of memorandums or addendums to existing student and staff handbooks. While there may be extenuating circumstances that require the school leader's discretion, policies and procedures ensure that all are treated equitably.

ENSURING THAT OTHERS ARE ACTING ETHICALLY

A leader can ensure that others are acting ethically by **communicating expectations** regarding ethical behavior. The leader can provide staff with **documents and training** that explain these expectations. Employees should acknowledge receipt of such documentation by signing to confirm that they have received them as well as signing in at training sessions to confirm participation. The leader can also **monitor employee behavior**. This can be done in person by walking around and observing performance or remotely by instructing others on the leadership team to observe employee behavior or monitoring with security cameras. Security cameras are useful in areas that are most prone to unethical conduct, such as places where money is exchanged, entrances and exits, records storage, and areas on campus that are not frequently trafficked. Additionally, the leader can implement **consequences for unethical behavior** and address such behavior swiftly. Employees may be encouraged to behave ethically to avoid consequences for unethical behavior.

CONSEQUENCES OF UNETHICAL BEHAVIOR

Consequences for an employee's unethical behavior can vary, depending on the severity of the offense. For a minor offense, the employee may receive a **verbal or written reprimand** to be included in his or her personnel file. This type of situation may require a formal conference with the school leader or other school district staff. More severe offenses can result in **suspension**, **reassignment**, or **termination of employment**. For example, if an employee has behaved in an unethical manner involving exchange of money, he or she may be reassigned to a position that does not require interaction with money. Severe offenses can result in the suspension or revocation of state licensure. Ethical offenses that involve breaking the law can also result in **legal consequences** such as fines, probation, or even imprisonment as determined by city, state, and federal law.

STEPS TO TAKE WHEN ETHICS HAVE BEEN BREACHED

If a school leader has been made aware of an ethical violation, it is his or her responsibility to act immediately. In many cases, there are **procedures or guidelines** that a school leader should follow, as determined by the school district. These procedures may include notifying district personnel, initiating an investigation, conferencing with the offending employee, drafting a formal note of reprimand, and other actions. There should also be guidance from the school district on notifying **outside authorities or organizations**, such as law enforcement or Child Protective Services. In some instances, district personnel or an entity acting on their behalf handle the situation and the school leader takes on a role of **support and facilitation**. It is important for a school leader to take reports of unethical behavior seriously and act quickly and appropriately. Additionally, the school leader should maintain thorough **documentation** of the events and timelines for audit purposes.

JUSTICE AND FAIRNESS
SOCIAL JUSTICE

Social justice refers to the **fair and equitable treatment of all people**, regardless of their status in society. Factors such as socioeconomic status, race, ethnicity, place of residence, and others influence the **privileges** that certain people may have in society. These privileges, or lack thereof, can be reflected in the school system as well. The concept of social justice as it relates to education means that all students, regardless of their social status, socioeconomic status, race, ethnicity, religion, sexual orientation, or any other identifying factor, are entitled to an **equitable education** and access to **educational resources**. For example, it is considered a social injustice for children in poverty to have outdated textbooks and a lack of access to technology in schools. Social justice in education refers to advocating for children who are typically **marginalized and disenfranchised** so that they can receive the same educational opportunities as other children.

ADVOCATING FOR ALL CHILDREN

A school leader is in a unique position to be an **advocate for all children on campus**. First, the school leader needs to ensure that the **academic and extracurricular programming** is accessible to all children and reflective of the needs of all children on campus. Next, the school leader should ensure that all **special programming** is properly funded and implemented on campus. This can include programs such as Title I, special education, gifted and talented programs, English as a Second Language programs, career and technology programs, and many others. Finally, some inequities are the result of **governmental policy**, which affect the school. The school leader can use his or her voice and authority to influence policy and promote social justice in the school. Examples of these types of policy issues include school finance and funding, school zoning, school vouchers, and many others.

COMMUNICATION OF EXPECTATIONS FOR THE STAFF AND STUDENTS
IMPORTANCE OF COMMUNICATING EXPECTATIONS TO STAFF AND STUDENTS

The school leader must communicate expectations to staff and students to increase the likelihood that staff and students will meet those expectations. It is difficult for staff and students to meet expectations if they are unaware of them. This can result in **unintentional disregard of expectations**. For example, teachers may decide to leave campus during an instructional planning period. If the teachers are unaware that the school leader expects them to remain on campus even when they do not have class, it will be difficult for the school leader to hold them accountable for that behavior. Likewise, the school leader should communicate **expectations of behavior** to students before a presumed offense is committed. A school leader must effectively communicate expectations so that students and staff will know what behavior to demonstrate and so the school leader can hold them accountable for those behaviors.

91

COMMUNICATING EXPECTATIONS TO STAFF AND STUDENTS

A school leader has many opportunities to communicate expectations to staff and students. These expectations can be written and shared in **employee and student handbooks** or **codes of conduct**. These documents can be printed as well as made available online. The school leader may require that staff and students provide a signature acknowledging receipt of such documents. Additionally, expectations for behavior can be communicated or reinforced during **announcements**, in **assemblies or meetings**, and in **individual conversations**. Many school leaders post expectations for behavior on posters in school hallways and classrooms. These often take the form of classroom rules for behavior, hallway expectations, cafeteria expectations, and so on. When correcting behavior that does not meet expectations, the school leader can reinforce expectations for the offender. For example, the school leader may verbalize to an employee that he or she is late to work and remind him or her of the expected arrival time.

Transparency, Feedback, and Reflection

TRANSPARENT DECISION-MAKING BASED ON DATA

TRANSPARENT DECISION-MAKING

Transparent decision-making is the act of making sure that the process, logic, and rationale used to make a decision are **clear and open** to others. When decision-making is transparent, any **critical information** used to inform that decision is also readily available to others for review. This transparency allows others to understand **how the decision was made**. For example, if a school leader were to decide whether or not to eliminate the art program, a transparent decision-making process would allow stakeholders and team members to observe and understand how the school leader makes the decision. The process may start with publicly making known that the decision needed to be made. Then, data relating to the art program would be provided, including data related to any other programming that may be compared to the art program. Additional rationale could be documented, such as evaluating the position of the art program in relation to the school vision and goals. Based on this relevant information, observers of the decision-making process would be able to **understand** and even **predict** the decision that the leader would make.

USING DATA TO SUPPORT TRANSPARENT DECISION-MAKING

Data is essential to offering transparency in decision-making. Data is **objective**, which makes it less refutable. Stakeholders may question or contest a school leader's decisions in some cases, but are less likely to question or contest the **data influencing those decisions**. Data that is shared may include financial data, student performance data, or data related to school demographics such as enrollment, attendance, or discipline. When data is shared with stakeholders, it is easier for them to understand the **basis and determining factors** for decisions. For example, if a school leader decides to eliminate a school program based on poor student participation, the school leader can be transparent and provide the attendance and participation data for that program to the stakeholders. As a result, the stakeholders will understand that the decision is based on objective data. Additionally, basing decisions on data will encourage the school leader to make sound decisions based on concrete data whenever possible because the school leader will be aware that the decision-making process will be observed by stakeholders.

MOST EFFECTIVE DATA IN SUPPORTING TRANSPARENT DECISION-MAKING

STAFF

Providing data is an essential component of transparency in decision-making. The school leader can share data such as **school performance data** and **individual student data** to demonstrate how a decision was made. Teachers and staff understand and are able to look at student data as employees working directly with students. This data can help them understand why decisions are

92

made about certain curricular programs, school discipline procedures, and other aspects of the school program. Also, the school leader can use data to **support conversations with staff** regarding individual performance, which can lead to decision-making. For example, a school leader may determine that a third-grade reading teacher should be reassigned to a fourth-grade classroom. The leader can use student performance data and the teacher's performance evaluation data to explain the decision to the teacher. A school leader should always protect the **confidentiality** of students and personnel when applicable.

COMMUNITY STAKEHOLDERS

Providing data is an essential component of transparency in decision-making. When being transparent with stakeholders, the school leader must be careful to protect the **confidentiality** of school, student, and personnel data. As a result, the school leader should be selective about the data that is shared with stakeholders and the manner in which it is shared. Data that is already public and is used to make a decision can be helpful when sharing data with stakeholders. The school leader should be prepared to **explain** the data, the measures used to obtain it, and its implications. Although the school leader cannot share individual student and staff data, the school leader can share **aggregates of the data**. For example, the school leader may provide data of third-grade student performance on a recent benchmark assessment. Data that is shared with stakeholders should be **clear, easy to understand, and purposeful** so that it adds to the transparency of the decision-making process.

ALLOWING FOR FEEDBACK
IMPORTANCE OF GATHERING FEEDBACK

Feedback is the process of gathering information from an outside source to **evaluate** or **correct** a particular course of action. A school leader should seek feedback to ensure that he or she is on the correct path when making decisions. Without feedback, a school leader may proceed with a course of action, only to realize later that it was a mistake. For example, a leader may decide to host parent meetings on Wednesday evenings. After hosting the first meeting with poor turnout, the leader may find that many families in the community attend church on Wednesday evenings. Had the leader gathered feedback, a different time might have been chosen. Gathering feedback can help the school leader make corrections or alter a course in a timely manner. Additionally, gathering feedback from stakeholders demonstrates that the school leader is **humble** and **receptive to feedback**. Perceived humility in the leader can help in team building and relationship building with the staff and the community. Gathering feedback also increases **buy-in** from those providing the feedback, such as members of the leadership team, key community members, or school district office personnel.

GATHERING FEEDBACK

A school leader can gather feedback from stakeholders in various ways to aid in their decision-making. A primary way of gathering feedback is presenting ideas and plans to the **campus leadership team**. The leadership team may include assistant principals, deans, or other leaders on campus. This team is effective in providing feedback because they know the campus, students, and community well and have demonstrated leadership skills and thinking. For example, the leadership team may provide feedback on a lunch schedule based on their experiences from lunch duty in the cafeteria. Also, **supervising district personnel** are often available to provide feedback to the school leader, especially in confidential matters. The school leader can also solicit feedback from **students, parents, and community members**. This type of feedback can help the school leader see situations and potential decisions from other perspectives. For example, a student may provide feedback that the proposed after school program does not interest the student body. Also, gathering and implementing feedback from **stakeholders** can increase stakeholder buy-in and support of the school's vision and goals.

RESPONDING TO NEGATIVE FEEDBACK

When a leader solicits feedback from students, staff, or stakeholders, it is possible that the feedback may be **negative**. The negative feedback may be in relation to aspects of the school program or in relation to the leader. When a leader receives feedback, he or she must avoid an immediate **emotional response** to the feedback. First the leader must determine whether the feedback has **validity**. People providing feedback can sometimes speak out of anger or frustration and deliver the feedback in a harsh way. However, delivery of the feedback does not necessarily determine whether the feedback is valid. Consequently, the leader must reflect upon his or her practice and identify whether the feedback identifies an area of improvement for the leader or the school program. If so, the leader must acknowledge this weak area and take steps to improve it. When improvements have been made, if possible, the leader should seek feedback once again to determine if the concerns of the stakeholders have been addressed.

RESPONDING TO POSITIVE FEEDBACK

Positive feedback from stakeholders can be encouraging for the school leader. Sometimes this feedback is solicited and other times it is volunteered. Positive feedback can be used for **reflection and improvement**. First, the leader needs to determine the **validity** of the feedback. Some people may feel the need to offer flattery or unsubstantiated positive feedback in an effort to favorably position themselves. Therefore, a leader must not assume that his or her performance or the school's performance is favorable because one or two people offered a compliment. Next, the leader must not become **overconfident** in the area that has received positive feedback. Instead, the feedback should encourage the leader to continue the actions that led to the favorable outcome to continue to achieve good results. Positive feedback can also be **shared** with other staff so they can be assured that they are performing well in the identified area.

HONEST SELF-REFLECTION
CONDUCTING HONEST SELF-REFLECTION

Honest self-reflection is a component of growth and efficacy as a school leader. A school leader should set aside time to reflect on **personal performance as a leader**, based on identified leadership **expectations and standards**. There are many models of leadership that the school leader can use for comparison, but most school districts select or develop a **tool for leadership evaluation**. These evaluation tools include the expectations for leadership skills, performance, and behaviors. School leaders can use the tools to identify their own strengths and weaknesses. Also, any time a leader is reading professional materials such as books or articles related to leadership, it is an opportunity to reflect on how he or she measures against the skills identified in the resource. Often, stakeholders such as parents or community members offer criticisms of the leader. The school leader should reflect upon the **validity of those criticisms** to determine areas for improvement. For example, during a parent conference, a parent may complain that the leader is a poor communicator. Even though the parent may have made the statement in a moment of frustration or anger, the school leader should take the opportunity to reflect upon his or her communication skills and how those skills were used in that situation.

ADDRESSING WEAKNESSES REVEALED THROUGH SELF-REFLECTION

Once a leader has identified weaknesses through self-reflection, he or she can take several steps to **address** them. First, the school leader can read **books, articles, and other resources** related to the areas of weakness. For example, if the school leader has difficulty with time management, he or she can identify resources that can help to cultivate better time management skills. A leader can also participate in **training or professional development** related to the identified areas of weakness. A variety of professional organizations provide workshops and training related to various leadership competencies. The leader can also seek assistance from a **supervisor or other**

94

district staff person. A supervisor can offer suggestions or guidance for improvement in a deficient area. Additionally, the school leader can obtain **mentors and coaches** outside of the school organization that can provide objective skill building in the school leader's deficit areas. Mentors may be retired principals or other types of leaders who are in the school leader's network and are willing to share their expertise. Mentors do not typically require payment. In contrast, coaches are often hired to help with targeted skill-building and professional growth.

EFFECT OF LEADER'S SELF-REFLECTION ON THE LEADERSHIP TEAM

A leader's self-reflection can affect the leadership team in a number of ways. First, it sets an example as a school leader that **self-reflection** should be a part of leadership practice. This also demonstrates to the leadership team that the leader is aware that he or she is not perfect and is making efforts to **address identified weaknesses**. The leadership team should be comprised of people who help to **compensate** for the leader's weaknesses. Therefore, when a leader identifies his or her weaknesses, this can lead to **adjustment** of the leadership team. For example, if the leader determines that his or her leadership in math and science is weak, the leader may identify a person who is strong in math and science to be a part of the leadership team. Additionally, a leader's self-reflection can lead to **shifting roles and responsibilities** on the leadership team and reflection about the strengths and weaknesses of the entire team.

EFFECT OF LEADER'S SELF-REFLECTION ON STAKEHOLDERS

A leader's self-reflection can affect how he or she is **perceived** by stakeholders as well as the leader's **relationship** with stakeholders. When stakeholders observe the leader committing to self-improvement and making changes, they may conclude that the leader is humble and willing to improve the practice and the operation of the school. This can build hope and trust among stakeholders. For example, the leader may communicate to stakeholders that he or she is working on improving communication skills and is committed to doing a better job of returning phone calls and responding to emails. Similarly, engagement in self-reflection and self-improvement demonstrates that the leader is **responsive to feedback**. It is difficult to engage with a leader who believes that he or she knows everything, does not want feedback, and cannot receive criticism. In contrast, a leader who reflects and improves can encourage stakeholders to engage with the leader and the school, and relationships can be built between the leader and stakeholders.

Professional Influence for Systemic Change

CONNECTING THE SCHOOL COMMUNITY WITH FEDERAL, STATE, AND LOCAL POLICY, REGULATIONS, AND OTHER REQUIREMENTS

PARTICIPATING IN PROFESSIONAL EDUCATION ORGANIZATIONS AND ASSOCIATIONS

It is important for school leaders to participate in professional education organizations and associations. Many organizations have been created to **support educators** in various stages of their career. There are organizations primarily created for teachers in the classroom, even organizations specific to particular content areas. There are also organizations created specifically for **school administrators**. Additionally, school leaders may consider joining organizations related to the **field** in which they obtained their degree. These organizations provide training, information, and networking opportunities. Some offer legal help and protection as well. Most organizations charge a fee for membership, and members have access to a website, newsletters, training opportunities, job postings and leads, networking events, and much more. The information provided through these organizations can also help school leaders stay **current** on trends in education, changing laws and policies, and politics that affect the field of education. Additionally, **networking** within these professional organizations can provide opportunities for growth, advancement, and partnerships.

USE OF PROFESSIONAL INFLUENCE TO IMPACT THE SCHOOL

The school leader often has influence in the community due to the position of leadership. This **influence** comes from the connection to others who are in a position to support the school's vision and goals. Additionally, the size and diversity of a school leader's **network and contacts** can increase the power of that influence. The school leader's professional influence can be used to bring **positive attention and resources** to the school. For example, a school leader may know professional athletes, musicians, or actors within the community and can invite them to speak to or mentor the students on campus. Having such people on campus can inspire the youth and encourage them to succeed academically. The school leader can also use his or her influence to secure **opportunities for students** from businesses and organizations in the community, such as field trips, internships, or other educational opportunities. Finally, the school leader's professional influence can be used to **promote social justice** within the school and the community. For example, the school leader may advocate for a public library within the community.

SPHERE OF INFLUENCE

A sphere of influence refers to a leader's power to affect others, even without formal authority. School leaders have **authority** over staff and students. Staff can be reprimanded or terminated and students can be disciplined. Staff and students conform their behavior to the expectations of the leader because of the leader's authority over them. In contrast, the leader does not have authority over **parents, community members, district personnel, and other stakeholders**. However, the leader has the ability to **influence** these people through speech and other communication, as well as behavior. For example, a school leader cannot mandate that a neighborhood organization offer childcare services on campus after school because the school leader has no authority over that neighborhood organization. Instead, the school leader could use his or her influence to **encourage or persuade** the neighborhood organization to provide childcare services in partnership with the school. A school leader must recognize that when operating within the sphere of influence, skills such as understanding, compromise, persuasion, and clear communication are necessary to reach desired outcomes. This skillset differs from the skills used with those under the school leader's authority.

EDUCATING COMMUNITY STAKEHOLDERS ABOUT LOCAL EDUCATION PROCESSES

The purpose of educating community stakeholders about local education processes is to help them understand the reason for **local policies and procedures** and to help them engage in the **local education processes**. Community stakeholders who are uninformed or misinformed on local education processes may mistakenly assign responsibility or culpability to the school and school leader. Stakeholders should be aware of the **decision-makers** within the school district, the **processes** for decision-making, and how they can **participate** in those processes. This can help stakeholders to be effective in **enacting change** for decisions and processes that they do not agree with. For example, the school's dance program may be eliminated. Stakeholders may mistakenly believe that this was the school leader's decision when, in reality, the school district eliminated funding for these types of programs district-wide. Stakeholders should be educated regarding the **budgeting process** and how they can participate in the decision-making for district and school budgets.

EDUCATING COMMUNITY STAKEHOLDERS ABOUT STATE AND FEDERAL EDUCATION PROCESSES

The purpose of educating community stakeholders about state and federal education processes is to help them understand the reason for the **laws and policies** that govern the education system and to help them engage in the **state and federal processes**. Many school policies and procedures are developed in response to state and federal laws. When community stakeholders are aware of the laws that impact their children, they are more likely to engage in the processes to **effect change**. For example, a community may believe that their students should not be subject to

96

standardized testing. Those community members would need to be informed of the accountability laws that require assessment of students. Then the community members would be able to participate in the processes that could affect those laws in the future, such as voting.

FACILITATING DISCUSSIONS THAT MAY LEAD TO IDENTIFYING AREAS IN NEED OF IMPROVEMENT

VALUE OF FACILITATING DISCUSSIONS WITH STUDENTS

Students can help the school leader identify areas of the school in need of improvement from the **student perspective**. This perspective is invaluable when evaluating **school programming** and **school culture**. For example, the school leader may have instituted an art program for students based on the perception that students wanted more arts on campus. Students can inform the school leader how well that art program meets their needs. They may explain that the student body was interested in digital arts rather than classical arts, therefore making the school leader's art program ineffective. Students have to abide by the **rules and policies** that school leaders design and can often provide feedback on how effective those rules and policies are. Students can inform the school leader of aspects of the school that do not enhance school safety, are deemed unfair or inequitable, or are simply ineffective. Students are also helpful in providing solutions for areas of improvement on campus.

VALUE OF FACILITATING DISCUSSIONS WITH TEACHERS

Teachers can help the school leader identify areas of the school in need of **improvement** from their perspective. Teachers are responsible for **implementing** the school program the leader designs. As a result, they are often aware of needed areas of improvement that the school leader cannot see. When a school leader facilitates discussions on school improvement with teachers, they are in a position to **gather information** that they may not have discovered otherwise. For example, the teachers may point out a misalignment in the curriculum's scope and sequence and the assessment calendar, which causes the performance data to be skewed. This information can help the leader analyze data that has already been collected and devise a plan for revising the assessment calendar. Additionally, including teachers in this discussion increases buy-in. This process allows them to voice their concerns and to identify areas of the school program that need improvement for them to do their job more easily and effectively.

VALUE OF FACILITATING DISCUSSIONS WITH COMMUNITY STAKEHOLDERS

Community stakeholders can provide the school leader with the **community perspective** of school areas in need of improvement. The school is an integral part of the community and plays a significant role in **meeting the needs of community families**. Community stakeholders can inform the school leader of areas in which the school is not meeting those needs. For example, community members may inform the school leader that school dismissal procedures are inadequate and that the school is creating disruptive traffic congestion in the community at dismissal time. The school leader can work with community members to develop a plan that is appropriate for the school and respectful of the surrounding community. Engaging community stakeholders in discussions relating to the efficacy of the school program also creates **buy-in of the school vision and goals**, as well as building relationships between the school and the community.

VALUE OF FACILITATING DISCUSSIONS WITH DISTRICT PERSONNEL

Feedback from district personnel regarding areas of campus improvement is valuable. **District personnel** offer a unique perspective because they are able to view the school as it relates to the entire district's curricular program, mission, and goals. As a result, their perspective can help the school leader remain in alignment with **district expectations**. District personnel can also provide feedback based on how the school **compares** to other schools in the district. School leaders do not often have the opportunity to visit all the other schools within the district to gather ideas and best practices, but other district personnel can provide this perspective. Additionally, district personnel are often the people responsible for **evaluating** the school leader's performance. Addressing weak areas identified by district personnel can ensure that the leader is meeting the district's performance expectations.

ROOT CAUSE ANALYSIS

Conducting a root cause analysis involves identifying the root cause or underlying source of a problem. A **root cause analysis** begins with identifying the problem, then systematically identifying the source of that problem with the understanding that a sequence of events or chain of causes and effects may have led to the problem's manifestation. Conducting a root cause analysis is valuable because the **main source of the problem** can be addressed rather than just the symptoms. For example, the school leader may notice that math scores are below expectations. A further analysis of the data may indicate that the majority of the low performing students have their math class in the morning. A further analysis may indicate that a significant number of students arrive late to school every day and are missing the math instruction needed to perform well on the assessments. The school leader may conclude that addressing the tardiness may help to improve math scores. Root cause analysis helps the school leader to address the right problem in order to improve outcomes.

SWOT ANALYSIS

A SWOT analysis is a method of identifying the strengths and weaknesses of an organization in order to develop an **improvement plan**. SWOT stands for Strengths, Weaknesses, Opportunities, and Threats. The **strengths** of an organization are what provide the school with a competitive advantage over other schools. A school may be technology-rich, which is a strength. **Weaknesses** describe areas of disadvantage relative to other schools. A school may have a poor attendance rate in comparison to other schools. **Opportunities** are areas the school may be able to use by leveraging strengths to address weaknesses. The school may identify that the technology can be used to provide students with instruction at home when absent or to provide accelerated instruction when they return to school. **Threats** are aspects of the environment that the school has little or no control over but may negatively affect the school. The school may identify that the closure of a chemical plant has resulted in the layoff of many students' parents. Conducting a SWOT analysis is helpful in identifying areas of potential improvement, even for schools that are already high-performing.

AREAS OF SCHOOL PROGRAMMING THAT SHOULD BE EVALUATED FOR WEAKNESSES

All areas of school programming should be evaluated for weaknesses. **Academic performance** is most often evaluated because this is the basis for school accountability measures. A school leader should examine the alignment of curriculum to assessments, the quality of the instruction that is delivered, and the rigor at which it is delivered. However, other aspects should also be evaluated. These include school safety, school culture, parental and family engagement, and much more. For example, a school leader should determine if school safety procedures are up-to-date and should also assess the performance of students and staff during safety drills. **School culture** can be evaluated based on student and staff perceptions as well as by the experiences and feedback of visitors on campus. Also, the school leader can identify whether the school is achieving **family engagement** on campus, if it is in the desired areas, and if it is producing the desired outcomes. There are always aspects of the school program that can be improved, so the school leader should have a mindset of continuous improvement.

USING DATA TO IDENTIFY AREAS OF WEAKNESS

Data is essential in the identification of weaknesses in the school program. Differences and changes in the data, identifying potential **areas of improvement**, may be observed. The school leader may identify **disparities** in the data between the school and others in the district. For example, the school leader may note that on a district benchmark assessment, his or her school had the lowest overall performance. Based on that data, the leader could develop a plan for improvement. Data may also reveal a disparity in performance on campus from one school year to the next, or between various groups of students. Other data that can be used to identify areas of needed improvement include student attendance data, discipline data, compliance in data reporting, staff performance or evaluation data, and more. All data collected on campus has the potential to indicate **needed improvements** in the school program. The school leader should analyze the data in comparison to other data as well as changes, trends, and gaps in the data.

ENCOURAGING STAKEHOLDERS TO LOBBY AND USE POLITICAL ACTIVISM TO BRING ABOUT CHANGE

ENCOURAGING STAKEHOLDERS TO LOBBY AND USE POLITICAL ACTIVISM TO BRING ABOUT CHANGE

The school leader has the influence to encourage stakeholders to lobby and use political activism to bring about change, especially in regard to social justice. The primary way that the leader can encourage engagement is by **educating** the community on present issues. The leader often has several opportunities to speak to community families en masse. These opportunities can be used to educate families about education trends and politics that will ultimately affect their community, school, and families. By **promoting awareness**, the leader can empower parents and community members to become active. The second way the school leader can encourage engagement is by showing community stakeholders how they can become **involved**. The school leader can invite community stakeholders to be active in bringing about change by writing letters, sending emails, making phone calls, or engaging with political leaders.

PRECAUTIONS TO TAKE WHEN ENGAGING IN POLITICAL ACTIVITIES

In the school leader's efforts to advocate for students and for social justice, the school leader must engage carefully. Most school districts have **guidelines** for how a school leader can represent him or herself in the community while representing the school district. These guidelines usually apply in regard to supporting specific political parties or candidates, persuading others how to vote in elections, and various other activities. A school leader must identify what actions they are allowed or not allowed to take while in the position of leader. Outside of school hours, the leader may have additional freedom to engage in such activities, but must still be aware of how his or her **influence and authority** are used in such activities. The school leader should consult with the school district or the leadership of their professional organizations regarding the implications of **political engagement** prior to doing so.

GACE Practice Test

1. A school leader is developing school goals for the campus for the new academic school year. Which of the following should be included in the goals to best support a culture of learning?

    a. Increased student attendance rates
    b. Improved teacher evaluation ratings
    c. Decreased student dropout rate
    d. Increased student completion of advanced placement courses

2. When developing a vision for the school, which of the following sources of information is most critical to consider?

    a. School, local, state, and federal policies
    b. Past school performance indicators
    c. Feedback from students, staff, and other stakeholders
    d. Performance of similar schools

3. Which of the following is the most crucial question to consider when developing school goals?

    a. Are the school goals based on accurate data?
    b. Are the school goals achievable?
    c. Are the school goals aligned with the school vision?
    d. Were stakeholders given the opportunity to participate in the development of the school goals?

4. A school leader unveiled the new school vision and goals for the academic year at a community meeting. Several parents and community members were not pleased with the presentation and were vocal in their opposition of the leader's plan. Which of the following was the most likely cause of poor community support for the school vision and goals?

    a. The vision and goals were not aligned.
    b. The goals were not rigorous enough to meet state and federal accountability standards.
    c. Stakeholders were not included in the development of the vison and goals.
    d. The community members do not support the school leader.

5. The math teachers on campus suggest to the school leader that improved academic performance in math should be one of the school's goals. The school leader agrees and decides to create a measurable goal for student math performance. Which of the following is the best example of a measurable math performance goal?

    a. 95% of eighth-grade students will demonstrate growth in their math class.
    b. All eighth-grade students will be successful in their math class.
    c. Eighth-grade students will earn at least a B average in their math class.
    d. 90% of Eighth-grade students will earn at least a B average in their math class.

6. A school leader and the leadership team have begun developing a plan for implementing the school goals. The leader has identified the necessary action steps, the persons responsible for each step, and the time frames in which each step should be taken. Which of the following is the most appropriate next step for finalizing the plan?

    a. Identify the resources needed for each step and evidence of implementation
    b. Share the plan with persons who will be responsible for completing an action step.
    c. Present the plan to staff.
    d. Plan future meetings with staff to monitor progress in implementing the plan.

7. A school leader has created a committee of staff members on campus, including the administrative team, school counselors, teacher leaders, and support staff, that will serve as an advisory board for accomplishing the school vision. The most likely result of this action would be that:

    a. the decision-making process will be slowed down because more people are involved.
    b. staff turnover will be reduced.
    c. the leader will be viewed as a poor decision-maker.
    d. staff will be supportive of the vision and will help to accomplish their assigned roles.

8. Which of the following best describes shared leadership?

    a. Authoritarian leadership
    b. The delegation of authority and responsibility to other team members
    c. Consulting others before making decisions
    d. Publicly recognizing stakeholders that demonstrate leadership

9. Which of the following is the best evidence of effective monitoring of progress toward the vision and goals?

    a. The leader implements clear checkpoints and milestones for goal activities.
    b. The leader provides regular updates to stakeholders regarding progress toward the vision and goals.
    c. Student performance data shows evidence of growth.
    d. An advisory committee meets regularly to provide feedback to the leader regarding the vision and goals.

10. A school leader conducts a data review and realizes that the school will not meet an important milestone in the action plan for accomplishing one of the school goals. Which of the following actions should be taken first?

    a. Begin developing a revised action plan.
    b. Communicate goal progress with the appropriate stakeholders to identify the barriers and challenges that prevented the milestone from being met.
    c. Identify who was responsible for the failure and offer corrective action.
    d. Host a community meeting to share an update with all stakeholders.

11. Which of the following is the best evidence of clear and effective communication regarding the school vision and goals?

    a. Stakeholders who understand the vision and goals can articulate them in their own words.
    b. Stakeholders can memorize the school vision and goals.
    c. Stakeholders offer suggestions for revision of the school vision and goals.
    d. Stakeholders support the school vision and goals.

12. Which of the following actions would be most effective for ensuring that shared vision and goals are implemented consistently?

a. Publishing regular updates regarding goal progress in the school newsletter and on the school website

b. Identifying barriers and challenges to vision implementation as quickly as possible and revising plans to address them

c. Delegating responsibility to others to assist with vision implementation, monitoring goal progress regularly, and holding all staff members accountable for fulfilling their roles in the implementation plan

d. Meeting regularly with internal and external stakeholders to solicit feedback and ideas regarding vision and goal implementation

13. A school leader is developing a process for continuous improvement on campus. Which of the following actions should the school leader take first?

a. Develop evaluation procedures and set checkpoints for evaluation.

b. Train staff on the continuous improvement process.

c. Select a low performing area that needs to be addressed.

d. Identify strategies for addressing low performing areas.

14. A school leader conducts a needs assessment for the school using student academic performance data, student attendance data, student focus groups, and teacher focus groups. The leader then decides to conduct an anonymous survey of community stakeholders. The primary benefit of this action is that:

a. the leader will increase buy-in from the community.

b. surveying the community will increase community engagement.

c. the school leader will be able to explain past school performance.

d. the school leader will have multiple sources of data to conduct a thorough needs assessment.

15. Which of the following is the best way to identify strategies for facilitating change?

a. Host student and teacher focus groups to solicit suggestions and ideas.

b. Conduct pilot programs and collect data to determine efficacy.

c. Study research-based and proven best practices.

d. Meet with community stakeholders to solicit suggestions and ideas.

16. A goal for XYZ High School is to increase teachers' and students' technology skills. Which of the following decisions best demonstrates that the leader is aligning resources to achieve the goal?

a. Require all staff communications to be paperless.

b. Purchase updated computers for teachers and students and provide training for using them.

c. Conduct regular professional development for teachers related to technology skills.

d. Offer a new course to students that teaches basic computer skills.

17. A school leader wants to enlist support for change on campus. Which of the following actions should be taken first?

a. Communicate the intended change effectively to all stakeholders.
b. Create an advisory committee.
c. Find supporters with influence over other stakeholders to help spread the word about the change.
d. Administer an anonymous survey to see how stakeholders feel about the proposed change.

18. Which of the following barriers would interfere the most with achieving a goal of increased student achievement in math?

a. A shortage of calculators
b. A lack of community support
c. The adoption of a new math textbook
d. The unexpected resignation of a math teacher

19. Which of the following best defines equity?

a. Providing all students with the same amount of resources and support
b. Providing students with the resources and support that meet their individual needs
c. Providing at-risk students with additional resources and support
d. Providing accommodations for students who receive special education services

20. Which of the following would provide the most valid indication of a culture of high expectations?

a. Setting campus goals above minimum standards
b. Hosting award ceremonies for high- achieving students
c. Recognizing the Teacher of the Year publicly
d. Holding regular community meetings to discuss school performance with stakeholders

21. When selecting professional development for staff, which of the following should a leader consider first?

a. The cost of the professional development
b. Whether the professional development has been effective on other campuses
c. The areas of deficit of staff based on observations and evaluations
d. The alignment of the professional development with the campus vision and goals

22. A school leader has decided to hire an instructional coach to support the teachers' growth. Which of the following is the most likely result of this decision?

a. The instructional coach will help the leadership team supervise and evaluate teachers.
b. The instructional coach will make the decisions regarding professional development and training on campus.
c. Having an instructional coach will eliminate the need for professional development and training on campus.
d. The instructional coach will provide individualized, targeted support to teachers to help them to grow.

23. Which of the following actions best demonstrates that a school leader is open to changing positions on an issue?

a. The school leader lets staff vote on decisions.
b. The school leader has an advisory committee made up of teachers, students, and community members.
c. The school leader holds regular community meetings to provide updates on school activities.
d. The school leader makes time to take phone calls from parents outside of school hours.

24. What is the primary purpose of professional learning communities?

a. To hold teachers accountable
b. To make it easier to monitor teaching and learning
c. To facilitate collaboration among teachers
d. To set and achieve instructional goals

25. What is the primary benefit of conducting teacher evaluations?

a. Evaluations can provide feedback to staff members so that they can grow professionally.
b. Evaluations are needed to determine who is not performing to expectations.
c. Evaluations can help identify the professional development and coaching that teachers need.
d. Evaluations can be used to remove an underperforming teacher from their position.

26. A teacher complains to the principal that the feedback from their most recent evaluation was not fair because it did not provide a well-rounded view of their performance. Which of the following is the best action that the principal can take to address this concern?

a. Conduct additional observations of the teacher at various days of the week, times of the day, and in varied circumstances.
b. Explain why the evaluation was accurate.
c. Find other staff members who can confirm what was written in the teacher's evaluation.
d. Show the teacher that all protocols and policies were followed in conducting the evaluation.

27. A school leader wants to create a risk-taking environment for teachers where they feel comfortable improving their practices for teaching and learning. Which of the following actions should the school leader take to accomplish this goal?

a. Create a system of peer evaluations.
b. Allow teachers to choose their own professional development opportunities.
c. Create a digital data dashboard so teachers can share achievement data with one another.
d. Place a suggestion box in the teachers' lounge.

28. A principal has received notice that the current standards will be phased out and a new set of standards will be adopted for the upcoming school year. Which of the following actions should the principal take first regarding curriculum development and revision?

a. Set aside money in the school budget for purchasing new curriculum.
b. Create a committee to advise the principal on curriculum adoption.
c. Plan dates for training teachers about the new curriculum.
d. Identify what standards are changing and how the current curriculum and resources align to the new standards.

29. The Individuals with Disabilities Education Act (IDEA) is a law that:
a. requires teachers to be highly qualified.
b. ensures that all children with disabilities have free and appropriate education.
c. mandates that elementary schools have pre-kindergarten programs.
d. allows students with disabilities to be exempt from state and federal testing.

30. Which of the following actions taken by a principal best addresses the problem of having primarily novice teachers on staff?
a. Increased teacher observations and feedback
b. Facilitating collaborative teaching and team teaching
c. Monitoring data closely
d. Providing tutorials for students after school

31. Which of the following best describes rigorous instruction?
a. Rigor in academic instruction refers to curriculum and instruction that is challenging to students.
b. Rigor in academic instruction refers to honors, advanced placement, and dual credit courses.
c. Rigor in academic instruction refers to appropriate grading and feedback on student work.
d. Rigor in academic instruction refers to teaching above student grade levels.

32. What is the primary reason that curriculum and instruction must be aligned to assessment?
a. School leaders must be able to justify why they select curriculum and resources.
b. Teachers must know what to teach in the classroom.
c. Assessments that are not aligned with curriculum and instruction will not accurately measure what students learned.
d. Alignment of curriculum and assessments makes it easier to analyze and compare student performance data.

33. Which of the following pieces of information would be most relevant when determining how to differentiate instruction for students?
a. Previous academic performance, special needs (such as a physical or learning disability), and learning style
b. Previous academic performance, demographics, and socioeconomic status
c. Student interests, career goals, and grade point average
d. Student interests, parental input, and learning style

34. A school leader is monitoring the curricular programs to determine whether student needs are being met. Which of the following would provide the most valid indication that the curricular programs are meeting student needs?
a. Assessment data shows that students are meeting minimum performance standards.
b. Parent survey data demonstrates that parents are pleased with the curricular programs.
c. Teacher observations are positive, overall.
d. Assessment data shows that most students are demonstrating academic growth.

35. A high school principal has created instructional teams comprised of teachers from each core content area and fine arts. These teams plan instruction together and incorporate concepts from the various subjects in each of their classrooms. This strategy is an example of what type of instruction?

    a. Differentiated instruction
    b. Rigorous instruction
    c. Cross-curricular instruction
    d. Professional learning communities

36. What trends in student achievement data would be the best indicator that there are problems in curriculum alignment?

    a. Students perform well on campus-based tests but perform poorly on college entrance exams.
    b. Students earn satisfactory grades on school report cards but perform poorly on standardized tests.
    c. Students with disabilities perform poorly on campus-based tests.
    d. Students who have a history of high academic performance show little to no growth on standardized tests.

37. A school principal has reviewed assessment data and is concerned about the quality of learning on campus. Which of the following would be the best source of data for the principal to examine next?

    a. Student survey data
    b. Teacher survey data
    c. Classroom observation data
    d. Class size and student to teacher ratios

38. Which of the following is the best example of summative assessment?

    a. Standardized tests
    b. Homework assignments
    c. Practice assignments completed in class
    d. Projects

39. A group of community members meet with the principal to share concerns that the community does not believe the principal is effectively communicating data about progress toward the school vision and goals to them. The community members explain that many of them are not able to attend meetings held at the school. Which of the following solutions should the principal suggest to the community members?

    a. Change the dates and times that community meetings are held so that more people can attend.
    b. Have community members who attend the meetings inform others who did not attend about what was discussed at the meeting.
    c. Refer community members to the school website where the meeting minutes are posted.
    d. Develop a variety of ways to communicate in addition to the community meetings, such as via email, a school newsletter, and regular phone calls.

40. Several teachers on campus have expressed concerns to the principal that there is too much focus on standardized assessment. The teachers suggest that they develop authentic assessments for student learning. Which of the following is the best example of authentic summative assessment?

a. Benchmark tests
b. Student choice of completing a project, essay, or performance
c. Oral exams
d. Allowing students to complete homework assignments at their own pace

41. An assistant principal is reviewing a reading teacher's gradebook and notices that the students have very few grades entered for the marking period. The assistant principal is concerned and plans on meeting with the reading teacher. Which of the following questions is most important for the assistant principal to ask the teacher during this meeting?

a. Are you aware of the grading policy in the faculty handbook?
b. How many grades do you plan on assigning for the marking period?
c. How do you document student mastery of objectives?
d. Do you need help with grading assignments?

42. A principal is planning for the upcoming school year. Which of the following factors would most directly impact student learning?

a. The number of math and reading teachers on staff and the size of the classes that they teach
b. The benchmark testing schedule for the academic year
c. The time that school starts each day
d. The number of computers purchased

43. A school leader is developing a plan for improving teaching on campus and has identified several effective teachers in the math department. How should the school leader best incorporate these teachers into the plan?

a. Request that the teachers mentor low-performing teachers.
b. Allow the teachers to continue teaching using their current best practices.
c. Recognize the teachers for their effective performance.
d. Allow the teachers to identify areas in which they would like to grow and provide resources and support.

44. A school leader is developing a plan for effective use of an annex building on the school property. Which of the following staff members would be able to best assist the school leader in developing this plan?

a. A lead teacher
b. The plant operator
c. An assistant principal
d. The district superintendent

45. Fire code regulations mandate that a fire drill should be conducted on campus monthly. It is the last day of the month and the principal realizes that a fire drill has not yet been conducted for the month. However, students are taking a mock standardized assessment. What action should the principal take?

    a. Conduct the fire drill immediately.

    b. Contact the fire inspector and inform them that the school was unable to conduct a fire drill for the month.

    c. Document why the fire drill was not conducted for the month and provide the documentation if requested.

    d. Contact the fire inspector to request an exception for the month.

46. The technology teacher informs the school leader that the computers in the computer lab are outdated and make it difficult to provide technology instruction to students. What action should the principal take first?

    a. Ask the technology teacher to choose a computer model to purchase to replace the outdated computers.

    b. Allocate money in the budget to purchase new computers for the computer lab.

    c. Refer to the campus technology plan to identify the timeline for replacing computers in the lab.

    d. Request a district technology support staff member to service the computers in the computer lab.

47. Students of XYZ High School will each receive a laptop for school use at the beginning of the school year. The school dean is tasked with developing an acceptable use policy for students. What is the primary benefit of creating an acceptable use policy for students?

    a. To encourage students to take care of the devices

    b. To help students learn how to use technology to engage in instruction

    c. To teach students how to conduct themselves online

    d. To clearly communicate how the device should be used and the consequences for not abiding by the policy

48. The dean of instruction is preparing to implement an online literacy program that the school district has just purchased. Which feature of the literacy program platform best aligns with the school's mission to use data to make instructional decisions?

    a. The program assesses students' reading levels bi-weekly.

    b. The program tracks students' growth over time and compares their actual growth to expected growth.

    c. The program autogenerates reports of student engagement and sends them to parents.

    d. The program provides all teachers and administrators with access to a data dashboard that includes all data collected through the program.

49. A middle school principal has been informed that there will be a cut in the school budget in the area of technology capital for the upcoming school year. Based on this information, which of the following represents the best action that the school principal could take?

    a. Do not offer a technology class for students for the upcoming school year.

    b. Assess the current technology on campus and determine how to use current assets for next school year's instruction.

    c. Apply for local grants to compensate for the budget cut.

    d. Ask the community for donations of technology equipment.

50. The fine arts teacher would like to construct a mural outside of the art building. The school leader believes it is a good idea, but does not have the funds to purchase the supplies required to complete the mural. What recommendation should the school leader make to the art teacher?

    a. Host a fundraiser to obtain money to purchase supplies.
    b. Ask the Athletic Director to use money from the athletics fund.
    c. Charge art students an art fee to obtain money for the mural.
    d. The art teacher cannot construct the mural this school year.

51. Which of the following represents the primary source of school funding?

    a. Allotments from the federal government
    b. Grants
    c. Donations
    d. Property taxes

52. A high school principal ensured that the campus was fully staffed with highly qualified teachers at least a month before the start of the school year. What is the primary benefit of this effort?

    a. Teachers who are hired early have more time to prepare for the school year.
    b. Personnel budgets must be submitted before the school year begins.
    c. All teachers will have an opportunity to participate in trainings and professional development prior to the start of the year.
    d. Teachers who are hired later in the year have classroom management issues.

53. Which of the following factors may directly affect a school leader's ability to recruit and retain highly qualified teachers?

    a. The number of recruitment fairs that a school leader attends
    b. The percentage of experienced teachers already on campus
    c. The school culture
    d. The available technology on campus

54. Which of the following best represents a threat to a physically safe campus environment?

    a. Inefficient arrival and dismissal procedures
    b. High student-to-teacher classroom ratios
    c. High teacher turnover
    d. Electrical hazards

55. Which of the following best represents a threat to an emotionally safe campus environment?

    a. Bullying
    b. Crowded classrooms
    c. High teacher turnover
    d. High rates of student suspensions

56. A leader must ensure that the school's physical plant, equipment, and support systems operate safely, efficiently, and effectively. Which of the following strategies best helps the school leader fulfill this responsibility?

    a. Walking the campus two times a day to check for safety
    b. Soliciting feedback about the campus from teachers and staff
    c. Selecting the appropriate staff to manage the physical plant
    d. Reviewing all inspection reports monthly

57. Which of the following circumstances would require that a school leader contact a child protective agency?

    a. A teacher reports to the school leader that one of her students has shown the teacher their bruises.
    b. A teacher reports to the school leader that a student who usually performs well academically has suddenly declined in academic performance.
    c. The school leader sees a child in the cafeteria throwing their lunch away and refusing to eat.
    d. The school leader witnesses a child bullying another child in the hallway.

58. Several community members have expressed concern to the school principal about the rate of teen suicide and believe that the principal should be proactive in promoting the mental health and wellbeing of students on campus. The school leader believes this is a helpful suggestion. Which of the following would be the best action to take to address the community members' concern?

    a. Write an article in the school bulletin about teen suicide.
    b. Begin a counseling and wellness program on campus that refers students to community agencies and resources.
    c. Hang posters in the school hallways promoting a 24-hour suicide hotline.
    d. Ban social media use on campus to prevent cyberbullying.

59. In which of the following situations can family and community stakeholders be most helpful?

    a. Identifying internships for students
    b. Evaluating teacher performance
    c. Analyzing student data
    d. Conducting teacher training

60. Which of the following strategies is most effective for communicating school and student success to families and the community?

    a. Publishing a monthly school newsletter
    b. Sending weekly automated calls
    c. Sending letters home with students
    d. Hosting monthly community meetings

61. Which of the following strategies would be most effective for communicating with stakeholders who speak a different language?

    a. Hire translators and provide translation machines at community events.
    b. Hire a bilingual principal.
    c. Translate all written communications.
    d. Ask students to translate for their parents.

62. A school leader is approached by a journalist to contribute to a news segment about preparing students for an upcoming standardized test. Which of the following actions should the school leader take first?

  a. Prepare a statement for the news segment.
  b. Contact the school district media department.
  c. Schedule a date for the interview.
  d. Identify students who can also participate in the news segment.

63. Which of the following factors should a school leader consider first when scheduling a parent meeting?

  a. The languages that the parents speak
  b. The availability of funds to serve refreshments
  c. The day of the week and time of the day to host the meeting
  d. The school leader's schedule

64. A group of parents expressed concern to the school leader that they did not feel involved in the decision-making processes at the school. Which of the following actions could the school leader take to address their concerns?

  a. Place a suggestion box in the front office of the school.
  b. Create a parent focus group.
  c. Invite parents to register as volunteers at the school.
  d. Create an email newsletter to distribute to parents monthly.

65. Which of the following is an example of a community partnership?

  a. Student club members pick up litter in the community on the weekends.
  b. A local business sets up a table at parent meetings to inform parents about their services.
  c. Local businesses provide mentors to students in the areas of business and entrepreneurship.
  d. The principal invites a local business owner as a guest speaker for a teacher in-service.

66. A group of teachers who are unhappy with some of the policies on campus have organized into an informal group. They have begun inviting other teachers and staff to meet with them to discuss campus concerns. The school leader becomes aware of the group. Which of the following is the best response to the formation of this group?

  a. Invite the group to meet with the school leader to discuss their concerns.
  b. Create a new campus policy banning the formation of groups without permission.
  c. Administer a survey to the staff to gather their opinions about campus policies.
  d. Require that the group only meet off campus outside of school hours.

67. Which of the following actions best illustrates how a school leader engages with the community in a proactive manner?

  a. The school leader attends all local school board meetings.
  b. The school leader attends the community holiday parade.
  c. The school leader hosts an award ceremony for students at the school.
  d. The school leader purchases advertisement space in the local community newspaper.

68. A new student arrives in the country from Switzerland, speaks French, and is enrolled in XYZ High School. The only languages spoken at the school are English and Spanish. Which of the following actions should the school leader take in order to accommodate the needs of this student?

  a. Research Swiss culture.
  b. Pair the student with a peer to help the student get acclimated.
  c. Hire a translator to help communicate with the student.
  d. Meet with the student and their family to discuss their needs.

69. A school leader has recently been appointed to school principal of ABC Elementary School. Which of the following actions would best help the new principal learn more about the community that the school serves?

  a. Research the community online.
  b. Review student demographic and academic performance data.
  c. Meet with a variety of stakeholders of the community.
  d. Meet with current staff to ask questions about the community.

70. Which of the following best illustrates the connection between the school community and local employment trends?

  a. A school begins to offer health care courses and training in response to a need for more healthcare workers in the community.
  b. The school librarian partners with the neighborhood library to share resources.
  c. A school sets a goal to increase the graduation rate.
  d. A school increases the number of dual-credit college courses offered on campus.

71. Which of the following best illustrates the connection between the school community and local education trends?

  a. A school creates an internship program for students interested in working in the healthcare industry.
  b. Recruiters from local colleges set up booths in the school cafeteria during lunch time to inform students about their school choices.
  c. Graduates of the local community college mentor high school seniors.
  d. A school offers a college math preparation course based on the math skills needed for success at the local community college.

72. A middle school is expecting a dramatic increase in the number of students requiring special education services for the upcoming school year. Which of the following should be the principal's primary concern?

  a. How this group of students will impact current student performance data
  b. The availability of human and fiscal resources needed to meet the needs of this group of students
  c. Community resources for this group of students
  d. The reason for the increase in the number of students requiring special education

73. Which of the following would be most likely to cause an administrator to look for outside resources in assisting students and their families?

    a. A student is having difficulty in math class.
    b. Two students participated in a physical altercation.
    c. A student and their family are struggling financially and are in need of food and clothing.
    d. A student will be the first in the family to graduate high school.

74. A school principal has decided to partner with a local community center to provide a basketball camp for students after school. The camp is free to students and the school will not pay the community center any funds for hosting the camp. Based on this agreement, what should the principal do next?

    a. Begin recruiting students for the camp.
    b. Draft a memorandum of understanding for both parties to sign.
    c. Send an email to the director of the community center reiterating the arrangement that was agreed upon.
    d. Find an organization that offers a football camp for students who do not want to play basketball.

75. Which of the following is an effective way to use community resources to support student learning?

    a. Invite local churches to host a back-to-school drive to provide students with school supplies.
    b. Partner with local businesses to provide free tutoring to students after school.
    c. Partner with local businesses to host field trips for students.
    d. Invite local businesspersons in the community to mentor students.

76. Which of the following is the most critical question to consider when using community resources in the classroom?

    a. Are the resources aligned with the curriculum?
    b. Are there enough resources for all students?
    c. Are teachers familiar with these resources?
    d. Are the resources expected to be returned?

77. The first year of a mentoring pilot program has been completed. The first year was free for the school, but the school will have to pay a fee if the mentoring program is to continue for subsequent years. Which of the following would best inform the principal's decision about whether to continue the program?

    a. The number of students that participated in the program
    b. Student feedback on the program
    c. Community feedback on the program
    d. Student performance indicators related to the campus goals

78. Which of the following best represents a mutually beneficial relationship between a school and a community organization?

   a. A neighborhood grocery store donates bottled water to the basketball team for home games.
   b. The school hosts a clothing drive for a local homeless shelter once a year.
   c. A local church has permission to use the school library for meetings on Saturday mornings and the principal is permitted to make announcements to the attendees during the meetings.
   d. A medical clinic near the school offers free immunizations and physicals to students actively enrolled at the school.

79. A community group has requested the use of the school gymnasium for an upcoming event. Which of the following should the principal consider first before approving the request?

   a. Whether the group has a religious affiliation
   b. Whether the request is in accordance with school and district policy for use of school facilities
   c. Whether the event occurs during the school day
   d. The fee that should be charged for rental of the gymnasium

80. The principal has noted that Mr. Smith, a star teacher, arrives late to school every day. The assistant principal who supervises Mr. Smith informs the principal that no one bothers Mr. Smith about his late arrival because he does such a great job in the classroom. The assistant principal's action is a violation of:

   a. fairness.
   b. integrity.
   c. justice.
   d. trust.

81. Which of the following best represents transparent decision-making?

   a. The principal meets with a focus group prior to making a decision.
   b. The principal administers a survey and considers the data prior to making a decision.
   c. The principal informs the community that a decision needs to be made about eliminating the dance program and shares data that may impact the decision.
   d. The principal posts meeting minutes from committee meetings online.

82. Which of the following represents a potential conflict of interest?

   a. A potential contractor for remodeling the gymnasium is a relative of the school principal.
   b. The assistant principal's son attends the school where they work.
   c. The principal owns a house in the community that the school serves.
   d. The math software that the district adopted was used in a school district where the principal served prior.

83. Which of the following laws dictates how student information can be used in an educational setting?

   a. HIPAA
   b. FERPA
   c. NCLB
   d. ESSA

84. Which of the following actions is NOT an example of a school leader functioning as an instrument of social justice?

   a. Writing a letter to the State Board of Education regarding education funding
   b. Participating in a community rally to protest the construction of a railroad through the neighborhood
   c. Becoming a paid member of an education organization for urban school leaders
   d. Campaigning in the school cafeteria for a political candidate in an upcoming election

85. A student reports to the principal that a teacher helped him with answers on the state standardized test. Which of the following should the principal do next?

   a. Investigate to find out if the student is telling the truth.
   b. Confront the teacher accused of cheating.
   c. Document the complaint in case the school is audited.
   d. Report the allegation to the district testing department.

86. Which of the following is the best way that a school leader can ensure equitable treatment of students and staff?

   a. Develop policies and procedures and adhere to them.
   b. Create advisory committees with representatives from a variety of diverse demographics.
   c. Create a diversity and inclusion statement for the school.
   d. Address student and staff complaints swiftly.

87. During a classroom observation, a school leader notices that a student is sitting in the corner of the classroom and is not engaged in the lesson. The teacher does not attempt to engage the student during the lesson. When the school leader meets with the teacher about the observation and asks about the student, the teacher responds that there was no point in trying to get that student to participate because they were going to fail no matter what. The teacher's response shows that they do not agree with which educational philosophy?

   a. Teach students to be life-long learners.
   b. Education is the key to success.
   c. All students can learn.
   d. Educate the whole child.

88. Which of the following is indicative of a school that is focused on encouraging intercultural awareness in students?

   a. Social studies classrooms are required to include one research project per year that focuses on different cultures.
   b. The principal invites African American guest speakers to the campus for Black History Month.
   c. The principal publishes a statement about diversity and inclusion on the school website.
   d. The principal adds American Sign Language to the foreign language course offerings.

89. The dean of students informs the school principal that discipline data shows that a disproportionate number of Black students have been suspended from school for the first semester when compared to the general population of students. Which of the following represents the best action that the principal could take?

    a. Identify a mentoring program for Black students on campus.
    b. Assess the school culture to determine if there are negative assumptions or beliefs that impact teaching and learning.
    c. Send an email to teachers that no Black students can be suspended for the second semester.
    d. Identify teachers who should attend classroom management training.

90. Which of the following represents an effective step that a school leader can take to change negative assumptions about teaching diverse populations?

    a. Conduct diversity training with all staff.
    b. Create a mentoring program on campus.
    c. Publish an official statement on diversity and inclusion.
    d. Only hire teachers that represent the student demographics.

91. Which of the following situations represents an issue of ethics?

    a. The football coach obtained a sponsorship from a local restaurant to provide snacks for students during football practice.
    b. A group of students make a request to form a club for students who were adopted.
    c. The debate sponsor uses money collected from students for fees to pay for his lunch but replaces the money after school.
    d. A pastor from a local church donates table linens to the drama department for an upcoming banquet.

92. ABC Elementary School receives permission to participate in a television news media segment about keeping children active. The principal would like all of the students in the soccer club to participate in the filming of the news segment. What should the principal do first?

    a. Inform the teachers that the media will be on campus.
    b. Meet with the students to set expectations for behavior when they are being filmed.
    c. Inform the community that the school will be participating in the news segment.
    d. Ensure that all students who plan to participate have a media release form signed by a parent on file.

93. A parent of a student with a disability informs the principal that they overheard two teachers making fun of their child's disability during dismissal. Which of the following is the most appropriate response that the principal should make to the parent?

    a. Inform the parent that they have permission to pick their child up from school early.
    b. Inform the parent that the teachers will be disciplined.
    c. Assure the parent that the described behavior is not tolerated, and an investigation will occur.
    d. Assure the parent that the teachers will no longer have dismissal duty.

94. Which of the following represents the most effective way that a leader can ensure the staff members they supervise act in an ethical manner?

    a. Writing and distributing policies and procedures
    b. Actively monitoring employee behavior
    c. Requiring employees to sign a form to acknowledge receipt of the staff handbook
    d. Responding to reports of unethical behavior immediately

95. All of the following demonstrate that the school leader conducts self-reflection EXCEPT:

    a. reading books and articles related to the field of education and leadership practice.
    b. keeping a journal.
    c. evaluating one's self using the personnel evaluation rubric.
    d. attending a mandated training.

96. The school principal informs the leadership team that she will participate in a six-week program to improve her leadership skills. This action best illustrates that:

    a. the principal is a model for continuous professional growth.
    b. the principal has weaknesses that need to be addressed.
    c. the principal is self-reflective.
    d. the principal is an effective leader.

97. The athletics director received notice that there will be random drug testing of all student athletes next week. The principal discovers that the athletics director acted against policy and advised all of the coaches to inform students of the upcoming drug test. Which of the following actions should the principal take next?

    a. Give the athletics director a written reprimand for breaching policy.
    b. Document the infraction in the athletics director's personnel file.
    c. Inform the athletics department of the information breach.
    d. Remove the athletics director from their position.

98. The school participates in a health education program that provides sex education to middle school students and offers contraceptives to students. A teacher is opposed to this program and becomes very vocal in the community about the dangers of having this program on campus. The principal begins to receive numerous phone calls and emails about the program. Which of the following actions would best help the principal refocus attention to vision and goals?

    a. Issue a public statement regarding the value of health education and the alignment of the program with the school's vision.
    b. Meet with the teacher who is opposed to the program to reach an agreement.
    c. Ignore the phone calls and emails.
    d. Hold a community meeting to discuss the program with stakeholders.

99. A school principal reflects on their personal performance during the most recent school year. Based on data and their own reflection, the principal noticed that many of the plans that were created at the beginning of the school year were not implemented properly because they were not able to get all of the action items done. Which of the following action plans might help the principal improve their time management in the future?

    a. Use data to make more effective decisions.
    b. Prioritize activities that are most directly related to the campus vision and goals.
    c. Hold members of the leadership team accountable for their task completion.
    d. Increase the number of hours that they spend on campus.

100. The campus testing coordinator has noticed that many of the teachers have been lax about following testing procedures when administering standardized tests to students. The testing coordinator knows that failure to adhere to testing procedures could result in consequences for individual staff members, the campus, or even the students. What next step should the testing coordinator take to address this concern?

    a. Conduct training to address common testing procedure violations.
    b. Send an email to staff warning them of the potential consequences if they violate testing procedures.
    c. Modify the campus testing plan to omit teachers who are likely to commit testing violations.
    d. Maintain documentation of violations in the event of an audit.

Answer Key and Explanations

1. D: The question tests the school leader's understanding of goals directly related to a culture of learning in contrast with other aspects of school performance. Participation in and completion of advanced placement courses is directly related to student learning and reflects high expectations for student academic performance.

2. A: All the information sources are valid and useful, but a school leader must ensure that the vison and goals of the school align with school, local, state, and federal policies first. After that alignment is confirmed, other information sources can be considered to develop the school's vision and goals.

3. C: All of these questions are important to consider when developing school goals. However, aligning the school goals to the school vision is most critical. The school vision describes how the school is envisioned to be in the future and the school goals are the steps that will enable the school to accomplish that vision.

4. C: It is important to involve stakeholders in the development of the school vision to help incorporate their varied perspectives into the vision and to increase buy-in for the vision. Without buy-in, community members and stakeholders may oppose the school vision and withdraw their support and resources for the school and school leadership.

5. D: Measurable goals can be quantified, and non-measurable goals cannot be quantified. This goal is measurable because calculating the percentage of students who earned at least a B average in their math class can reveal whether or not the goal was met. It also identifies how students are expected to perform in order to reach the goal. When goals are measurable, it is easy to determine whether or not the goal has been met.

6. A: The components of an effective plan include action steps, persons responsible, time frames, milestones, resources needed, and evidence of implementation. The plan will include the resources needed to accomplish the plan so that these resources are planned for and obtained, thus preventing delay in the plan's accomplishment. The evidence of implementation should be included in the plan so that ongoing monitoring can take place. Depending on the aspect of the plan, evidence of implementation could include documents, visible indicators, or regular meetings.

7. D: Different roles on campus can help accomplish the vision. The school leader can ensure the success of the school vision by engaging the internal community and including diverse perspectives in the implementation of the vision. This strategy increases buy-in and utilizes staff members' roles to accomplish the vision. For example, the administrative team can lead projects and delegate tasks to others, school counselors can support the psychosocial needs of students to support their academic success, teacher leaders can lead and support the instructional staff, and support staff can support the logistics and communication of the plans.

8. B: A leader demonstrates shared leadership by assigning persons particular leadership responsibilities and granting them the authority to fulfill those leadership responsibilities. When sharing leadership, responsibilities are not dependent on job titles and can thus be delegated to any staff members who are capable of fulfilling the role. While sharing leadership can also involve including others in decision-making processes, shared leadership is best exemplified when a leader distributes power and authority to others.

9. A: A leader effectively monitors goal progress by implementing clear checkpoints and milestones for goal activities. Each goal should be broken down into smaller goals, or milestones, that can be reviewed at regular intervals. This allows the leader to analyze progress toward the goal on a timeline so that, if there is not sufficient progress toward the goal, there is time to intervene and make changes to the action steps.

10. B: Goal progress should be communicated effectively and in a timely manner, especially to those who are instrumental in achieving the goal. The school leader should communicate progress toward a goal, whether positive or negative. When there is regression in progress or a lack of progress, two-way communication should occur with appropriate stakeholders to determine what unexpected barriers and challenges to accomplishing the goal need to be addressed. Communicating regression in progress toward a goal is necessary so that corrections can be made.

11. A: When a school leader has clearly and effectively communicated the school vision and goals, others will be able to describe the vision and goals in their own words. They will be able to communicate the vision and goals to others and explain the rationale behind the vision and goals. Stakeholders who understand the vision and goals will propose ideas and actions that are aligned to the vision and will understand how they can participate in or contribute to achieving the vision.

12. C: Shared leadership, regular monitoring of progress, and accountability of everyone participating in implementation are key elements to consistent goal implementation. Sharing leadership creates buy-in for the vision and empowers others to take action so that the leader is not solely responsible for making progress toward the vision. Regular monitoring of goal progress using milestones and timelines keeps everyone on pace for implementing the goals and vision. The leader must also hold people accountable because each person must do their part in order for the plan to be implemented successfully and according to schedule.

13. A: The process of continuous improvement is the ongoing act of assessing performance and adjusting efforts in order to improve that performance. In order to implement a process of continuous improvement, there must be procedures of evaluation developed and implemented at regular checkpoints. Based on these regular evaluations, the leadership team can identify areas of improvement and initiate interventions and actions based on those identified areas. In schools, the regular evaluation of progress toward the campus vision and goals can be developed into a process of continuous improvement. However, campus leaders must focus on both the strengths and weaknesses of the campus in this process. Deficient areas can be improved to perform to standard, while areas performing at standard can be innovated for improvement.

14. D: All the choices are benefits of gathering the data, but the primary benefit is obtaining multiple sources of data to accurately identify the strengths, needs, gaps, and areas of improvement for the school. The school leader chose a combination of quantitative and qualitative data to accurately assess school performance and the cultures, values, attitudes, and beliefs that impact that performance. It is important to use data from multiple sources to develop the school vision and goals because using only one source of data may portray a limited or skewed picture of the school. Using multiple sources of data can confirm the validity of data and provide a more complete picture of the complex dynamics of a school campus.

15. C: To address weak areas, it is better to implement strategies that are backed by research and have been proven to yield good results. This can save the campus the time, effort, and resources that would be wasted if untested and unproven strategies were implemented unsuccessfully. When a leader is looking for strategies to implement to foster change on campus, using research-based and proven best practices is beneficial because there will be a clear direction as to how to successfully implement the strategy and a realistic idea of what results to expect. When untested strategies are implemented, the outcome is less certain. Untested strategies also often take more research and a process of trial and error, or a learning curve, to implement, both of which can delay the implementation of change.

16. B: The goal is for both teachers and students to improve their computer skills; providing training to teachers or a new course for students does not fully address the school goal. Purchasing updated computers for students and teachers and training them to use the devices best demonstrates that the leader is using school resources to support the school goal.

17. A: Leaders intent on fostering change or being agents of change are required to strategically communicate the intended change and gather supporters for that change. First, the leader needs to communicate the intended change effectively. Many people are unwilling to support changes because they fear the unknown. The leader should communicate not only what is to be changed but also how the changes affect the various staff members and how the changes are aligned to the school vision and goals.

18. D: Although each of these options could negatively impact the math performance goal, the loss of a math teacher directly impacts student learning and performance. Student performance in math is directly related to the quality of instruction that students receive in the classroom, meaning that the absence of a qualified math teacher for any length of time can be impactful. Additionally, the unexpected loss of a teacher can be a difficult obstacle to address in a timely manner. It is likely that losing a math teacher would negatively impact the goal.

19. B: All students are expected to meet the standards outlined by the state and federal government. School leaders are responsible for providing students with the instruction, resources, and support necessary to meet these standards. Equity refers to providing students with the resources and support that meet their individual needs. When leaders implement equity in schools, this may mean that some students receive more resources and support or different resources and support than others. This need may be due to a lack of educational opportunity, physical or intellectual disabilities, or other circumstances. Leaders must be aware of what students need so that the right resources and support can be used to support these students. All students will need resources and support to enrich their education, but practicing equity means that students will receive the appropriate amount of resources based on their identified needs.

20. A: In a culture of high expectations, staff and students strive towards high goals and excellence. A leader can create a culture of high expectations by setting campus goals above minimum standards. For example, if the expectation is that a school has at least a 90% attendance rate, the leader may set a goal of 95% for the school's attendance rate. Expecting students and staff to perform above minimum expectations creates a culture of high expectations.

21. D: All of these factors are important to consider, but the leader must first ensure that the professional development will help staff meet the vision and goals that have already been established. A leader needs to be deliberate in selecting professional development for staff members so that the professional development is purposeful in helping staff achieve the campus goals and vision.

22. D: A coach is a professional who helps a teacher develop the skills necessary to do their job effectively. A coach is a staff member who does not supervise or evaluate the person being coached. This helps to foster a relationship of trust between the coach and the teacher. A coach will identify a teacher's areas of strength and weakness based on a predetermined rubric or set of expectations.

Then the coach will provide one-on-one support to the teacher to help improve targeted areas. A coach may provide books and resources, recommend professional development sessions, model effective teaching methods, observe the teacher in practice to provide real-time feedback, assist in the lesson planning process, and guide the teacher in self-reflection and critical analysis processes. A coach provides individualized, targeted support to teachers and helps them to grow, usually in a shorter period of time than other forms of professional development support.

23. B: Creating an advisory committee and meeting with the committee regularly demonstrates that the leader is willing to hear other perspectives and opinions prior to making decisions. A school leader may believe one course of action is correct but then change their mind after receiving feedback from an advisory committee. A school leader can demonstrate a willingness to change by getting information from a variety of sources prior to making decisions.

24. C: Professional learning communities allow staff with shared roles or responsibilities to collaborate in a way that meets the needs of teachers and students. These communities are usually goal-driven and encourage the sharing of ideas and responsibilities. Professional learning communities are used in a variety of ways, but the primary purpose is to facilitate collaboration among educators.

25. A: The primary benefit of evaluating staff members is to provide an opportunity for leaders to identify areas of strength and weakness among the staff and to provide constructive feedback to staff members so that they can grow professionally. Leaders can use these evaluations to determine what additional support and resources need to be provided to support or improve the performance of staff members.

26. A: Leaders should use as many opportunities as possible to observe staff performance in order to have a well-rounded view of their performance. The opportunities may include various days of the week, times of the day, and varied circumstances. A leader should be intentional and deliberate about seeking different opportunities to observe staff at a variety of times in a variety of circumstances in order to obtain a fair and holistic view of staff performance.

27. B: When teachers are given the power to choose their own professional development opportunities, they are given the opportunity to reflect on their own practice, identify their strengths and weaknesses, and participate in professional development that they believe is relevant. This contributes to building a risk-taking environment because teachers will be able to examine their own beliefs, values, and practices concerning teaching and learning and determine where they would like to improve.

28. D: All curriculum and resources should be aligned to standards. Therefore, if standards change, it is likely that the curriculum will need to be revised and new resources purchased. However, before changes in the curriculum can be made, the principal will need to know how the new standards differ from the previous standard. This will help the principal determine if minor revisions to the curriculum are needed or if a new curriculum will need to be adopted.

29. B: The Individuals with Disabilities Education Act (IDEA) is a law that makes a free, appropriate, public education available to eligible children with disabilities throughout the nation and ensures special education and related services will be provided for those children. This law governs how states and public agencies provide educational services to children with disabilities. Congress reauthorized the IDEA in 2004 and most recently amended it through Public Law 114-95, the Every Student Succeeds Act, in December 2015 (U.S. Department of Education).

30. B: Novice teachers need increased support. Facilitating collaboration between teachers and encouraging team teaching provides support for teachers while simultaneously improving the quality of instruction delivered to students. Monitoring data, conducting observations, offering feedback, and providing tutorials to students are beneficial actions, but are reactive to deficits in instruction. The principal is being proactive by facilitating collaborative teaching so that students will receive good instruction in the classroom.

31. A: Rigor in academic instruction refers to curriculum and instruction that is challenging to students. Rigorous instruction challenges students academically, but also intellectually and even personally. Rigorous instruction is often complex and challenges students to think deeply and critically. Rigor does not mean excessively hard or difficult. However, rigor does involve instruction that is stimulating and engaging. Rigorous instruction often requires students to make connections across academic content areas and apply concepts to the real world.

32. C: Curriculum and instruction must be aligned to assessment because what is taught must be measured and what is measured must be taught. If instruction is not aligned to the assessment, it is likely that there will be no measurement of how well students mastered what was taught. Additionally, if instruction is not aligned to the assessment, it is likely that students will be assessed on concepts and material that they have not been taught. Neither of the scenarios is fair or beneficial to students.

33. A: Differentiated instruction refers to providing customized or tailored instruction to students to meet their diverse learning needs. Previous academic performance, special needs (such as a physical or learning disability), and learning styles are good ways to determine how to differentiate instruction to meet student needs. Other sources of data, such as interests, career goals, and others can be helpful, but are not always relevant.

34. D: Effective curricular programs will help students grow academically. Meeting academic performance standards may not be a good indicator of appropriate curricular programs if there is a population of students on campus who are consistently exceeding the performance standards on assessments. Meeting only minimum standards would be a cause of concern and these students would need a curricular program that extends their learning and supports their academic growth. In contrast, an effective curricular program would foster academic growth for all students.

35. C: Cross-curricular instruction is the deliberate making of connections between various content areas so that students may apply their knowledge in more than one content area at a time. For example, students may examine the historical setting of a story in a reading class, utilize math strategies in a science class, or discuss geometric principles in an art class. Cross-curricular instruction is beneficial for students because it demonstrates the relevance of their content knowledge.

36. B: When students have satisfactory academic performance in class (reflected through items such as classroom assignments, teacher-created tests, and projects), but fail to meet satisfactory performance on standardized tests, that is an indication that what is taught in the classroom is not aligned with what is tested. This data trend shows that students are performing well based on the curriculum, but the curriculum does not adequately prepare students for what is assessed on the standardized test.

37. C: The school leader observing classroom instruction also provides opportunities to observe students in the learning process. Classroom observations can provide valuable information about instructional delivery, teacher quality, and student performance. Reviewing classroom observation data in conjunction with student academic performance data can provide the school leader with a more well-rounded understanding of the quality of learning on campus.

38. A: Summative assessment is assessment that is used to evaluate student learning for mastery. Summative assessment usually occurs at the end of an instructional unit or a designated period of time, such as a grading period or school year. These assessments are aligned to objectives or standards and are usually high stakes, which means they may count for a significant grade or may determine a student's progress in their educational career. A summative assessment may be a midterm or final exam, a research project, a unit test, or a standardized exam. The results of summative assessments may determine a student's grade promotion or earning of course credit. Results from summative assessments may also determine a school's performance according to accountability standards. Summative assessment results are often used by school leaders for instructional planning and goal setting for the subsequent school year.

39. D: A leader should communicate with parents and the community about progress toward goals frequently and in a variety of ways. This can include community meetings, but communication should not be limited to in-person meetings. The leader can provide a newsletter or bulletin that will update the community about school performance, upcoming events, and ways to get involved with the school to help achieve the school goals. Many schools feature phone systems that can mass call students' homes, which can be used to communicate announcements regarding school goals and progress toward those goals. Similarly, school leaders can mail letters to parents containing updates regarding the school goals.

40. B: Traditional methods of assessment usually involve a standardized test with closed questions that require students to select an answer from several choices. Authentic assessment allows students to demonstrate mastery of content and objectives in different ways within the context of the subject matter. This may include project assessments, writing assessments, and performance assessment. The goal of authentic assessment is to provide students with the opportunity to authentically demonstrate that they have mastered the content.

41. C: Grades should reflect student mastery of objectives. The assistant principal needs to know if the reading teacher is assessing students properly to assign grades and if so, determine why measurements of student progress and mastery are not entered into the gradebook in a timely manner.

42. A: The number of math and reading teachers and the size of their classes most directly impact student learning. Research has demonstrated that class size is an influencing factor of student performance and that reducing class sizes to assist struggling students has also shown to be effective. School start time, testing intervals, and access to technology indirectly impact student learning.

43. D: A school leader should focus on improving all teaching on campus, even teaching that is already considered effective. This reinforces a culture of high expectations on campus and demonstrates to high-performing teachers that they are valued. When a school leader is committed to improving all instruction on campus, even instruction that is considered effective, all staff are encouraged to grow professionally for the benefit of students.

44. B: The plant operator oversees the operation of the school campus from a facilities standpoint. This staff member will have information related to the physical layout of the facility, its intended use, accessibility, and many other aspects of the physical building that will be helpful in determining how the building can be used appropriately.

45. A: School leaders must abide by policies set forth by local safety departments. In this case, a fire drill may be disruptive to the school day, but it is a priority and must be conducted. In the future, the principal should plan when to conduct fire drills in advance rather than waiting and possibly failing to conduct them.

46. C: The campus technology plan will include information such as when the computers were purchased, how they should be maintained, and when the computers should be replaced. If it is time to replace the computers, the school leader needs to identify what funds in the budget can be used to purchase new computers. If it is not time to replace the computers, the school leader may request technical support for improving the functionality of the computers.

47. D: An acceptable use policy is a document that dictates how students use the school's physical technology device, hardware, software, and Internet and network access. An acceptable use policy is a document that is usually signed to indicate that the user acknowledges the terms of technology use and understands the consequences of not abiding by those terms.

48. D: The online literacy program collects valuable data, but the data must be accessible by instructional decision makers for them to be able to make data-driven instructional decisions. Collecting data without being able to access it is not effective for data-driven decision making. In order for data to be useful, it must be easily accessible by those who need it in a timely manner. In this scenario, teachers and administrators would be able to access all the data in one location, which would facilitate using that data to make decisions using that data.

49. B: Although a technology budget cut is bad news, the principal would want to assess the current technology equipment on campus first. If the campus is already technology rich, the budget cut may not result in a drastic impact to instruction for the upcoming school year and little to no action may be necessary. After assessing the current technology equipment on campus, the principal can determine if the equipment meets the needs for the upcoming school year and, if not, how to make adjustments.

50. A: Fundraisers are a common way for schools to secure money and resources outside of school budgets. Fundraisers should always be conducted within the policies and procedures outlined by the school campus and the school district.

51. D: School funding comes from a variety of sources. The federal government provides some funding, but this funding is usually unsubstantial and may fluctuate due to the changing budget decisions at the federal level. The state governments also provide funding to schools based on income and/or sales taxes. The majority of school funding is gained from property taxes within the school district. Both residences and commercial properties are taxed, and a portion of those taxes are allocated to school districts. Schools and school districts often seek grants and donations from foundations to supplement the school's budget.

52. C: The beginning of the school year is a critical time that can impact the success of the entire school year. Therefore, a leader should strive to have 100% of staff in place before school starts. Important trainings and professional development occur prior to the start of the year. A teacher who is hired later will miss these important trainings, which can impact their efficacy in the classroom and their ability to build relationships with the rest of the instructional team.

53. C: The school culture can create a welcoming environment for new teachers, or it can repel them. When the school culture is positive, focused on students, and driven by excellence, teachers will want to be a part of that culture. They will be motivated by the positive culture and will recruit others to join the team. On the other hand, if the school culture is negative, then teachers and staff will likely have negative attitudes as well. Teachers will seek a way out of that school environment

125

rather than encouraging others to join the team. This negative culture can negatively affect students' academic performance and behavior. If a potential teacher candidate observes a negative school culture, they may be unwilling to work at that campus.

54. D: A physically safe environment is free from dangers, both seen and unseen, that would pose a threat to the physical safety of anyone exposed to the environment. A physically safe environment is in good repair, accessible to all, and accommodating in relation to the nature in which the environment is designated for use.

55. A: An emotionally safe environment is an environment where everyone can learn. It is free from all obstacles, negative emotions, and conflicts due to preventative strategies and quick resolutions. When an environment is not emotionally safe, children can feel fear, anxiety, and a host of other negative emotions. In an emotionally safe environment, both adults and children feel comfortable participating in the learning environment and interacting with one another. There is an absence of peer-to-peer conflict, peer-to-adult conflict, and bullying.

56. C: It is most important for the school leader to identify the appropriate staff to manage the physical plant. This staff member has the primary responsibility to ensure the safe functioning of everything on campus; therefore, the leader must choose the right staff member for the job and monitor the performance of that staff member. While it is important for the school leader to personally inspect their campus on a regular basis, management of the physical plant must be delegated to an appropriate staff member to ensure that the campus is maintained appropriately.

57. A: Child Protective Services is a service provided by state agencies to protect the welfare of children. This agency investigates allegations of child abuse or neglect and provides services to children if such allegations are proven valid. As a school leader, there will be instances in which the school leader or a school staff member has reason to believe that a child is being neglected or abused. Whenever there is suspicion of abuse or neglect, it is each staff member's responsibility, including that of the school leader, to submit a formal report to Child Protective Services for investigation.

58. B: Although there are many factors and influences outside of the school that can lead a young person to commit suicide, the school and its staff can serve as a resource and support for students who experience suicidal thoughts. A school leader should ensure that there are systems in place on campus that allow students to express their needs so that they can be referred for services. This may include having walk-in counseling hours or open-door policies with key staff members.

59. A: Almost all aspects of the school program can be supported with community resources. However, stakeholders cannot participate in confidential matters involving personnel or anything else that may violate FERPA laws. Local community organizations can prove to be valuable in a wide array of areas that benefit the school, its staff, and the students, including connecting students with businesses in the community to participate in internships.

60. D: Letters and automated calls are acceptable forms of communication, but communication is most effective when parents and community members have the opportunity to engage in two-way conversation. Hosting a meeting gives participants a chance to ask questions and provide feedback to school leadership.

61. A: In diverse communities, school leaders often encounter language barriers when attempting to communicate with parents of students or other community members. While it is helpful when a school leader is fluent in more than one language, there are often a variety of languages that are spoken in these communities. There can be translators, including sign language interpreters, or

126

translation machines available at community meetings when appropriate. There are also many businesses that offer translation services for documents and real-time translation for meetings and conferences.

62. B: There are times when the school leader will need to effectively communicate with the media for both positive and negative reasons. The school leader should first follow the protocols and procedures outlined by the school district when communicating with the media, especially in situations in which the media attention is negative for the school or district. Some school districts centralize media communication and do not permit school leaders or other staff to communicate with the media without express approval.

63. C: When scheduling parent meetings for large groups of parents, the school leader should consider the time of the day and the day of the week that these meetings are to be held. The goal of these meetings is to effectively communicate with parents in a group setting, so the school leader needs to ensure that the scheduled time and day of the meeting accommodates the majority of parents for maximum attendance.

64. B: The school leader can form a parent focus group in order to gather feedback and opinions on decisions to be made at the school. A focus group would allow multiple parents to participate and would foster two-way communication. Two-way communication allows both parties to participate and contribute. One-way communication methods can gather input from others or deliver information, but they do not allow stakeholders to actively participate in the decision-making process.

65. C: Utilizing community services builds partnerships and relationships between the school and the community, which can have long-range benefits for both parties. When businesses provide mentors for students, they are engaged in activities over time that can have a positive impact on the school community.

66. A: A school leader must identify key stakeholders within the school community, including those with competing perspectives. The school leader should meet with the group of disgruntled teachers, also, to facilitate two-way communication. The school leader will have an opportunity to listen to and address the group members' concerns, while the teachers will have an opportunity to hear the rationale for certain policies and procedures.

67. B: Participating in school- and district-sponsored events is not always the same as engaging with the greater community. Community stakeholders can include members of the community who do not have children enrolled in the school district but are contributors to the community as a whole. These stakeholders may include business owners, community organization leaders, and residents near the school. Additionally, community engagement involves opportunities for two-way communication between the school leader and community members. Attending the community parade gives the school leader an opportunity to represent the school at a community event and engage with community stakeholders. This increases the school leader's visibility in the community and demonstrates that the school is a part of the community that it serves.

68. D: If possible, the school leader should communicate directly with the student and their family to learn about the student's academic, social, and emotional needs. Schools and school districts have policies and procedures for supporting students whose first language is not English so that these students can receive the support that they need to be academically successful.

69. C: Meeting with a diverse group of stakeholders from the community will give the new principal a well-rounded perspective of the community. Researching the community online, reviewing student data, and talking with staff are all effective methods of collecting information, but speaking directly with community members is a better source of more insightful information.

70. A: The school provides education and training to students that will make them employable in the community workforce. As a result, the school can supplement or adjust school programming to respond to the needs of the community, such as training students in particular employment fields that are experiencing a shortage within the community. Many schools, especially secondary schools, partner with their local community colleges and community organizations to identify employment trends in order to support the local community and increase the likelihood that graduates can obtain employment.

71. D: It is beneficial to the school community, the community at large, and postsecondary education institutions to align education expectations between secondary school and postsecondary school. The communication between postsecondary institutions and school leaders can help identify the skills necessary to succeed in college, trends in degree programs, and career paths. This type of communication can also lead to the integration of higher education programming on school campuses, such as dual-credit enrollment or training and certification programs.

72. B: Although the principal should be concerned with a variety of ways that this influx of students may impact the current instructional program, the primary concern should be how equipped the school is to provide this special population of students with an appropriate education. Human resources may include teachers and paraprofessionals. Fiscal resources may include furniture, equipment, technology, and other physical resources needed to support instruction.

73. C: Depending on school budget and resources, student needs that are not directly related to student safety and academic performance may not be able to be addressed using school resources. Many community resources used to support schools are targeted toward students in need. These types of resources may address physical needs of students and their families, such as providing food, clothing, toiletries, haircuts and grooming, or helping adults find jobs.

74. B: A memorandum of understanding is a contract that is used between two parties to outline the details of an agreement in which no money is exchanged. It is an agreement of services to be provided. The verbiage of the memorandum of understanding can be the same as that which is used in a traditional contract. However, the language is often simpler because the sole purpose of the document is to state the exchange of services with no monetary compensation. The purpose of the memorandum of understanding is to document the services to be provided. This type of documentation can be helpful for both parties in providing evidence that the services were agreed upon and delivered.

75. B: Community resources can be used in a variety of ways, such as providing school supplies for students, facilitating field trips, and providing mentorship. However, providing tutorial services to students most directly supports student learning. Tutoring students directly impacts student academic performance in class, whereas the other community resources support students' economic and psychosocial needs that may only impact learning indirectly.

76. A: Community resources used in the school must align with school programming. As a result, resources that will be used in the classroom must align with the curriculum. While it is important to consider a variety of other factors prior to incorporating community resources into the curriculum, it is imperative that the resources are aligned with the school vision and goals, which include the curriculum.

77. D: Although the other sources of information can be helpful, the principal must ensure that all funds allotted in the school budget are aligned with the campus vision and goals. When school funds are utilized, there must be a return on the investment that aligns with the vision and goals for the school. Programs and resources that do not align with the school vision and goals must be deprioritized or even eliminated.

78. C: This scenario best represents a mutually beneficial relationship. The church has the benefit of having a meeting place and the principal has the benefit of communicating directly with community members on a regular basis. The other activities help to build positive relationships between the school and the community, but are one-sided.

79. B: School districts and state laws may provide guidelines for how school facilities can be utilized by the community. These regulations normally dictate the timeline for requests, any fees that should be assessed, and the types of activities that can occur on school property.

80. A: Mr. Smith's performance in the classroom does not excuse him from meeting other professional expectations. The assistant principal's response implies that Mr. Smith would be held accountable for his late arrival if he were not doing a good job in the classroom. It is unfair to allow Mr. Smith to arrive late without allowing other teachers to do the same. Integrity is most often applied to situations of morality, while justice is most often applied to situations in which the appropriateness of consequences is questioned. In this scenario, it is implied that the violation of policy for arrival time is based upon teaching performance, which would indicate that teachers who do not perform as well may be held to strict adherence to the policy. There is no discussion of morality or administered consequences in this scenario, only the unequal application of the policy.

81. C: Transparent decision-making is the act of making sure that the process, logic, and rationale used to make a decision are clear and available to be communicated to others. When decision-making is transparent, any critical information used to inform that decision is also readily available to others for review. This transparency allows others to understand how the decision was made.

82. A: A conflict of interest is a situation in which the school leader can obtain personal gain or harm from a decision they make as school leader. If it is determined that hiring the contractor who is related to the principal would bring the principal personal gain, then the situation could be deemed a conflict of interest.

83. B: FERPA stands for the Family Educational Rights and Privacy Act. It is a federal law that protects student information and education records.

84. D: A school leader cannot use their professional influence or position to solicit votes for a candidate on campus. Public school educators have a right to engage in the political process outside of school, but these activities cannot interfere with their job duties or cause a conflict of interest.

85. D: Testing procedures may vary, but there are specific guidelines for reporting testing violations. The principal should report the alleged testing violation to the appropriate authorities so that it can be handled according to proper procedure. Confronting the accused teacher or attempting to investigate the allegation could impair the investigation. Documenting the complaint may be a step that the principal will need to take after the allegation has been reported per protocol.

86. A: The best way that the school leader can ensure equitable treatment of students and staff is to develop policies and procedures and adhere to them. When there are policies and procedures in place, the school leader can refer to these to determine their course of action when dealing with students and staff. Policies and procedures help leaders proactively ensure that students and staff are treated equitably because they serve as guidelines for behavior and are not subjective. Creating an advisory committee can assist with developing these policies and procedures, but doing so does not shape the behavior of all staff and students. Additionally, while it is advisable that a school leader addresses student and staff complaints swiftly, this is a reactive response and likely occurs after someone has already been treated in an inequitable manner.

87. C: When a person finds value and worth in each student, they exemplify the educational philosophy that all students can learn. Some students may need more support or different resources, but they still have the capacity to learn. This teacher's statement that the student would fail anyway is in direct opposition to this philosophy.

88. A: This action best represents an effort to develop a culture of knowledge about and comfort with cultures other than the students' own. Whereas knowledge doesn't always have highly noticeable effects on the school culture in the short-term, it has long-term impact on the community because it helps to break down ignorance about other cultures. Students who know something about another culture are much more willing to interact with people from that culture, rather than avoid peers who are not like themselves. This is particularly helpful when implemented as a schoolwide policy rather than occurring in individual classes because it will have a greater impact on the entire culture of the school. Black History Month should be celebrated, but it only provides perspectives from one culture and doesn't necessarily encourage interaction between various cultures. Publishing a statement about diversity and inclusion likely does not show a strong enough gesture to encourage real change. Adding ASL to course offerings is also not likely to reach a broad enough audience to have a huge change, although it is great to have those options available.

89. B: The disproportionate number of students suspended from school based on race may indicate that there are beliefs influencing how teachers relate to students. The school principal needs to identify if there is evidence of this in the school culture and whether campus policies perpetuate negative beliefs.

90. A: All staff can benefit from diversity training so they can challenge any negative assumptions that they may have about various populations of students or staff. School leaders must take caution not to allow negative assumptions and beliefs to impact the hiring process or the implementation of policies and procedures on campus.

91. C: The use of school funds represents a common ethical situation. All school funds should be used according to policies and procedures outlined by the school board. Using school funds for personal use is a violation of ethics.

92. D: Many school districts require parents to provide express permission for their child to appear in photographs and videos for media purposes. Other school districts indicate that consent is implied unless there is written documentation expressly forbidding their child to appear in content for media. In either circumstance, the school leader needs to confirm that each student who will participate has permission from a parent or guardian to do so.

93. C: The school leader's responsibility is to investigate the accusation that has been made to determine next steps. An investigation is needed because the school leader cannot take immediate action in response to the teachers' actions based solely on the report of the parent. Whether the teachers will be disciplined or not, the school leader should not discuss such discipline of personnel with others.

94. B: The best way to ensure that others are acting ethically is to actively monitor employee behavior. This can be done in person by walking around and observing performance, instructing others on the leadership team to observe employee behavior, and monitoring using security cameras. Security cameras are useful in areas that are most prone to unethical conduct, such as places where money is exchanged, entrances and exits, records storage, and areas on campus that are not frequently trafficked. While it is recommended to have policies and procedures for ethical behavior in place, the school leader must actively monitor adherence to those policies and procedures.

95. D: Attending a mandated training session indicates that the leader failed to identify that the training was needed for themselves, but instead needed to be directed by someone else to attend. Self-reflection involves reflecting on one's own performance in comparison to a set of leadership expectations and standards.

96. A: The principal's announcement that they are committing to an ongoing training program indicates that they are committed to professional growth. This is a model to the other members of the leadership team.

97. C: The principal's initial responsibility is to report the infraction to the athletics department because the breach of confidential information may require the drug testing plan to be revised. After the principal reports the breach, they may determine how to address the personnel matter with the athletics director.

98. D: The principal should take action that allows stakeholders to participate in the process of refocusing attention to campus vision and goals. A community meeting would allow for two-way communication so that the principal can hear the concerns of the community and so that the community can hear about the alignment of the program to the campus vision and goals.

99. B: The principal noted that they were not able to implement plans properly because they did not have time. Action items in the plan were not accomplished, indicating that this is a time management issue and the leader needs to set appropriate priorities for accomplishing tasks. Simply adding hours to one's work week does not mean that those hours will be spent completing the right tasks. School leaders must become efficient at prioritizing their activities to achieve school goals. Additionally, the leader is concerned with self-improvement, so holding others accountable is not an appropriate solution in this instance.

100. A: Widespread testing violations indicates that the staff would benefit from additional training regarding testing procedures. There may be misconceptions or gaps in information that may need to be addressed in the training.

Constructed Response

Essay Questions

SCENARIO 1

XYZ High School has been identified as an underperforming school for the past two years. During the most recent school year, the principal implemented a rigorous plan for improving student academic performance. This plan was presented and approved by the community prior to implementation. Student-performance data collected throughout the school year suggested that the school was on track to meet performance expectations. However, due to the complexity of how school performance was calculated, the school ultimately showed improvement but did not meet performance expectations. Describe how the school principal can clearly communicate the explanation for the school performance results to the community.

SCENARIO 2

A middle school principal has noticed that, of the five elementary schools that most of the middle school students matriculate from, two of the elementary schools consistently promote students with significant deficits in math to middle school. The principal has decided that this must be addressed if student performance at the middle school is to improve. Identify and describe at least three steps the principal can take to address the math deficits of incoming students.

SCENARIO 3

XYZ High School has been traditionally known for its fine arts program. However, the school has been underperforming for several years. There is pressure from the school district and from state agencies to reallocate funds from fine arts programs to state-assessed subjects like math and reading. The community is unhappy about a proposal to decrease support of the fine arts program in lieu of increased tutorials and resources for math and reading. The principal must determine the goals for the school year and use these goals to align human and fiscal resources. Determine whether the fine arts program should be included in the school goals for the year and explain why or why not.

SCENARIO 4

The dean of instruction at a high school recently administered a benchmark assessment to tenth-grade students in the area of math. The data showed that 93% of the students mastered the math objectives that were assessed. The dean compared this performance to the math goal for the grading period and noted that current student performance exceeded the milestone of 90% that had been set at the outset of the school year. Describe at least two recommendations that the dean of instruction should make to the principal in response to this data.

SCENARIO 5

A teacher leader provided the principal with feedback related to the professional-development opportunities that had been offered to teachers on campus. Many of the teaching staff were unhappy with the mandatory training sessions and believed that these sessions were not beneficial in improving instructional practice, nor were they responsive to teacher needs. The teacher leader requests that the principal consider adjusting the campus's approach to professional-development delivery. Describe at least three suggestions that the principal can offer the teacher to address their concerns about professional development.

SCENARIO 6

The principal has noted that, based on classroom observations and interim assessment data, students with limited English proficiency are not performing well overall, and the greatest deficits are in English language arts. The group of students with limited English proficiency make up about 15% of the student population and speak a total of twelve languages amongst the group. Create a three-step plan to address this need.

SCENARIO 7

A professional learning community made up of reading teachers and a campus reading specialist met to analyze and discuss the most recent data from a reading benchmark assessment. The data showed that the majority of students failed to perform satisfactorily. The reading specialist asked the teachers if the benchmark scores were reflective of student performance in the classroom. The reading teachers indicated that most students were passing their reading classes. The reading specialist is concerned about the discrepancy between classroom performance and assessment performance for students. Identify two possible reasons for the discrepancy between grades and test scores.

Essay Sample Responses

SCENARIO 1

The school performance results may be confusing and disappointing to the community because they vetted the plan in advance and interim campus assessment data indicated that the plan was working and that the school was performing well. In order to clearly explain the school performance results to the community, the principal will first need to focus on explaining how school performance ratings are calculated. Then the principal needs to explain the difference between data collected at the campus level, using assessments such as benchmark exams, and data that is collected from standardized tests. The principal should provide a clear description of how school performance ratings are calculated, such as which students are included in the data calculations, the impact of students who belong to special populations, and other factors that may impact how school ratings are calculated. Also, the principal can compare the campus-based data and the official student-performance data from the standardized tests to identify any discrepancies and provide an explanation for those discrepancies.

SCENARIO 2

The first step the principal can take is to create a coalition of elementary and middle school principals in the community. Together the principals can collaborate, share resources, and vertically align their curricular programs so that all students matriculating from the elementary schools will have the same educational opportunities and be academically prepared to attend middle school. The next step the principal can take is to partner with the principals of the two elementary schools that are promoting students with math deficits to middle school. The principal can first find out why students are having deficits in this area. These reasons may include teacher turnover, changes in curriculum, or other factors that the principals may be able to identity and address. Lastly, the middle school principal can develop a plan to prepare incoming students for middle school. For example, the principal can create a summer school program that provides targeted instruction in math for incoming students from the local elementary schools.

SCENARIO 3

The principal must consider that campus performance as assessed by state and federal guidelines is of utmost priority. Campus performance and school accountability are often based upon core subject areas, such as math and reading. There is much research that supports the value of fine arts programs in schools. However, if a campus is not performing in core subject areas, then fine arts cannot be prioritized. As a result, the principal will need to develop school goals that will directly impact the school's performance rating based on state and federal standards. This will also mean that school resources will be aligned to these goals and may not be used for fine arts. Creating goals focused on these subject areas does not necessarily mean that the fine arts program will be eliminated, but the resources for the program may have to come from external sources, such as the community, grants, fundraisers, and donations.

SCENARIO 4

The student progress data is commendable and exceeds the expected performance for the marking period. However, it is noted that the benchmark assessment only measured student performance on selected math objectives, not all objectives. The dean of instruction should recommend to the principal that the data be further disaggregated to identify student performance on specific math objectives and develop intervention strategies for students based on specific objectives. Additionally, because the data indicates that most students are performing well, the dean of instruction can recommend that teachers provide instruction and intervention that can help

134

students exceed minimum passing requirements. All recommendations made should demonstrate that there is a culture of continuous improvement, even if expectations are currently being met.

SCENARIO 5

The teacher leader's feedback indicates that the current professional-development plan does not address teacher needs, does not incorporate teacher input, and does not directly impact teaching and learning. To address these concerns, the principal can suggest that teachers have an opportunity to attend professional-development sessions that are hosted outside the school organization. Often, professional teacher organizations and education entities offer a variety of trainings and conferences that may better meet the individual needs of instructional staff. Allowing the teachers to choose their professional development can help them to find training solutions that meet their unique needs. Additionally, the principal can suggest offering multiple professional-development sessions for teachers to choose from. These offerings can be presented conference style, where some sessions are for all teachers and other sessions are attended by choice. This suggestion also allows teachers to choose the sessions that are beneficial to them and allows the principal to ensure that all sessions are aligned to campus goals. Finally, the principal may suggest that teachers complete a survey indicating the areas in which they need support. This data can help the principal identify relevant professional-development sessions for teachers both as individuals and collectively.

SCENARIO 6

First, the principal should meet with the English language arts teachers to gather more data about the needs of this group of students in the classroom environment. Even though they are all English language learners, it should not be assumed that all the students are experiencing the same challenges within the classroom. Next, the principal should consult with the staff and committees that are assigned to monitor the support of English language learners. There are specific policies and procedures that are in place to meet the needs of English language learners on campus and these must be adhered to. The staff should ensure that all instructional supports as outlined in committee documentation are up to date and that the teachers are appropriately and consistently implementing the recommendations made by the committee. There is also opportunity to revise and update the documents to better meet the needs of the students. Finally, the principal may need to provide additional training for teachers regarding the support of English language learners in the classroom, such as using effective instructional strategies and supplemental instructional resources.

SCENARIO 7

One possible reason for the discrepancy is that the reading teachers are not accurately grading student reading performance in the classroom. While classroom grades should be reflective of student mastery of objectives, they often are not. Grade inflation may occur if students are given grades for class participation, assignment completion, or other activities and performance indicators that are not reflective of student mastery of objectives. If students are given grades or awarded points for non-academic activities or behaviors that are not indicators of objective mastery, classroom grades can be inflated. Another possible reason for the discrepancy is that the curriculum is not appropriately aligned to the standards that are assessed. If this is the case, students may perform satisfactorily in class on the standards and objectives taught by the teacher, but they will not have received instruction related to the standards and objectives on the test, causing them to perform poorly. If a test does not assess what is taught in the classroom, then there will be discrepancies between classroom grades and test grades.

How to Overcome Test Anxiety

Just the thought of taking a test is enough to make most people a little nervous. A test is an important event that can have a long-term impact on your future, so it's important to take it seriously and it's natural to feel anxious about performing well. But just because anxiety is normal, that doesn't mean that it's helpful in test taking, or that you should simply accept it as part of your life. Anxiety can have a variety of effects. These effects can be mild, like making you feel slightly nervous, or severe, like blocking your ability to focus or remember even a simple detail.

If you experience test anxiety—whether severe or mild—it's important to know how to beat it. To discover this, first you need to understand what causes test anxiety.

Causes of Test Anxiety

While we often think of anxiety as an uncontrollable emotional state, it can actually be caused by simple, practical things. One of the most common causes of test anxiety is that a person does not feel adequately prepared for their test. This feeling can be the result of many different issues such as poor study habits or lack of organization, but the most common culprit is time management. Starting to study too late, failing to organize your study time to cover all of the material, or being distracted while you study will mean that you're not well prepared for the test. This may lead to cramming the night before, which will cause you to be physically and mentally exhausted for the test. Poor time management also contributes to feelings of stress, fear, and hopelessness as you realize you are not well prepared but don't know what to do about it.

Other times, test anxiety is not related to your preparation for the test but comes from unresolved fear. This may be a past failure on a test, or poor performance on tests in general. It may come from comparing yourself to others who seem to be performing better or from the stress of living up to expectations. Anxiety may be driven by fears of the future—how failure on this test would affect your educational and career goals. These fears are often completely irrational, but they can still negatively impact your test performance.

> **Review Video: 3 Reasons You Have Test Anxiety**
> Visit mometrix.com/academy and enter code: 428468

Elements of Test Anxiety

As mentioned earlier, test anxiety is considered to be an emotional state, but it has physical and mental components as well. Sometimes you may not even realize that you are suffering from test anxiety until you notice the physical symptoms. These can include trembling hands, rapid heartbeat, sweating, nausea, and tense muscles. Extreme anxiety may lead to fainting or vomiting. Obviously, any of these symptoms can have a negative impact on testing. It is important to recognize them as soon as they begin to occur so that you can address the problem before it damages your performance.

> **Review Video: 3 Ways to Tell You Have Test Anxiety**
> Visit mometrix.com/academy and enter code: 927847

The mental components of test anxiety include trouble focusing and inability to remember learned information. During a test, your mind is on high alert, which can help you recall information and stay focused for an extended period of time. However, anxiety interferes with your mind's natural processes, causing you to blank out, even on the questions you know well. The strain of testing during anxiety makes it difficult to stay focused, especially on a test that may take several hours. Extreme anxiety can take a huge mental toll, making it difficult not only to recall test information but even to understand the test questions or pull your thoughts together.

> **Review Video: How Test Anxiety Affects Memory**
> Visit mometrix.com/academy and enter code: 609003

Effects of Test Anxiety

Test anxiety is like a disease—if left untreated, it will get progressively worse. Anxiety leads to poor performance, and this reinforces the feelings of fear and failure, which in turn lead to poor performances on subsequent tests. It can grow from a mild nervousness to a crippling condition. If allowed to progress, test anxiety can have a big impact on your schooling, and consequently on your future.

Test anxiety can spread to other parts of your life. Anxiety on tests can become anxiety in any stressful situation, and blanking on a test can turn into panicking in a job situation. But fortunately, you don't have to let anxiety rule your testing and determine your grades. There are a number of relatively simple steps you can take to move past anxiety and function normally on a test and in the rest of life.

> **Review Video: How Test Anxiety Impacts Your Grades**
> Visit mometrix.com/academy and enter code: 939819

Physical Steps for Beating Test Anxiety

While test anxiety is a serious problem, the good news is that it can be overcome. It doesn't have to control your ability to think and remember information. While it may take time, you can begin taking steps today to beat anxiety.

Just as your first hint that you may be struggling with anxiety comes from the physical symptoms, the first step to treating it is also physical. Rest is crucial for having a clear, strong mind. If you are tired, it is much easier to give in to anxiety. But if you establish good sleep habits, your body and mind will be ready to perform optimally, without the strain of exhaustion. Additionally, sleeping well helps you to retain information better, so you're more likely to recall the answers when you see the test questions.

Getting good sleep means more than going to bed on time. It's important to allow your brain time to relax. Take study breaks from time to time so it doesn't get overworked, and don't study right before bed. Take time to rest your mind before trying to rest your body, or you may find it difficult to fall asleep.

> **Review Video: The Importance of Sleep for Your Brain**
> Visit mometrix.com/academy and enter code: 319338

Along with sleep, other aspects of physical health are important in preparing for a test. Good nutrition is vital for good brain function. Sugary foods and drinks may give a burst of energy but this burst is followed by a crash, both physically and emotionally. Instead, fuel your body with protein and vitamin-rich foods.

Also, drink plenty of water. Dehydration can lead to headaches and exhaustion, especially if your brain is already under stress from the rigors of the test. Particularly if your test is a long one, drink water during the breaks. And if possible, take an energy-boosting snack to eat between sections.

> **Review Video: How Diet Can Affect your Mood**
> Visit mometrix.com/academy and enter code: 624317

Along with sleep and diet, a third important part of physical health is exercise. Maintaining a steady workout schedule is helpful, but even taking 5-minute study breaks to walk can help get your blood pumping faster and clear your head. Exercise also releases endorphins, which contribute to a positive feeling and can help combat test anxiety.

When you nurture your physical health, you are also contributing to your mental health. If your body is healthy, your mind is much more likely to be healthy as well. So take time to rest, nourish your body with healthy food and water, and get moving as much as possible. Taking these physical steps will make you stronger and more able to take the mental steps necessary to overcome test anxiety.

> **Review Video: How to Stay Healthy and Prevent Test Anxiety**
> Visit mometrix.com/academy and enter code: 877894

Mental Steps for Beating Test Anxiety

Working on the mental side of test anxiety can be more challenging, but as with the physical side, there are clear steps you can take to overcome it. As mentioned earlier, test anxiety often stems from lack of preparation, so the obvious solution is to prepare for the test. Effective studying may be the most important weapon you have for beating test anxiety, but you can and should employ several other mental tools to combat fear.

First, boost your confidence by reminding yourself of past success—tests or projects that you aced. If you're putting as much effort into preparing for this test as you did for those, there's no reason you should expect to fail here. Work hard to prepare; then trust your preparation.

Second, surround yourself with encouraging people. It can be helpful to find a study group, but be sure that the people you're around will encourage a positive attitude. If you spend time with others who are anxious or cynical, this will only contribute to your own anxiety. Look for others who are motivated to study hard from a desire to succeed, not from a fear of failure.

Third, reward yourself. A test is physically and mentally tiring, even without anxiety, and it can be helpful to have something to look forward to. Plan an activity following the test, regardless of the outcome, such as going to a movie or getting ice cream.

When you are taking the test, if you find yourself beginning to feel anxious, remind yourself that you know the material. Visualize successfully completing the test. Then take a few deep, relaxing breaths and return to it. Work through the questions carefully but with confidence, knowing that you are capable of succeeding.

Developing a healthy mental approach to test taking will also aid in other areas of life. Test anxiety affects more than just the actual test—it can be damaging to your mental health and even contribute to depression. It's important to beat test anxiety before it becomes a problem for more than testing.

> **Review Video: Test Anxiety and Depression**
> Visit mometrix.com/academy and enter code: 904704

Study Strategy

Being prepared for the test is necessary to combat anxiety, but what does being prepared look like? You may study for hours on end and still not feel prepared. What you need is a strategy for test prep. The next few pages outline our recommended steps to help you plan out and conquer the challenge of preparation.

STEP 1: SCOPE OUT THE TEST

Learn everything you can about the format (multiple choice, essay, etc.) and what will be on the test. Gather any study materials, course outlines, or sample exams that may be available. Not only will this help you to prepare, but knowing what to expect can help to alleviate test anxiety.

STEP 2: MAP OUT THE MATERIAL

Look through the textbook or study guide and make note of how many chapters or sections it has. Then divide these over the time you have. For example, if a book has 15 chapters and you have five days to study, you need to cover three chapters each day. Even better, if you have the time, leave an extra day at the end for overall review after you have gone through the material in depth.

If time is limited, you may need to prioritize the material. Look through it and make note of which sections you think you already have a good grasp on, and which need review. While you are studying, skim quickly through the familiar sections and take more time on the challenging parts. Write out your plan so you don't get lost as you go. Having a written plan also helps you feel more in control of the study, so anxiety is less likely to arise from feeling overwhelmed at the amount to cover.

STEP 3: GATHER YOUR TOOLS

Decide what study method works best for you. Do you prefer to highlight in the book as you study and then go back over the highlighted portions? Or do you type out notes of the important information? Or is it helpful to make flashcards that you can carry with you? Assemble the pens, index cards, highlighters, post-it notes, and any other materials you may need so you won't be distracted by getting up to find things while you study.

If you're having a hard time retaining the information or organizing your notes, experiment with different methods. For example, try color-coding by subject with colored pens, highlighters, or post-it notes. If you learn better by hearing, try recording yourself reading your notes so you can listen while in the car, working out, or simply sitting at your desk. Ask a friend to quiz you from your flashcards, or try teaching someone the material to solidify it in your mind.

STEP 4: CREATE YOUR ENVIRONMENT

It's important to avoid distractions while you study. This includes both the obvious distractions like visitors and the subtle distractions like an uncomfortable chair (or a too-comfortable couch that makes you want to fall asleep). Set up the best study environment possible: good lighting and a comfortable work area. If background music helps you focus, you may want to turn it on, but otherwise keep the room quiet. If you are using a computer to take notes, be sure you don't have any other windows open, especially applications like social media, games, or anything else that could distract you. Silence your phone and turn off notifications. Be sure to keep water close by so you stay hydrated while you study (but avoid unhealthy drinks and snacks).

Also, take into account the best time of day to study. Are you freshest first thing in the morning? Try to set aside some time then to work through the material. Is your mind clearer in the afternoon or evening? Schedule your study session then. Another method is to study at the same time of day that you will take the test, so that your brain gets used to working on the material at that time and will be ready to focus at test time.

STEP 5: STUDY!

Once you have done all the study preparation, it's time to settle into the actual studying. Sit down, take a few moments to settle your mind so you can focus, and begin to follow your study plan. Don't give in to distractions or let yourself procrastinate. This is your time to prepare so you'll be ready to fearlessly approach the test. Make the most of the time and stay focused.

Of course, you don't want to burn out. If you study too long you may find that you're not retaining the information very well. Take regular study breaks. For example, taking five minutes out of every hour to walk briskly, breathing deeply and swinging your arms, can help your mind stay fresh.

As you get to the end of each chapter or section, it's a good idea to do a quick review. Remind yourself of what you learned and work on any difficult parts. When you feel that you've mastered the material, move on to the next part. At the end of your study session, briefly skim through your notes again.

But while review is helpful, cramming last minute is NOT. If at all possible, work ahead so that you won't need to fit all your study into the last day. Cramming overloads your brain with more information than it can process and retain, and your tired mind may struggle to recall even previously learned information when it is overwhelmed with last-minute study. Also, the urgent nature of cramming and the stress placed on your brain contribute to anxiety. You'll be more likely to go to the test feeling unprepared and having trouble thinking clearly.

So don't cram, and don't stay up late before the test, even just to review your notes at a leisurely pace. Your brain needs rest more than it needs to go over the information again. In fact, plan to finish your studies by noon or early afternoon the day before the test. Give your brain the rest of the day to relax or focus on other things, and get a good night's sleep. Then you will be fresh for the test and better able to recall what you've studied.

STEP 6: TAKE A PRACTICE TEST

Many courses offer sample tests, either online or in the study materials. This is an excellent resource to check whether you have mastered the material, as well as to prepare for the test format and environment.

Check the test format ahead of time: the number of questions, the type (multiple choice, free response, etc.), and the time limit. Then create a plan for working through them. For example, if you have 30 minutes to take a 60-question test, your limit is 30 seconds per question. Spend less time on the questions you know well so that you can take more time on the difficult ones.

If you have time to take several practice tests, take the first one open book, with no time limit. Work through the questions at your own pace and make sure you fully understand them. Gradually work up to taking a test under test conditions: sit at a desk with all study materials put away and set a timer. Pace yourself to make sure you finish the test with time to spare and go back to check your answers if you have time.

After each test, check your answers. On the questions you missed, be sure you understand why you missed them. Did you misread the question (tests can use tricky wording)? Did you forget the information? Or was it something you hadn't learned? Go back and study any shaky areas that the practice tests reveal.

Taking these tests not only helps with your grade, but also aids in combating test anxiety. If you're already used to the test conditions, you're less likely to worry about it, and working through tests until you're scoring well gives you a confidence boost. Go through the practice tests until you feel comfortable, and then you can go into the test knowing that you're ready for it.

Test Tips

On test day, you should be confident, knowing that you've prepared well and are ready to answer the questions. But aside from preparation, there are several test day strategies you can employ to maximize your performance.

First, as stated before, get a good night's sleep the night before the test (and for several nights before that, if possible). Go into the test with a fresh, alert mind rather than staying up late to study.

Try not to change too much about your normal routine on the day of the test. It's important to eat a nutritious breakfast, but if you normally don't eat breakfast at all, consider eating just a protein bar. If you're a coffee drinker, go ahead and have your normal coffee. Just make sure you time it so that the caffeine doesn't wear off right in the middle of your test. Avoid sugary beverages, and drink enough water to stay hydrated but not so much that you need a restroom break 10 minutes into the test. If your test isn't first thing in the morning, consider going for a walk or doing a light workout before the test to get your blood flowing.

Allow yourself enough time to get ready, and leave for the test with plenty of time to spare so you won't have the anxiety of scrambling to arrive in time. Another reason to be early is to select a good seat. It's helpful to sit away from doors and windows, which can be distracting. Find a good seat, get out your supplies, and settle your mind before the test begins.

When the test begins, start by going over the instructions carefully, even if you already know what to expect. Make sure you avoid any careless mistakes by following the directions.

Then begin working through the questions, pacing yourself as you've practiced. If you're not sure on an answer, don't spend too much time on it, and don't let it shake your confidence. Either skip it and come back later, or eliminate as many wrong answers as possible and guess among the remaining ones. Don't dwell on these questions as you continue—put them out of your mind and focus on what lies ahead.

Be sure to read all of the answer choices, even if you're sure the first one is the right answer. Sometimes you'll find a better one if you keep reading. But don't second-guess yourself if you do immediately know the answer. Your gut instinct is usually right. Don't let test anxiety rob you of the information you know.

If you have time at the end of the test (and if the test format allows), go back and review your answers. Be cautious about changing any, since your first instinct tends to be correct, but make sure you didn't misread any of the questions or accidentally mark the wrong answer choice. Look over any you skipped and make an educated guess.

At the end, leave the test feeling confident. You've done your best, so don't waste time worrying about your performance or wishing you could change anything. Instead, celebrate the successful

completion of this test. And finally, use this test to learn how to deal with anxiety even better next time.

Important Qualification

Not all anxiety is created equal. If your test anxiety is causing major issues in your life beyond the classroom or testing center, or if you are experiencing troubling physical symptoms related to your anxiety, it may be a sign of a serious physiological or psychological condition. If this sounds like your situation, we strongly encourage you to seek professional help.

Thank You

We at Mometrix would like to extend our heartfelt thanks to you, our friend and patron, for allowing us to play a part in your journey. It is a privilege to serve people from all walks of life who are unified in their commitment to building the best future they can for themselves.

The preparation you devote to these important testing milestones may be the most valuable educational opportunity you have for making a real difference in your life. We encourage you to put your heart into it—that feeling of succeeding, overcoming, and yes, conquering will be well worth the hours you've invested.

We want to hear your story, your struggles and your successes, and if you see any opportunities for us to improve our materials so we can help others even more effectively in the future, please share that with us as well. **The team at Mometrix would be absolutely thrilled to hear from you!** So please, send us an email (support@mometrix.com) and let's stay in touch.

> **If you'd like some additional help, check out these other resources we offer for your exam:**
> **http://MometrixFlashcards.com/GACE**

144

Additional Bonus Material

Due to our efforts to try to keep this book to a manageable length, we've created a link that will give you access to all of your additional bonus material.

> **Please visit**
> http://www.mometrix.com/bonus948/gaceedleader **to access**
> **the information.**